Concepts in Context

Edited by
Felix Boteram, Winfried Gödert, Jessica Hubrich

BIBLIOTHECA ACADEMICA

Reihe

Informations- und Bibliothekswissenschaften

Band 1

ERGON VERLAG

Concepts in Context

Proceedings of the
Cologne Conference on Interoperability and Semantics
in Knowledge Organization
July 19th - 20th, 2010

Edited by
Felix Boteram, Winfried Gödert, Jessica Hubrich

ERGON VERLAG

This proceedings volume is published with the financial support of the German Research Foundation and the Cologne University of Applied Sciences.

Cover image: Logo of the CrissCross project, designed by Hans-Joachim Hubrich

Bibliographic information published by the Deutsche Nationalbibliothek
The Deutsche Nationalbibliothek lists this publication in the
Deutsche Nationalbibliografie; detailed bibliographic data are available
in the Internet at http://dnb.d-nb.de.

Gedruckt auf alterungsbeständigem Papier.
Satz: Matthias Wies, Ergon-Verlag GmbH
Umschlaggestaltung: Jan von Hugo

www.ergon-verlag.de

ISBN 978-3-89913-871-9

Content

Preface

The Cologne Conference on Interoperability and Semantics in Knowledge Organization entitled "Concepts in Context" was held at the Cologne University of Applied Sciences on July 19th and 20th, 2010. It aimed not only at reporting on the projects *CrissCross* and *Reseda*, being accomplished at the Institute of Information Management at the Cologne University of Applied Sciences, but also at presenting several ideas and models that are related to their content. Well-known national and international information specialists could be brought together to inform about their actual work concerning semantic representation, interoperability and information retrieval and to discuss perspectives for future developments. The first day was designed as final workshop of the CrissCross project which was funded by the German Research Foundation and conducted by the Cologne University of Applied Sciences in cooperation with the German National Library.

When we planned the conference, information institutions like libraries had become more and more aware that their intellectually created data could provide essential elements for establishing a *Semantic Web* as envisioned by Tim Berners-Lee. Against this background, semantics as well as interoperability of data had gained new significance. Ever since, in many places the term *Semantic Web* with its focus on the semantics in its appellation has been replaced by the term *Linked Data*. Many information institutions want to secure that their existing data become an integral part of the *Linked Data Cloud*. Accordingly, the number of indexing languages that have been published in the language of the *Simple Knowledge Organization System (SKOS)* have increased. Services are under way that want to take benefit of the new Web representation formats. All these activities mainly emphasize the representational level of data; the adequacy and interoperability of the semantics provided by encoding schemes for the Web are explored and their potential for different applications is tested. However, a Semantic Web can only become reality if the semantics inherent in the data, i.e. the meaning of the modelled concepts, their relations and conceptual interoperability, are also examined in view of the requirements of the Semantic Web and – where necessary – improved. This proceedings volume considers all these aspects making it valuable for researchers as well as practitioners.

After a general thematic introduction by *Winfried Gödert* on the central topics of the proceedings, *Dagobert Soergel* proposes a method for mapping knowledge organization systems based on deep semantics. Best practice examples, planned applications as well as models for semantic interoperability and standardization are discussed by several contributors. *Jan-Helge Jacobs, Tina Mengel* and *Katrin Müller* describe the mapping of the German subject headings authority file *Schlagwortnormdatei (SWD)* to the *Dewey Decimal Classification (DDC)* conducted in the CrissCross project. Supplemental, *Helga Karg and Yvonne Jahns* present issues of translingual retrieval based on a linking between the German SWD, the French indexing language *Rameau* and the English indexing language *LCSH.* Taking up results of theoretical reflections of the CrissCross project, *Jessica Hubrich* correlates types of inter-system relations to specific search functionalities in retrieval scenarios. The feasibility of standardized mapping types is examined by *Stella Dextre Clarke* with regard to different mapping strategies and projects.

By establishing semantic interoperability, enhanced access points are provided. Other possibilities for improving the efficiency of information retrieval are discussed in two additional articles. *Philipp Mayr, Philipp Schaer* and *Peter Mutschke* present three science model driven retrieval services for Digital Libraries: co-word analysis based query expansion, re-ranking via Bradfordizing and author centrality. *Claudia Effenberger* and *Julia Hauser* report on a small research project of the German National Library which exploited the advantages of versioning DDC classes for information retrieval.

A contemporary issue with high potential for future development is addressed by the topic *Functional Requirements for Subject Authority Data (FRSAD)* as follow-up to the *Functional Requirements for Bibliographic Records (FRBR). Gordon Dunsire* describes recent work on registering *Resource Description Framework (RDF)* versions of the entities and relations from FRBR and FRSAD. *Maja Žumer* sketches FRSAD and presents comments on the world-wide reviewing process. Shortcomings and possible expansions of the FRSAD model are discussed in two final articles. Whereas *Michael Panzer* examines alignments between FRSAD and the *Simple Knowledge Organization System (SKOS), Felix Boteram* focuses on the question how to integrate semantic interoperability between concept schemes into FRSAD based on considerations made within the projects CrissCross and Reseda.

We would like to thank all who contributed to this proceedings volume. We are indebted to the German Research Foundation. Without its support neither the conference nor the proceedings volume would have been possible.

Cologne, June 2011

Felix Boteram
Winfried Gödert
Jessica Hubrich

Programmatic Issues and Introduction[1]

Winfried Gödert

Concepts in Context is the topic of these proceedings. With this topic two central terms are mentioned, which are treated in individual contributions. The term "concept" refers to entities of meaning, which are integrated in a structure and a specific context to represent knowledge. Designing knowledge organization and information retrieval systems requires constant considering how concepts and context should be modelled appropriately for efficient and user-friendly forms of searching and finding. This becomes all the more important, the more searching and finding should go beyond the mere pattern matching approach and integrate the semantic level.

We are all impressed by the sheer amount of information that can be reached by the *World Wide Web*. There are countless valuable repositories and access tools for all media types. But up to now no substantial progress has been made when it comes to supporting semantic searching, especially when we consider multilingual aspects or questions of combined searches over heterogeneously indexed collections or repositories. Even the success of a search engine like *Google* is mainly based upon its ingenious ranking algorithm and affiliated business plan, but not supported by any means of contextualizing the search concepts. The given description is well accepted and both considerations and efforts are undertaken in order to improve the situation. The vision of the *Semantic Web* entails high expectations, but although some models for the formal representation of semantic data have already been developed, the concept has indistinct outlines. For the model to comply with the requirements of semantic retrieval further clarification of the central terms "concept" and "context" and of the possibilities of their formal representation are indispensable. However we understand and define the Semantic Web, it cannot be constructed from scratch. It must be based on existing material, for example existing indexing languages, ideally by a more precise understanding and formally correct representation of concepts and their content.

With this description the metaphor of bridge-building is addressed, a metaphor well-suited for describing interoperability of indexing languages. Bridge-building has become a popular metaphor within the political and societal context, at the latest since our new head of state, *Christian Wulff*, declared his commitment to bridge-building. At the end of our *CrissCross*

1 This text is a revised, written version of the opening words spoken by Winfried Gödert at the conference on July 19th, 2010 in Cologne.

project we recognize our obligation to the task of building bridges. The central challenge of the project consisted of two bridge-building tasks. First, a method for linking the elements of the German *Schlagwortnormdatei* to the classes of the German translation of the *Dewey Decimal Classification* had to be developed, which would take into account the context of both: topical headings and DDC classes. Second, the joins, the bridges had to be constructed for all 160,000 headings and 50,000 classes. All in all, we were constantly confronted with the task of harmonizing the practical work with theoretical reflections to achieve best possible results, a further aspect of bridge building – especially in the environment of an university of applied sciences. If regarded separately, each part threatens to fall into insignificance.

To invoke our metaphor, we might ask, which further bridge-building tasks describe the design of improved indexing and retrieval environments for future purposes. We could mention for example:

- Bridges understood as relations between semantic entities, headings and classes in indexing languages
- Bridges between best practice findings and new ideas
- Building bridges between findings of different disciplines, for example harmonizing the findings of knowledge organization with findings of formal knowledge representation.
- RDF-triples as example of newer forms of representation for typed relations between data entities in the context of linked data developments
- Definition of knowledge structures by representation of knowledge entities in semantically structured networks with possibilities of switching from one network to another along typed relations

Constructing new inventories containing both, new entities and new relations seems impossible. Instead new ideas of automatic indexing and collaborative approaches following well-defined rules, have to be implemented.

One of the speakers of our conference, *Stella Dextre Clarke*, recently stated in a contribution to an anthology devoted to future directions of information science:

> Designing a vocabulary for a specific retrieval application had always been a challenge. But to make it work across multiple networked applications adds a new dimension of complexity. The networks have opened up an array of different resources, systems and applications, and users want to search them all, at one pass. Indexing vocabularies can no longer be designed in isolation, if they are to serve in the interconnected world. Interoperability between systems is not just a buzzword; there is a real demand. [...] But eight years into the twenty-first century, at least one question is wide open: will developers of new applications, vocabularies and systems be content to follow the standards to realize the interoperability ad-

> vantages, or will practices continue to diverge as new technologies stimulate innovative approaches to knowledge organization?[2]

Herewith the concept of interoperability is addressed, a concept which comes close to bridge-building between entities of semantically structured vocabularies. Technically speaking interoperability means a standard for interchanging and processing of data. When considering semantically interpretable data this conception is often extended to ideas of semantic equivalence in order to improve retrieval systems. This extension is by no means trivial. To justify this extension and to embed it into the general conceptual framework when designing retrieval systems, some requirements have to be met. Without going into details I will briefly mention some points:

- Retrieval systems contain indexing data of utmost heterogeneity.
- Modelling semantic interoperability should be based on a conception of semantic equivalence or as a connection from entities of satellite systems to entities in a core ontology.
- It should be further studied whether it is possible to harmonize cognitive understanding and machine interpretation and what kind of improved retrieval could be realized by this harmonization.
- User-oriented systems should offer colloquial or even slang forms for verbal access as well as machine readable forms of representation for inference systems.
- The concept of semantic interoperability should be modelled within a formal structure with defined logical properties of relations between semantic entities allowing machines to draw inferences for retrieval purposes.
- Multilingual requirements should be kept in mind.
- When defining relations connecting conceptual entities, the resulting inventories should go beyond traditional thesaurus relations. Suggestions may be derived from former studies including ideas of building facetted or syntactical indexing devices.
- The benefit of enhanced relational inventories for retrieval systems has to be studied further.
- The requirements of formal models for representing semantic data like SKOS or RDF should be taken into account, desirable enhancements of the models should be proposed.
- Transformation – especially in form of relational enrichment – and future use of existing indexing languages seems to be more realistic than creating entirely new ones.
- Prospects and limitations of automatic procedures should be studied.

2 Dextre Clarke 2009: 56 and 57.

All these points may contribute to a transformation process which may lead to a transition from term based forms of information retrieval to concept based forms. One of our most visionary future goals would be the creation of indexing systems allowing for a conceptual navigation making use of an enriched inventory of conceptual relations and an appropriate selection mechanism supporting retrieval and exploration by drawing logically valid inferences along specified relations.

Many details have to be elaborated further, a very essential brace for all necessary efforts is the interoperability of concepts in context or by building bridges between semantically represented knowledge, the topic of this proceedings volume.

To conclude my introductory words, let me once more cite *Stella Dextre Clarke*:

> Gone are the preoccupations with keeping knowledge organization schemes and other tools down to a manageable size. Gone too are most of the difficulties of getting hold of the published literature. In their place we are now grappling with how to make easily navigable and searchable an increasingly diverse and complex network of systems, languages and resources.[3]

References

Dextre Clarke, Stella G. (2009). The last 50 Years of Knowledge Organization: A Journey Through My Personal Archives. In: Gilchrist, Alan (ed.). Information Science in Transition. London: Facet Publ. 45–62.

[3] Dextre Clarke 2009: 59.

Conceptual Foundations for Semantic Mapping and Semantic Search

Dagobert Soergel

Abstract: This article proposes an approach to mapping between Knowledge Organization Systems (KOS), including ontologies, classifications, taxonomies, and thesauri and even natural languages, that is based on deep semantics. In this approach, concepts in each KOS are expressed through canonical expressions, such as description logic formulas, that combine atomic (or elemental) concepts drawn from a core classification. Relationships between concepts within or across KOS can then be derived by reasoning over the canonical expressions. The canonical expressions can also be used to provide a facet-based query formulation front-end for free-text search. The article illustrates this approach through many examples. It presents methods for the efficient construction of canonical expressions (linguistic analysis, exploiting information in the KOS and their hierarchies, and crowdsourcing) that make this approach feasible.

1. *Introduction*

This article lays the foundation for developing the conceptual infrastructure for large-scale semantic interoperability across multiple collections using different Knowledge Organization Systems (KOS) such as ontologies, classifications, thesauri, and dictionaries in multiple languages and universal semantic-based search, especially facet-based search, either directly or through a query formulation front-end. Even mapping between natural languages is included. The focus lies on deep semantic match rather than syntactic interoperability.

Among the applications such an infrastructure would support are the following:

1. Semantic-based, especially facet-based, cross-language search across digital libraries, Web search engines, etc. based on any combination of cataloger-assigned subject metadata, social tags, and free text. Facet-based search may work through a front-end that lets the user formulate a query using a faceted classification and then maps to a query for the target system, which may use words and phrases from the text or social tags. This would support for instance:
   - Facet-based search across all collections in the European Library by mapping between the classifications and subject heading lists used by European National Libraries

- Mapping between KOS in the framework of FAO's Agricultural Ontology Server

2. Support for metadata creation (cataloging) by catalogers or users (assisted social tagging)
3. Support for creating new specialized or general KOS

All are supported by mapping between any two participating KOS through the canonical expressions in the hub. The long-range goal is the creation of a Web service where a KOS with canonical expressions can be uploaded and mappings to specified target KOS are returned.

The remainder of this article is organized as follows:

Section 2 introduces the idea of a KOS concept hub that consists of canonical expressions for compound concepts to enable mapping between KOS and formulating queries in terms of a KOS (controlled vocabulary queries) or enriched free-text queries. Section 2 illustrates this idea with simple examples.

Section 3 further illustrates this idea through examples from the knowledge bases of a hypothetical concept hub and applications with more complex examples.

Section 4 discusses the crucial issue of implementation. Here the key principle is that the canonical expression for a concept can be created locally, but through the canonical expression the concept is linked to other concepts globally. The Herculean task deriving canonical expressions to represent millions of concepts is made manageable through knowledge-based, computer-assisted or fully automated methods and through the use of crowdsourcing. This section also briefly discusses how to handle shades of meaning and multiple perspectives on the same topic and its structure.

Section 5 gives some historical background where these ideas come from and relationships to other work and Section 6 concludes the article.

2. *Mapping KOS through a hub*

Figure 1 illustrates the idea of mapping KOS through a hub in a nutshell.

In the proposed system, mapping and interoperability are achieved by representing concepts from all participating KOS through canonical expressions, such as a description logic formula using atomic concepts and relationships. This means that once some systems, for example, the Dewey Decimal Classification (DDC), the Library of Congress Classification (LCC) and the Library of Congress Subject Headings (LCSH), are represented in the hub through canonical expressions, uploading the Universal Decimal Classification (UDC) with canonical expressions for its concepts

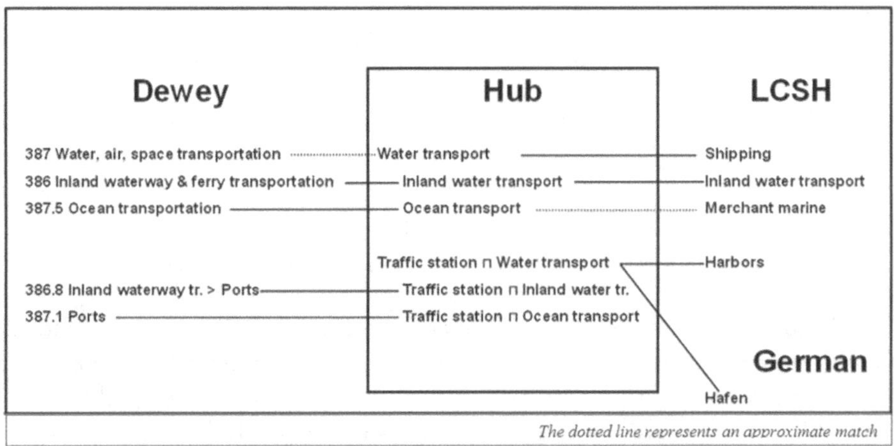

Figure 1: KOS mapping through a hub

would enable mapping between UDC and the other three schemes. Later in the article I will address the issue of feasibility and deal with the question how to produce canonical expressions for half a million classes in the Library of Congress Classification.

The atomic (elemental) concepts are taken from an extensible faceted core classification of atomic concepts which forms the backbone of the proposed system. As will be seen in later examples, the core classification is augmented with a set of relationships to enable more precise canonical expressions.

Mapping from KOS to KOS can be achieved by reasoning over these canonical expressions. In the simplest case, two concepts to be mapped have the same canonical expression. So to map German *Hafen* to LCSH, go from *Hafen* into the hub to find its canonical expression *Traffic station ⊓ Water transport*, and then go from that canonical expression into LCSH to find *Harbors*; the German concept and the mapped-to LCSH concept are on the same level. Mapping from DDC class 386.8 to LCSH is more complex: Going from 386.8 into the hub, we find the canonical expression *Traffic station ⊓ Inland water transport*. Going from there to LCSH, we find that there is no LCSH concept for that canonical expression. The LCSH term *Harbor* refers to traffic stations for any water transport (inland or ocean) while the DDC class 386.8 is restricted to traffic stations for inland water transport. But not all is lost; we can still find a mapping from DDC 386.8 to LCSH. The core classification shows that *Inland water transport* has above it *Water transport*, therefore we can reason that the canonical expression *Traffic station ⊓ Inland water transport* has above it *Traffic station ⊓ Water transport*; that expression leads to LCSH *Harbors*. So DDC 386.8 maps to the broader

LCSH concept *Harbors*. This simple example (cf. Figure 2) illustrates the power of the hub approach.

LCSH:	Harbors	= Traffic station ⊓ Water transport
German:	Hafen	= Traffic station ⊓ Water transport
DDC:	386.8 Inland waterway transportation > Ports	= Traffic station ⊓ Inland water transport

Figure 2: Examples for mapping from a German subject heading list and from the Dewey Decimal Classification to the Library of Congress Subject Headings

The beauty of the hub approach is that once several KOS, say A, B, and C, have been processed into the system (by finding the canonical expression for each of their concepts), a new KOS D can be included and mapped to A, B, and C (and vice versa) without the person working on D having any knowledge of A, B, or C. All that is needed is deriving the canonical expressions for the concepts in D, a <u>local</u> operation. Once that is done, the concepts of D are linked into a <u>global</u> network. The unifying force is the common core classifications.[1] The more concepts are processed into the system the more concepts can be handled partially or entirely automatically.

The core classification is envisioned as extensible. For example, in the Art and Architecture Thesaurus (AAT), *harbor* and *port* are differentiated. *Harbor* refers to a place where ships can safely rest, and *port* refers to the facilities to load and unload cargo etc. To express these AAT concepts, two elemental concepts, *Vehicle parking* and *Terminal facilities,* need to be added to the core classification under *Traffic station* (see Figure 3). These concepts are now available for general use. The core classification must be open to representing many perspectives and points of view; that can be accomplished by including many facets and by allowing alternate hierarchies under one concept. Problems arise when a term has shades of meaning. For example, a term may have slightly different meaning in different scientific schools – it may have the same broad concept but may assume a different meaning at a more specific level. Or a term may take on slightly different meanings over time. Or term A from language LA and term B from language LB are considered translation equivalent yet have subtle differences in meaning and connotations. In these cases the core classification must include highly differentiated concepts with appropriate comparative definitions under one umbrella concept. In time, the core classification would become a comprehensive universal faceted classification.

1 We eschew here the complexity of multiple core classifications that are mapped to each other, which is entirely possible.

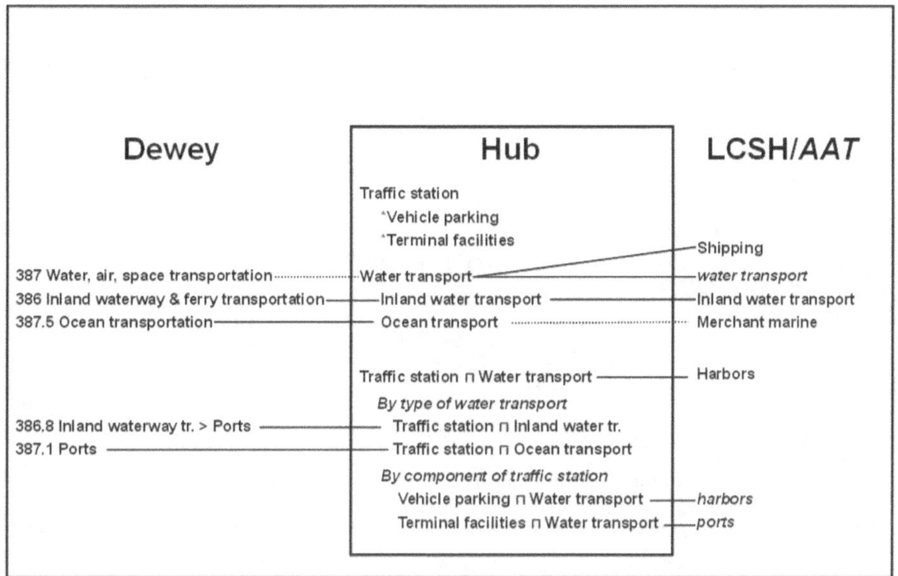

Figure 3: Amending the core classification

The hub can be used to formulate queries for any type of question. The user may just type in a free-text query; the system would use its database to represent the free-text query in a canonical expression in the hub. Or the user would be offered a facet-based search interface and, with guidance, formulate the query directly as a canonical expression. Either way, the system would map from the hub to a query formulation in the target system, be it a class number (or OR-combination of class numbers), a Boolean combination of controlled vocabulary descriptors, or an enriched free-text query for a Web search engine such as Google.

Figure 4 shows the general process of query formulation through a hub, Figure 5 gives an example. Section 3 gives more complex examples.

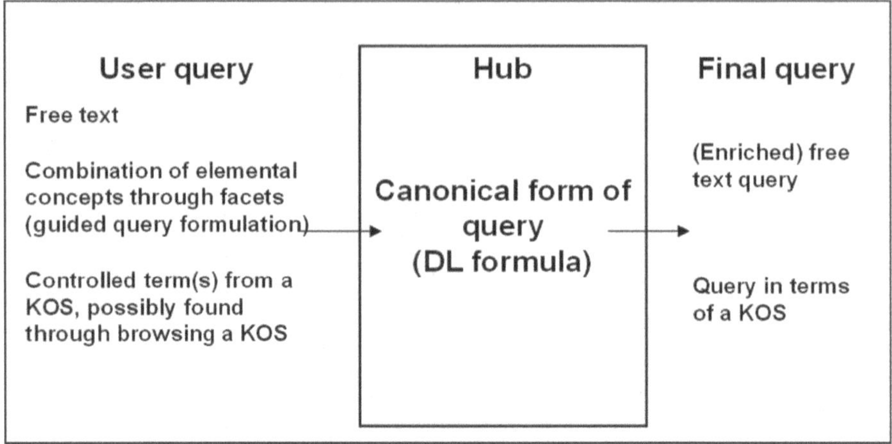

Figure 4: Mapping user queries through a hub

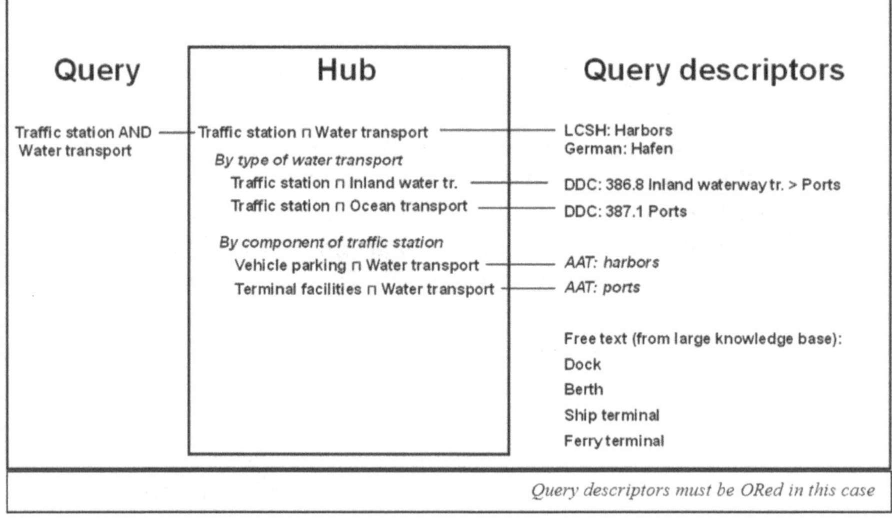

Figure 5: Query formulation through a hub

3. *Examples of Mapping KOS through a hub*

3.1 *Examples from the Library of Congress Classification (LCC) and the LC Subject Headings (LCSH)*

Figures 6a – d show the core classification, the canonical expressions for some LCC and LCH concepts, and the resulting mappings through a hub. Figures 7a and b illustrate how the system starts from a query formulated as a canonical expression and finds through the hub the LCC classes and LCSH subject headings one should use.

L00 Transportation and traffic L10 Traffic system components L13 Traffic facilities L15 Traffic stations L17 Vehicles L30 Modes of transportation L33 Air transport L37 Water transport	**P00 Buildings, construction** P23 Buildings P27 Architecture P43 Construction **R00 Engineering** R30 Acoustics R37 Soundproofing **T70 Military vs. civilian** T73 Military T77 Civilian

L10 and L30 are facets within L00, T70 is a general facet, facet structure of P00 and R00 not shown

Figure 6a: Sample core classification for LCC and LCSH

HE550-560 Ports, harbors, docks, wharves, etc.	= L15 Traffic stations ⊓ L37 Water transport ⊓ Civilian
NA2800 Architectural acoustics	= P27 Architecture ⊓ R30 Acoustics
NA6300-6307 Airport buildings	= L15 Traffic stations ⊓ L33 Air transport ⊓ P23 Buildings ⊓ T77 Civilian
NA6330 Dock buildings, ferry houses, etc.	= L15 Traffic stations ⊓ L37 Water transport ⊓ P23 Buildings ⊓ T77 Civilian
TC350-374 Harbor works	= L15 Traffic stations ⊓ L37 Water transport ⊓ R00 Engineering
TH1725 Soundproof construction	= P23 Buildings ⊓ P43 Construction⊓ R37 Soundproofing.
TL681.S6 Airplanes. Soundproofing	= L17 Vehicles ⊓L33 Air transport ⊓ R37 Soundproofing.
TL725-726 Airways (Routes). Airports and landing fields. Aerodromes	= L13 Traffic facilities ⊓ L33 Air transport
VA67-79 Naval ports, bases, reservations, docks	= L15 Traffic stations ⊓ L37 Water transp. : T73 Military
VM367.S6 Submarines. Soundproofing	= L17 Vehicles ⊓ L37 Water transport ⊓ R37 Soundproofing ⊓ Military.

Figure 6b: LC classes with decomposition into semantic factors

Aeroplanes-Soundproofing	= L17 Vehicles ⊓ L33 Air transport ⊓ R37 Soundproofing
Airports-Buildings	= P23 Buildings⊓ L15 Traffic stations ⊓ L33 Air transport
Buildings-Soundproofing	= P23 Buildings ⊓ P43 Construction ⊓ R37 Soundproofing
Ships-Soundproofing	= L17 Vehicles ⊓ L37 Water transport ⊓ R37 Soundproofing.

Figure 6c: LC subject headings with decomposition into semantic factors

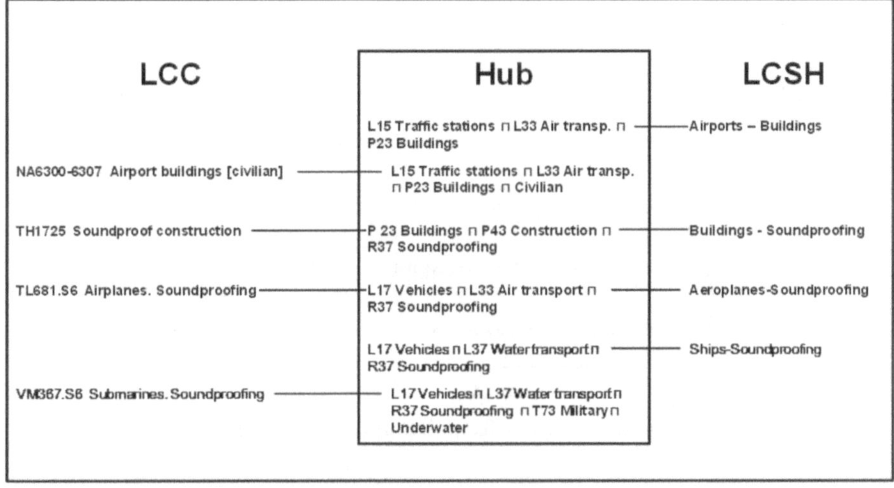

Figure 6d: Mapping between LCC and LCSH through a hub

Notice that in some cases there is a direct mapping between LCC and LCSH, and in other cases the concept in one scheme is narrower than the concept in the other scheme. In the examples, the LCC concept happens to be narrower in both cases. This can be easily seen from the canonical expressions. That in LCC *NA6300-6307 Airport buildings* actually means *civilian airport buildings* is something the editor just needs to know; *Military airports* would be in Class U *Military science.*

How we get all the canonical expressions to make mapping and query formulation possible is discussed in Section 4.2.

Figures 7a and b illustrate how from a query expressed through atomic descriptors (as constructed in a facet-guided search) the system finds the LCC classes and the LCSH headings to be used to find documents on the topic in a library using these schemes.

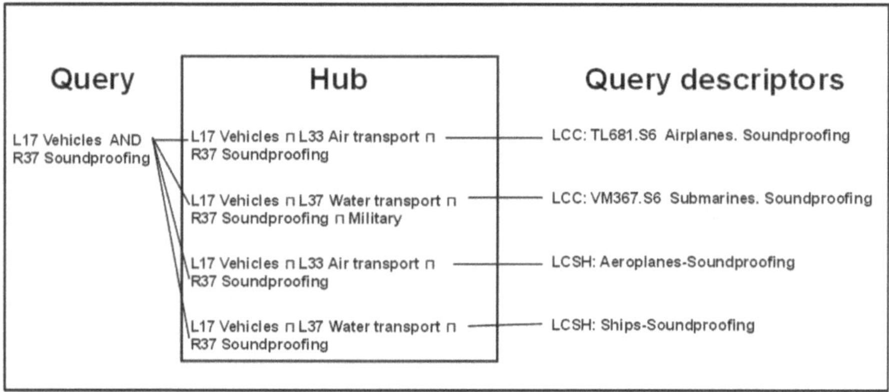

Figure 7a: Query formulation through a hub

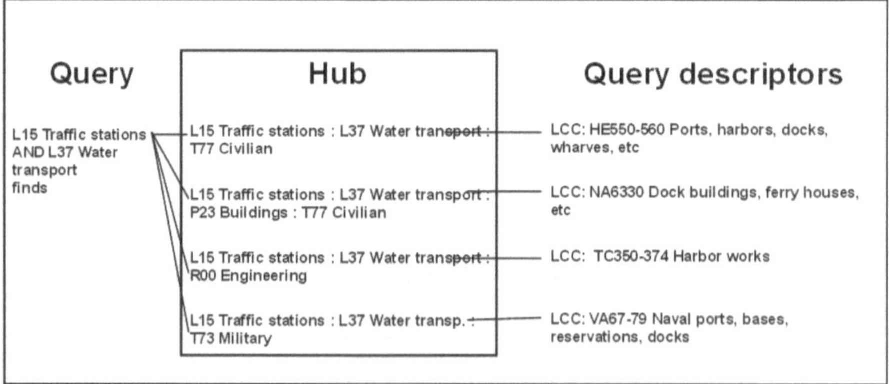

Figure 7b: Query formulation through a hub

3.2 *Examples illustrating the use of relationships in canonical expressions*

The examples in this section are taken from the following schemes:

- NALT National Agricultural Library Thesaurus
- LCSH Library of Congress Subject Headings
- DDC Dewey Decimal Classification
- SWD Schlagwortnormdatei (Germany)

They illustrate how canonical expressions can be made more precise by replacing the non-descript $\sqcap$ through specific relationships that carry more information. Figure 8 gives examples of mapping between DDC and SWD, and Figure 9 between LCSH and NALT. But many of the canonical expressions in the hub are the same, so we have a knowledge base that allows mapping from any of the four KOS to any other of the four KOS. Figure 10 gives a number of further examples.

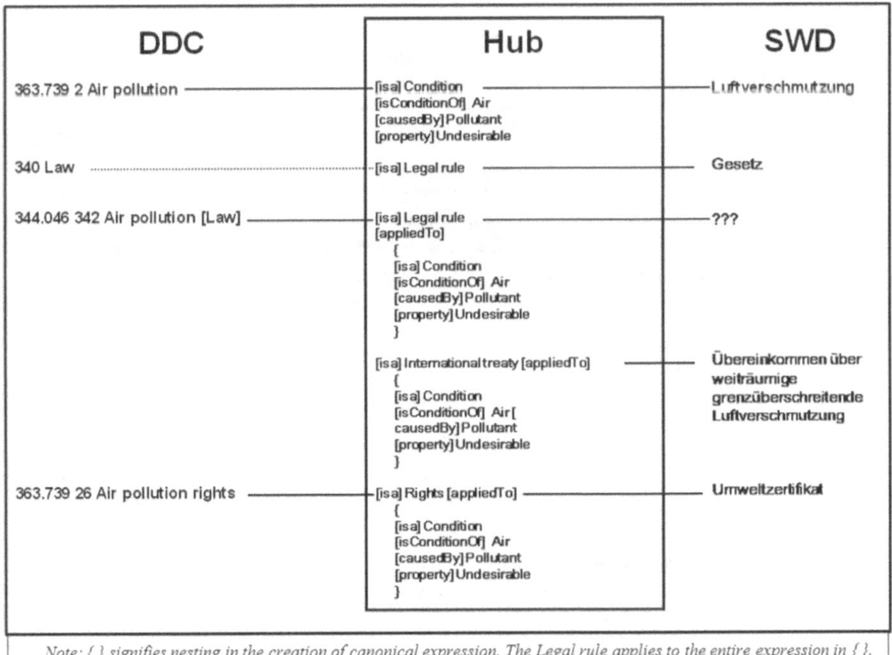

Note: { } signifies nesting in the creation of canonical expression. The Legal rule applies to the entire expression in { }.

Figure 8: Mapping through a hub. DDC and SWD.

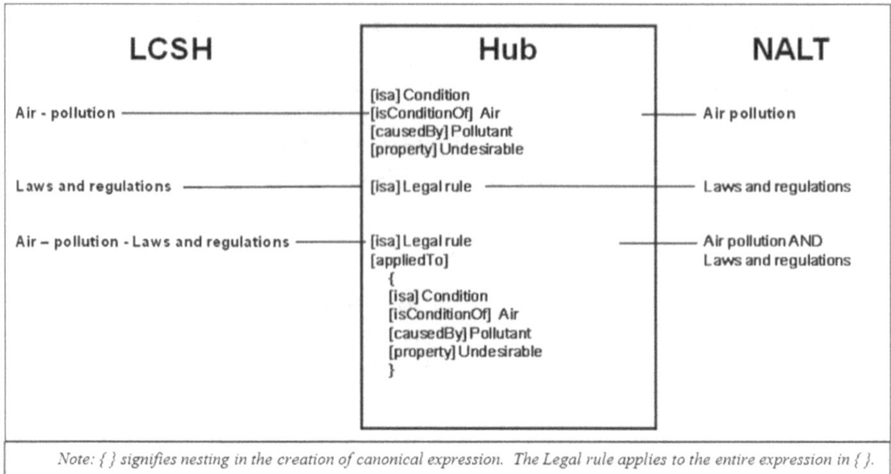

Figure 9: Mapping through a hub. LCSH and NALT.

LCSH term **Soil moisture** = [isa] Water [containedIn] Soil
NALT term **Soil water** = [isa] Water [containedIn] Soil
Mapping LCSH —► NALT Soil moisture —► Soil water

LCSH term **Greenhouse gardening** = [isa] Gardening [inEnvironment] Greenhouse [inEnvironment] Home
NALT terms
Home gardening = [isa] Gardening [inEnvironment] Home
Greenhouse = [isa] Greenhouse
Mapping LCSH —► NALT Greenhouse gardening —► Home gardening AND Greenhouse
Note: In LCSH, it is clear from the scope note and concept relationships that *Greenhouse gardening* refers only to home gardening in a greenhouse while NALT *Greenhouse* includes both home and commercial use.

LCSH term: **Salad greens** = [isa] Green leafy vegetable [usedFor] Salad
NALT term: **Green leafy vegetables** = [isa] Green leafy vegetable
Mapping LCSH —► NALT Salad greens —► **BT** Green leafy vegetables

LCSH term: **Emerging infectious diseases** = [isa] Disease [hasProperty] Infectious [hasProperty] Emerging
NALT term: **Emerging diseases** = [isa] Disease [hasProperty] Infectious ? [hasProperty] Emerging
Mapping LCSH —► NALT ???
Emerging infectious diseases —► Emerging diseases
Emerging infectious diseases —► **BT** Emerging diseases
Note: It is not clear whether in NALT all *emerging diseases* are infectious diseases. This needs to be clarified to arrive at the proper canonical expression and, through it, the proper mapping

Figure 10: More mapping examples. LCSH and NALT

Figure 11 shows an example where one DDC class maps to many narrower terms in the SWD but the SWD does not have a concept at the same level as the DDC class. The hierarchical relationships can be seen from the canonical expressions.

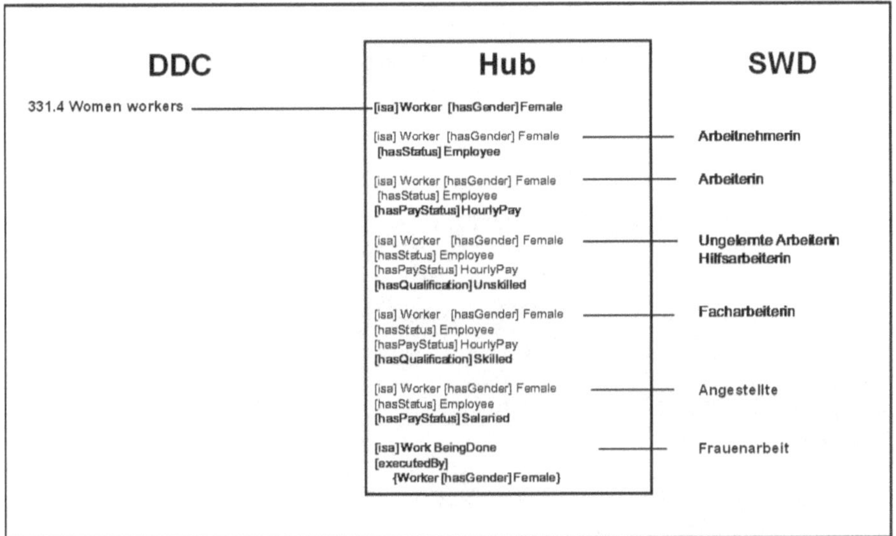

Figure 11: Mapping through a hub. One DDC to many NT SWD.

Figures 12a and b give examples from a different domain. They show how a proper knowledge base supports the formulation of comprehensive high-recall free-text queries. In these examples, the knowledge base contains

- Canonical expressions (conceptual knowledge)
- Broader Term and Narrower Term relationships (conceptual knowledge)
- Synonym relationships (terminological knowledge)
- Factual statements (the *<influences>* statement)

All three types of knowledge are used in creating the query formulation.

Physician	= [isa] Worker [profLevel] Doctoral [domain] Medicine
Oncologist	= [isa] Worker [profLevel] Doctoral [domain] Oncology
Ophthalmologist	= [isa] Worker [profLevel] Doctoral [domain] Ophthalmology

Physician	ST Doctor
Ophthalmologist	ST Eye doctor
Medicine	BT Health care
Medicine	Oncology
Medicine	Ophthalmology
[isa] Worker [profLevel] Doctoral	BT Professional
Income	ST Earnings
Income	NT Compensation
Compensation	ET Pay
Compensation	NT Wages

Fee schedule [usedBy] {Insurance company [domain] Health care}
<*influences*> Compensation [receivedBy] Physician

Figure 12a: Knowledge base used in query formulation

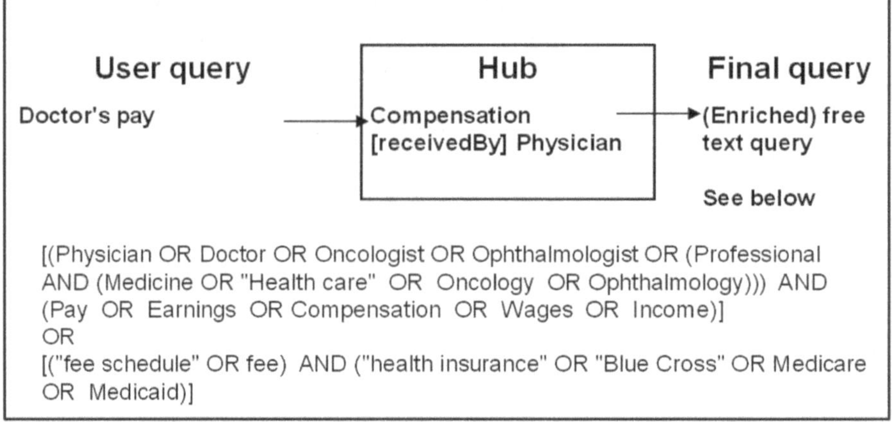

Figure 12b: Comprehensive query formulation through a hub

Figure 13 gives one last example of mapping through a hub, this time between

TGM	Thesaurus of Graphic Materials, Library of Congress
AAT Taiwan	TELDAP, Institute for Information Science, Academia Sinica
TGM	Thesaurus of Graphic Materials, Library of Congress

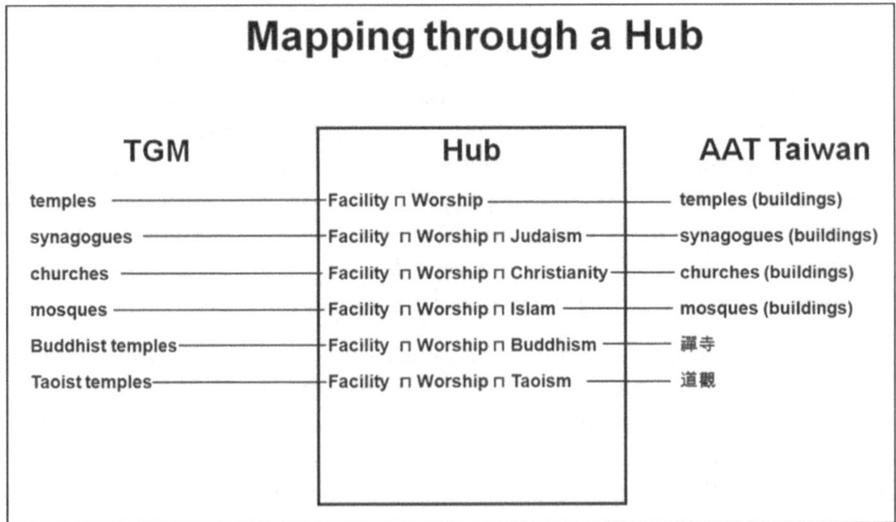

Figure 13: Mapping through a hub. TMG and AAT Taiwan

4. *Issues of implementation*

4.1 Knowledge base and general principles

The implementation of a comprehensive KOS mapping system[2] requires an ever growing classification and lexical knowledge base containing many kinds of data:

1. An extensible core classification: a faceted classification of atomic concepts and a set of relationships types seeded from sources with well-developed facets such as
   UDC
   the Alcohol and Other Drug (AOD) Thesaurus
   the Harvard Business Thesaurus
   the Art and Architecture Thesaurus
   various systems called ontologies
2. Linguistic knowledge bases such as WordNet, E-HowNet (Chinese), FrameNet, and mono-, bi- and multi-lingual dictionaries and thesauri
3. Many KOS such as LCC, UDC, DDC, DMOZ directory, LCSH, Schlagwortnormdatei, MeSH and UMLS, AGROVOC, Gene Ontology with each concept expressed through a canonical expression

2 Here KOS is construed broadly to include the various natural languages.

4. The KOS should over time be fused into one large multilingual knowledge base with many terminological and translation relationships and relationships linking terms to concepts, with an increasing number of concepts semantically represented by a canonical expression. This system would function as one integrated virtual database. This does not mean that all data need to be in one physical database; they could also be, for example, in a number of Linked Open Data sets. It would be advantageous (not an absolute requirement) for all data sets to implement a piece of one overarching database schema.

The core classification is extensible and should be continuously updated by many contributors. It must be able to express shades of meaning and, in the long run, usage information. It also needs to be able to accommodate alternate hierarchies to represent different points of view. As mentioned earlier, over time this would become a universal faceted classification. Ideally, there should be one central faceted classification of core concepts, but multiple mapped core classifications could be used.

Key to this system is that every KOS has assigned a canonical expressions to its concepts – let's call this a *semantically enhanced KOS* or *SEKOS*. It is then a simple matter of reasoning over the canonical expressions to map from any SEKOS to any other SEKOS (somewhat dependent on the core classifications used).

An objection to this approach is that creating the canonical expressions requires so much work as to be infeasible. There are three approaches that can be used together to answer this objection:

1. Use linguistic processing of the terms (including classification captions) that designate a concept to assist in identifying the semantic components of the concept.
2. Use the structure of existing KOS. If we have the canonical expression for a broad concept we already know something about what to do with the concepts below it; we can use hierarchical inheritance to assist in deriving new canonical expressions.
3. Use crowdsourcing; many people and organizations can contribute canonical expressions and other pieces of knowledge.

4.2 Linguistic processing and hierarchical inheritance

Figures 6a and 14a - e give examples of a hypothetical computer-assisted system for assigning canonical expressions to the classes of the Library of Congress Classification.

L00 Transportation and traffic L10 Traffic system components L13 Traffic facilities L15 Traffic stations L17 Vehicles L30 Modes of transportation L33 Air transport L37 Water transport	**P00 Buildings, construction** P23 Buildings P27 Architecture P43 Construction **R00 Engineering** R30 Acoustics R37 Soundproofing **T70 Military vs. civilian** T73 Military T77 Civilian
L10 and L30 are facets within L00, T70 is a general facet, facet structure of P00 and R00 not shown	

Figure 6a: Sample core classification for LCC and LCSH *(Repeated here for easy reference)*

LCC class	Canonical expression
HE Transportation	L00 Transportation and traffic ⊓ T77 Civilian
HE550-560 Ports, harbors, docks, wharves, etc.	*Inherited*: L00 Transportation and traffic ⊓ T77 Civilian *Added by editor*: L15 Traffic stations ⊓ L37 Water transport *Resolved to*: **L15 Traffic stations ⊓ L37 Water transport ⊓ T77 Civilian**

Figure 14a: Deriving canonical expressions for LCC

Figure 14a illustrates how canonical expressions can be derived for LCC: The editor works on LCC broad class *HE Transportation* and all its subclasses. The class HE *Transportation* would seem like a straightforward lexical mapping, but it is not. In LCC, everything having to do with *military* is in classes U and V, so HE is *civilian transportation*; knowing this, the editor assigns the canonical expression that captures the meaning of HE.[3] Next the editor works on *HE550-560 Ports, harbors, docks, wharves, etc.* First, by hierarchical inheritance in the LCC hierarchy, and using the knowledge just entered into the database, the system shows two atomic concepts (semantic factors), *L00 Transportation and traffic* and T77 *Civilian*. Linguistic analysis in this case does not reveal semantic structure, so the editor needs to contribute intellectual effort to add the atomic concepts *L15 Traffic stations ⊓ L37 Water transport.* The system then determines from the core classification that L00 is broader than L37 and keeps only the narrower concept L37 (eliminating redundant atomic concepts). The editor's knowledge that HE is *civilian*, once entered into the database, is carried forward (inherited down) to all classes in HE.

3 The editor working on creating canonical expressions for the concepts in a given KOS has to be familiar with that KOS.

Figure 14b is self-explanatory. It is assumed that *Airport* and *Buildings* are already in the database with their canonical expressions. The terms in the class label correspond to semantic components in the class, so linguistic analysis is helpful. The editor's knowledge is needed for adding *Civilian*; the editor must know that *military airport buildings* are in Class U *Military Science*.

LCC class	Canonical expression
NA6300-6307 Airport buildings	*From linguistic analysis and existing database* Airport = L15 Traffic stations ⊓ L33 Air transport Buildings = P23 Buildings *Checked by editor, editor adds*: T77 Civilian *Resolved to* **L15 Traffic stations ⊓ L33 Air transport ⊓ P23 Buildings ⊓ T77 Civilian**

Figure 14b: Deriving canonical expressions for LCC

In Figure 14c, the editor does not add *Civilian* because she knows that this class would also be applied to military airplanes.

LCC class	Canonical expression
TL681.S6 Airplanes. Soundproofing	*From linguistic analysis and existing database*: Airplane = L17 Vehicles ⊓ L33 Air transport Soundproofing = R37 Soundproofing *Checked by editor, editor adds*: Nothing *Resolved to* **L17 Vehicles ⊓ L33 Air transport ⊓ R37 Soundproofing**

Figure 14c: Deriving canonical expressions for LCC

LCSH subject heading	Canonical expression
Aeroplanes-Soundproofing	*From linguistic analysis and existing database:* Aeroplanes = Airplane [Spelling variant] *Therefore term is recognized as the same as* Airplanes. Soundproofing *Resolved to* **L17 Vehicles ⊓ L33 Air transport ⊓ R37 Soundproofing**

Figure 14d: Deriving canonical expressions for LCSH

Figure 14e is self-explanatory. This case is quite clear-cut; there is no need for an editor to check the result of the computer program. 70% of LCC classes are of this type.

LCC class	Canonical expression
Any class formed by geographical subdivision, such as NA6300-6307 Airport buildings **NA6305.E3 Egypt**	*Egypt* recognized using a dictionary of geographical names Inherits from subject class above it; simply add the country, **no editor checking needed.** L15 Traffic stations ⊓ L33 Air transport ⊓ P23 Buildings ⊓ T77 Civilian ⊓ **Egypt**

Figure 14e: Deriving canonical expressions for LCC

As can be seen from the examples in Figure 14a – e, a good deal of the work of deriving canonical expressions can be automated, using knowledge available in a database that is updated instantaneously as the editor makes decisions. The Library of Congress Classification has about half a million classes. About 70% of these are subdivisions by geography or language or form or similar recurring elements; these can be handled entirely automatically without checking by the editor. For another 23% the system can derive suggestions of semantic components by linguistic analysis of the term (caption) for the class; these need to be checked and often modified by the editor. Only 7% require intellectual effort unassisted by computer processing.[4]

In the process of creating canonical expressions the editor will encounter cases where an atomic concept is missing from the core classification and will add an atomic concept subject to be reviewed by the editor(s) of the core classification.

4.3 Distributed implementation. Crowdsourcing

Key principles of the approach are:

- Canonical expressions are created locally.
- The hub places each concept in a global structure.

The person or algorithm producing canonical expressions need to know only the core classification and the KOS to be transformed into a semantically enhanced KOS. They need not know the structure of the often large other KOS to which or from which the KOS being processed is to be mapped. Thus this approach lends itself to crowdsourcing; many small con-

4 Soergel 1990.

tributions can make a large and unified edifice. The organization that "owns" a KOS may take responsibility for creating canonical expressions for its KOS concepts, or they may give a stamp of approval to canonical expressions for their concepts created by others.

Ideally the system would offer a user-friendly interface anyone could use for computer- and knowledge-base-assisted creation of canonical expressions as illustrated in Section 4.2. There would need to be some system of editorial approval, not for inclusion of data into the system – any contribution would be accepted – but to offer users the ability to select data by their approval status. The core classification in particular would need editorial control because of its central importance.

5. *Relationship to other thought*

This proposal draws on many well-known ideas.

The idea of expressing concepts as combinations of atomic (or elemental) concepts has been around at least since the creation of the earliest Chinese characters (before 1,000 BC), many of which combined graphical elements each expressing a semantic component. It has been formalized by Leibniz[5], among others, introduced by Kaiser as a principle of creating subject catalogues[6] and systematized and promoted by Ranganathan[7] and the British Classification Research Group[8]. The best book is still Vickery's *Faceted Classification* from 1960[9]. Faceted classification and faceted search are increasingly used on the Web, especially on e-commerce sites. In 2008 a special issue of Axiomathes[10] was devoted to faceted classification. In *Beyond Facets: Semantic Roots and Modifiers* Soergel takes the idea to still more basic components.[11] In linguistics, the same idea is known as componential analysis.[12] Canonical expressions in a format called *semantic code*, which is similar to description logic, has been used in an early computer retrieval system at the Case Western Reserve University.[13] In the 1990s, the idea of expressing concepts as combinations of atomic (or elemental) concepts has

---

5 Wikipedia 2011b.
6 Kaiser 2011.
7 Ranganathan 1933, 1937.
8 Cf. http://www.iva.dk/bh/lifeboat_ko/CONCEPTS/classification_research_group.htm.
9 Vickery 1960.
10 Axiomathes 2008.
11 Soergel 1991.
12 Katz 1964; Wikipedia 2011a.
13 Melton 1958, Vickery 1959.

been formalized in *Description Logic* which provides a syntax for writing canonical expressions and tools for reasoning with them.[14]

The concept of a "switching language" for establishing mappings between many KOS has been around for quite a while, but it is not universally understood that a switching language must be in every area at least as detailed as any of the KOS to be mapped; we cite just one example, the Broad System of Ordering[15]. The same idea is called in linguistics, in the context of machine translation, *intermediate language*, a language into which a computer program could translate a French text and from which the program could translate into an English text, vastly simplifying translation between any pair of languages. This idea did not work out because the intermediate languages used were not expressive enough to capture all the information present in the French text required for proper choice of words and sentence structure in the English text.

The idea of using canonical expression as the switching language (our hub) is described in *A General Model for Indexing Languages* by Soergel[16] (without a claim of being first). It is implemented, in a limited way, in *Semantic matching with S-Match* by Shvaiko, Giunchiglia & Yatskevich.[17]

There is a great deal of work on ontology mapping or ontology matching (formerly known as thesaurus compatibility or convertibility). It is concerned primarily with methods for deriving pairwise mappings between KOS. This work is relevant for automatic or computer-assisted derivation of canonical expressions for elements of a KOS. An example of this is *Crowd Sourcing Through Social Gaming for Community Driven Ontology Engineering, Results and Observations* by Shvaiko, Giunchiglia & Yatskevich. Much material can be found on the website *http://ontologymatching.org/*. In *Classification and Review of Ontology Mapping Methods* Whitlow & Soergel[18] provide material for a classification and give a review of methods.

Collaborative development and crowdsourcing need no further introduction. It is now widely accepted that they can be used for ontology development provided proper assistance to contributors through a good interface and quality control. In *SemWeb. Proposal for an Open, Multifunctional, Multilingual System for Integrated Access to Knowledge Base About Concepts and Terminology* Soergel proposed a system for this purpose.[19] Sini et al. describe

14 For a good tutorial, see Baader 2005.

15 The website of *BSO – Broad System of Ordering* is available at: http://www.ucl.ac.uk/fatks/bso/. See also Soergel 1979.

16 Soergel 1972.

17 Shvaiko, Giunchiglia & Yatskevich 2010.

18 Whitlow & Soergel 2008.

19 Soergel 1996.

in *The AGROVOC Concept Server Workbench System*[20] a workbench for the collaborative development and maintenance of vocabularies with an elaborate system of authorizations. In the biomedical community collaborative work on ontologies is common. Some dictionaries on the Web, such as the Wiktionary[21], are produced through user inputs. Further examples are *Crowd sourcing through social gaming for community driven ontology engineering, results and observations* by Chua et al.[22] and *Crowdsourcing the assembly of concept hierarchies* by Eckert et al.[23]

6. *Conclusion*

This article proposes an approach to mapping between Knowledge Organization Systems (KOS), including ontologies, classifications, taxonomies, and thesauri and even natural languages, that is based on deep semantics. In this approach, concepts in each KOS are expressed through canonical expressions, such as description logic formulas, that combine atomic (or elemental) concepts drawn from a core classification. Relationships between concepts within or across KOS can then be derived by reasoning over the canonical expressions. The canonical expressions can also be used to provide a facet-based query formulation front-end for free-text search. The article argues that this approach is feasible by presenting methods for the efficient construction of canonical expressions (linguistic analysis, exploiting information in the KOS and their hierarchies, and crowdsourcing).

It is time to unify many disparate KOS development and KOS mapping efforts on a sound semantic footing and use the power of deep semantics to vastly improve support for users. The article argues that this is technically feasible. Whether it is politically and organizationally feasible is a different matter entirely. Implementation of such a system would require (1) a concerted effort of major players in the library world, in Web search, and in the ever increasing applications of ontologies in the sciences and (2) strong encouragement from funding agencies.

---

20 Sini et al. 2010.

21 Cf. http://en.wiktionary.org/wiki/Wiktionary:Main_Page.

22 Chua et al. 2010.

23 Eckert et al. 2010.

References

Web documents were accessed on May 31, 2011.

Axiomathes 2008. Theme Issue on Faceted Classification. In: Axiomathes 18 (2).

Baader, Franz. (2005). Description Logic Tutorial. Five Lectures at The 2005 Logic Summer School of the Research School of Information Sciences and Engineering at the Australian National University and at the ICCL Summer School 2006.

Slides of the 1st lecture are available at: http://lat.inf.tu-dresden.de/~baader/Talks/dl1.pdf.

Slides of the 2nd lecture are available at: http://lat.inf.tu-dresden.de/~baader/Talks/dl2.pdf.

Slides of the 3rd lecture are available at: http://lat.inf.tu-dresden.de/~baader/Talks/dl3.pdf.

Slides of the 4th lecture are available at: http://lat.inf.tu-dresden.de/~baader/Talks/dl4.pdf.

Slides of the 5th lecture are available at: http://lat.inf.tu-dresden.de/~baader/Talks/dl5.pdf.

Chua, Alloy Martin et al. (2010). Crowd Sourcing Through Social Gaming for Community Driven Ontology Engineering, Results and Observations. Poster. In: Fifth International Workshop on Ontology Matching collocated with the 9th International Semantic Web Conference ISWC-2010, November 7, 2010 Shanghai. Available at: http://disi.unitn.it/~p2p/OM-2010/om2010_poster13.pdf.

Eckert, Kay et al. (2010). Crowdsourcing the Assembly of Concept Hierarchies. In: JCDL. Proceedings of the 10th Annual Joint Conference on Digital libraries. 139–148.

Kaiser, Julius. (1911). Systematic Indexing. London: Pitman. OCR reprint. General Books 2010.

Katz, Jerrold J. (1964). Semantic Theory and the Meaning of "Good". In: Journal of Philosophy 61 (23) : 739-766.

Melton, John L. (1958). The Semantic Code. In: Perry, J[ames] W[hitney]; Kent, Allen (eds.). Tools for Machine Literature Searching: Semantic Code Dictionary, Equipment, Procedures. New York: Interscience Publishery. 221-279.

Ranganathan, Shiyali R. (1933). Colon Classification. 1st ed. Madras: Madras Library Association.

Ranganathan, Shiyali R. (1937). Prolegomena to Library Classification. 1st ed. Madras: Madras Library Association.

Ruckley, Ryan (aka ToneDuff). (2008) Crowd Sourcing the Semantic Web. Blog post. In: Nurd Land. Technical Postings from a Self confessed Geek [Blog]. Available at: http://nurdland.blogspot.com/2008/07/crowd-sourcing-semantic-web.html.

Shvaiko, Pavel; Giunchiglia, Fausto; Yatskevich, Mikalai. (2010). Semantic Matching with S-Match. In: De Virgilio, Roberto; Giunchiglia, Fausto; Tanca, Letizia (eds). Semantic Web Information Management. A Model-based Perspective. Berlin: Springer. 183-203.

Sini, Margherita et al. (2010). The AGROVOC Concept Server Workbench System: Empowering Management of Agricultural Vocabularies with Semantics. In: IAALD XIIIth World Congress,Montpellier (France), 26-29 April 2010. (Unpublished) [Conference Paper]. Available at: http://eprints.rclis.org/handle/10760/15187?mode=full.

Soergel, Dagobert. (1972). A General Model for Indexing Languages: The Basis for Compatibility and Integration. In: Subject Retrieval in the Seventies – New Directions. New York: Greenwood; College Park, Md.: University of Maryland, School of Library and Information Services. 36-61.

Soergel, Dagobert. (1979). The Broad System of Ordering -- A Critique. In: International Forum on Information and Documentation 4 (3) : 21-24.

Soergel, Dagobert. (1990). Investigating the Structure of LCC and LCSH. Developing a Knowledge Base. In: Annual Review of OCLC Research. July 1989 – June 1990. Dublin, OH: Online Computer Library Center. 54-55.

Soergel, Dagobert. (1991). Beyond Facets: Semantic Roots and Modifiers as Elements of a Conceptual Morphology. In: Proceedings of the 2nd American Society for Information Science/SIG-CR Classification Research Workshop. Held at the 54th ASIS Annual Meeting, Washington, DC, Oct. 27, 1991. Washington, DC: ASIS. 149-158. (Advances in Classification Research 3). Available at: http://www.dsoergel.com/cv/B36.pdf.

Soergel, Dagobert. (1996). SemWeb. Proposal for an Open, Multifunctional, Multilingual System for Integrated Access to Knowledge Base about Concepts and Terminology. In: Proceedings of the Fourth International ISKO Conference, 15-18 July 1996, Washington, DC. Frankfurt/Main: Indeks Verlag. (Advances in Knowledge Organization 5). 165-173. Available at: http://www.dsoergel.com/cv/B58.pdf.

Vickery, Brian C. (1959). The Structure of "Semantic Coding", a Review. In: American Documentation 10 (3) : 234-41.

Vickery, Brian C. (1960). Faceted Classification. A Guide to Construction and Use of Special Schemes. London: Aslib.

Whitlow, Abby; Soergel, Dagobert. (2008). Classification and Review of Ontology Mapping Methods. Course Paper. College Park, MD: University of Maryland, College of Information Studies. Available at: http://

www.dsoergel.com/WhitlowOntologyMappingReviewUMDLBSC7092008Sp.pdf.

Wikipedia. (2011a). Componential Analysis. Available at: http://en.wikipedia.org/wiki/Componential_analysis.

Wikipedia. (2011b). Gottfried Leibniz. Symbolic Thought. Available at: http://en.wikipedia.org/wiki/Leibniz#Symbolic_thought.

Insights and Outlooks: A Retrospective View on the CrissCross Project

Jan-Helge Jacobs, Tina Mengel, Katrin Müller

Abstract: This paper discusses goals, methods and benefits of the conceptual mapping approach developed by the CrissCross project, in the framework of which the topical headings of the German subject headings authority file Schlagwortnormdatei (SWD) have been mapped to notations of the Dewey Decimal Classification (DDC). Project-specific retrieval concepts for improving thematic access in heterogeneous information spaces are outlined and explained on the basis of significant examples.

1. CrissCross project

The CrissCross project started in 2006 and ended in autumn 2010. It has been conducted by the German National Library (Deutsche Nationalbibliothek) and the Cologne University of Applied Sciences (Fachhochschule Köln). Financially it has been supported by the German Research Foundation (Deutsche Forschungsgemeinschaft). The aim was to create a thesaurus-based and user-friendly research vocabulary to facilitate search in heterogeneously indexed collections by linking topical headings of the German subject headings authority file Schlagwortnormdatei (SWD) to notations of the Dewey Decimal Classification (DDC).

As subject access in networked information spaces is less effective due to the co-existence of different knowledge organization systems (KOS) various approaches have been developed to connecting KOS in order to create inter-system interoperability. CrissCross integrates two already established and widely used KOS by creating crosswalks to improve retrieval processes and, at the same time, ensure the continuous use of already existing indexing data.

1.1 DDC

The Dewey Decimal Classification (DDC) is the most widely used universal classification system. It has been translated into more than 30 languages and is used by 200,000 libraries in over 135 countries.[1] Since 2006 the German National Library has been using the DDC for subject indexing.

Due to increased translation activities, the perspective of the DDC, which in its beginning strongly emphasized the American point of view,

1 OCLC 2009.

has become more and more international. Classes have been added or have been expanded in their scope of meaning to achieve better accommodation of local needs (concerning e.g. cultural and social issues).

Since the DDC is structured by disciplines, concepts can appear in classes within more than one discipline. "Cardigans" for example are located in the fields "Costume and personal appearance" (391), "Sewing, clothing, management of personal and family life" (646), and "Clothing and accessories" (687).

The 22nd edition, which was the work basis for the mapping procedure, contains about 50,000 classes.[2] Additionally, number building allows for synthesizing new classes to represent not yet covered complex concepts. The classes of the DDC are represented by notations in Arabic numerals. By this, linguistic problems are avoided and the DDC becomes a globally usable system.

1.2 SWD

The German subject headings authority file Schlagwortnormdatei (SWD) is a universal indexing language that is being used for subject indexing in German speaking countries since 1988. It contains 550,000 headings divided into different categories, such as geographical names, topical headings (concepts and objects), headings for time and form, names of institutions (corporate bodies), and titles of works.[3] The topical headings are structured in 37 subject groups which again are divided in subgroups. Three types of relations describe the semantic relationships between the headings: equivalent, hierarchical and associative. However, according to an unpublished study which has been executed in 2004 by the Cologne University of Applied Sciences on behalf of the German National Library, almost 87 % of all topical headings had no associative relations and about 34 % had neither hierarchical nor associative relations at all. In the context of CrissCross about 160,000 topical headings of the SWD had to be mapped to classes of the DDC. (In the following, topical headings are referred to as headings or SWD headings.)

1.3 Methods

The outlined characteristics of the DDC combined with its widespread use and its universal scope enabled it to serve as the target system to which the headings of the SWD were being mapped.

2 Gödert 2002: 399.
3 Jahns 2009: 3.

In CrissCross, mapping practice was characterized by three guidelines:

1. *One-to-many strategy:* According to the discipline-based structure of the DDC, one SWD heading could be mapped to several classes in different disciplines. For example, the heading "Kaffee" (coffee) has been allocated to the following classes: `583.93 Gentianales` in the discipline "Plants (Botany)", `633.73 Coffee` in the discipline "Agriculture", and `641.3373 Coffee` in the discipline "Home & family management". By this means several aspects of one concept can be represented.
2. *Deep level mapping:* This was applied to ensure that the meaning of a heading could be represented as specific as possible. Although the 22nd edition of the DDC already provides 50,000 classes, there often was the need to display more complex subjects as the meaning of the SWD headings is often more specific than the already existing DDC classes. To describe for example the complex concept "breeding of coffee" (in the SWD expressed by the heading "Kaffeezüchtung"), the classes `633.73 Coffee` and `631.52 Production of propagational organisms and new varieties` were being synthesized to create the built number `633.732`. If there was no number building allowed, the SWD heading was mapped to the superordinate class.
3. *Degrees of Determinacy (D):* The relation between SWD heading and class is described by four *Degrees of Determinacy (D)*. These degrees range from full (D4) to partial coverage (D1) and indicate the conceptual congruency between heading and class. Due to the unidirectionality of the mappings with the DDC as the target system these degrees provide only information about the relation of a heading to a class and not vice versa.

   D4: A concept represented by a heading mapped with D4 is by this definition fully congruent to the connotation scope of the class. This is the only case where the relation between heading and class can be characterized as a bidirectional one.

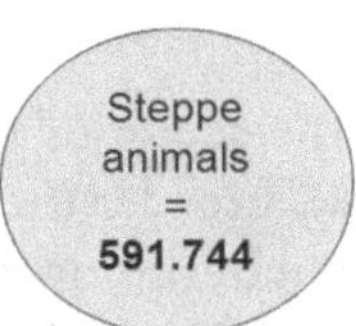

Figure 1: Full conceptual coverage between SWD heading "Steppentiere" (Steppe animals) and DDC class `591.744 Steppe animals`

D3: D3 represents a slight degradation of D4. Thus, the meaning of a heading approximates the connotation scope of a class to a large extent, but not fully.

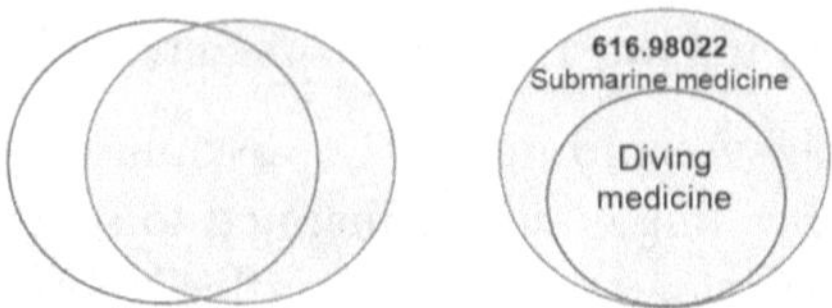

Figure 2: The heading "Tauchmedizin" (diving medicine) in relation to the class `616.98022 Submarine medicine`

D2: This degree indicates far less congruency than D3 and is for example used in cases where the SWD heading is only one concept among many others or if a heading has been matched to a superordinate class.

Figure 3: The SWD heading "Hausfrau" (housewife) is only one of a number of possible persons in the class `640.92 Home economists`

D1: D1 describes only slight conceptual congruency between heading and class.

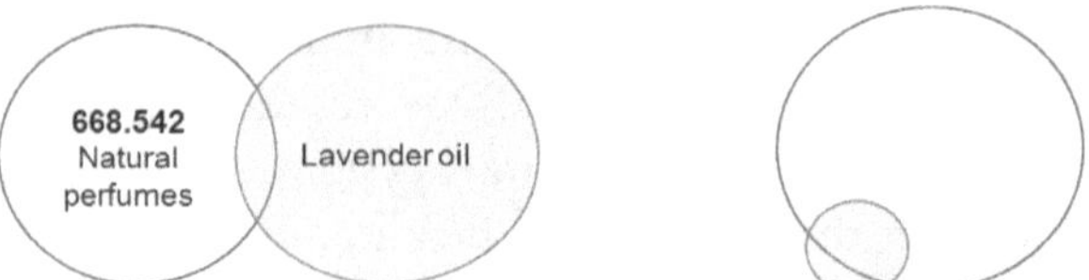

Figure 4: "Lavendelöl" (lavender oil) is mapped with D1 to `668.542 Natural perfumes` as it, among other aspects, serves as the basis for perfumes

1.4 *Mapping process*

The first step was to identify the scope of the heading. This was done by looking at synonyms (field 830), broader (field 850) and narrower headings (not visible in Figure 5) and by consulting reference books (field 808 contains the source of the heading). After that, the corresponding DDC classes had to be found out. Following the *one-to-many-strategy*, more than one class could be attached to a heading. These classes were verified by checking titles with the according notations in WorldCat and other library catalogues. Then the Degree of Determinacy had to be determined for each class. After that, notation plus Degree of Determinacy were inserted in the SWD record (field 816).

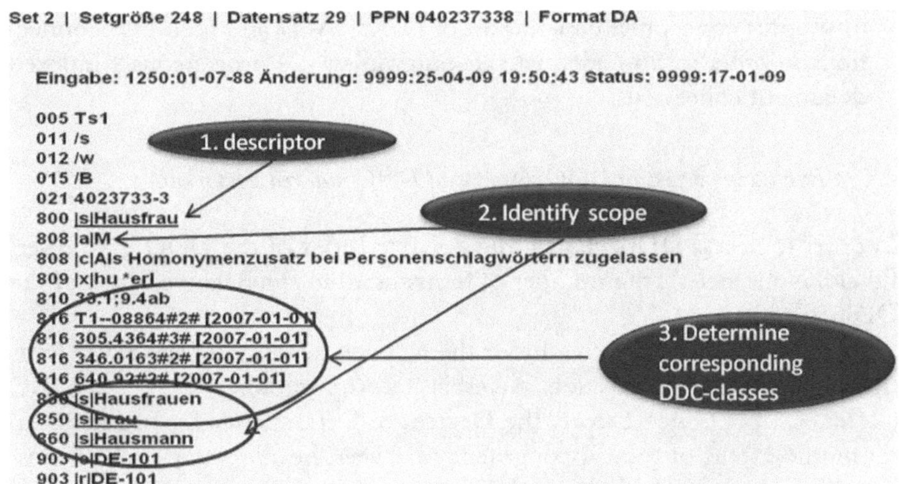

Figure 5: Screenshot of the record "Hausfrau" in the SWD database

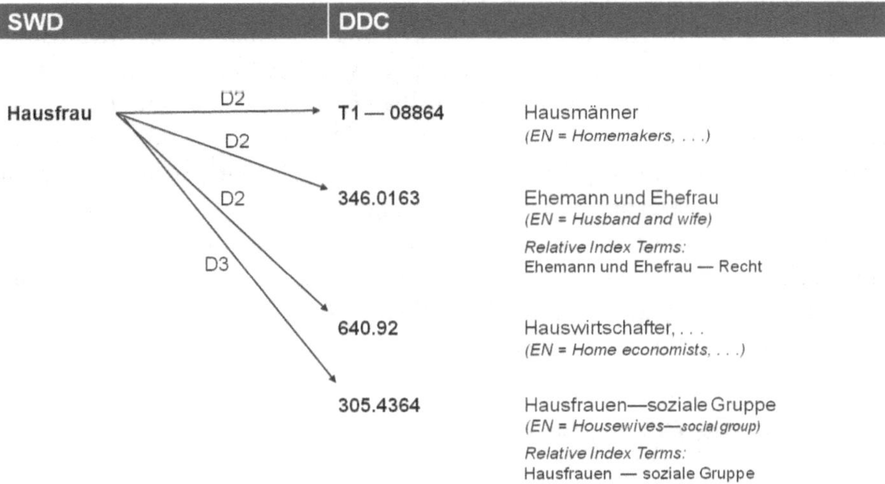

Figure 6: The SWD term "Hausfrau" with its corresponding DDC classes and the Degrees of Determinacy of the mappings

2. *Retrieval*

The mappings produced within the CrissCross project are first and foremost tools to optimize retrieval processes. Three main applications can be emphasized: Utilization of the mappings

- to enhance access to the DDC itself and to DDC-indexed documents,
- to structure document sets (search result lists) via mappings,

- to support conceptual exploration of DDC, SWD and their interconnections in order to find adequate access points to heterogeneously indexed document collections

2.1 *Enhancing access to DDC classes and DDC-indexed documents*

In order to access DDC classes, the Relative Index of the DDC is a powerful aid. Nonetheless, the number of terms listed in the Relative Index of the DDC is limited.

In addition to the Relative Index the mapped headings of the SWD (plus their synonyms) can function as verbal and topical access points to DDC classes. As mentioned before, the Degrees of Determinacy are meant to indicate the extent of topical congruency between heading and class. It must be taken into account that most of the mappings do not express an equivalence relationship between heading and class therefore the shift in scope has to be made transparent to the user.

An example for this would be the heading "Drehkran" (slewing crane) which is mapped with D2 to the DDC class `621.873 Cranes`. A user could thus be guided from the SWD heading "Drehkran" to the DDC number `621.873`. However, documents classified with this number do not always cover the subject "Drehkran". The most relevant documents about this subject can be expected when searching for "[SWD heading]:Drehkran AND [DDC number]:`621.873`". If the collection contains documents that are not indexed with SWD headings, alternative search strategies can be applied, e.g. by the combined search for "[title keyword]:Drehkran (or its synonyms) AND [DDC number]:`621.873`".

2.2 *Structuring document sets*

A query for a class number may produce many search results, whereas not all documents might be relevant to the user's information need. For example, the information seeker may look for a specific topic that is one amongst other topics represented by a DDC class or he may be primarily interested in documents that treat the topic of a DDC class comprehensively. In order to find documents that are most relevant to the overall topic of a DDC class, all documents indexed with an SWD heading that is mapped to this class with D4 or D3 could be ranked accordingly high. For example, documents indexed with the D3-mapped heading "Kran" (crane) can be considered most relevant for the DDC class `621.873 Cranes`, whereas documents indexed with a more specific heading such as "Drehkran" (slewing crane) could be ranked lower. Thus, document sets with a specific DDC number can be structured (and transparently presented as grouped search results) according to mapped headings and their Degree of Determinacy, whereas the practical relevance of the documents need not necessarily correspond with the order of their presentation. In order to narrow down the document set according to his individual information need, the information seeker may choose between the mapped headings of a DDC class.

A search result list for a heading query can also be structured with the help of CrissCross mappings. Such a hit list can be grouped according to the mapped DDC numbers. Thus, the document list would be structured by DDC disciplines or aspects.

If a query for an SWD heading retrieves too many documents, the user can narrow down the set of retrieved documents by selecting a specific DDC number in addition to the heading (= increase of precision). By picking one of the mapped DDC class numbers (or letting the system automatically choose the mapping with the highest Degree of Determinacy), a corresponding viewpoint or discipline is chosen and those documents are retrieved that treat the concept (expressed by the heading) in the context represented by the DDC class.

If the information seeker needs more recall when searching for an SWD heading, an additional search for mapped class numbers alone, truncation of class numbers or moving upwards in the DDC hierarchy may be some possibilities to mention, but in doing so, the decrease of precision in regard to the initial heading should also be kept in mind.

Table 1 shows a model search that makes use of the mappings to illustrate the surplus value of a CrissCross-powered search and its potential to refine search results. A possible ranking order is provided, in which a rough descending order of rank is expressed by numbers and subgroups that are expressed by letters.

The search entry is the SWD heading "Kabelbrücke" (cable-stayed bridge), which is mapped to the following DDC classes (with Degree of Determinacy and DDC discipline in brackets):

`624.23 Suspension and cable-stayed bridges` (D3, discipline: Engineering)

`725.98 Bridges, tunnels, moats` (D2, discipline: Architecture)

`388.132 Bridges` (D2, discipline: Transportation)

Ranking order	Conducted search	Search results
1a	SWD heading: Kabelbrücke AND DDC: 624.23 (D3)	No results
1b	SWD heading: Kabelbrücke AND DDC: 725.98 (D2)	No results
1b	SWD heading: Kabelbrücke AND DDC: 388.132 (D2)	No results
2	SWD heading: Kabelbrücke	9 potentially relevant documents
3a	DDC: 624.23 (D3)	1 document about bridges, not about cable-stayed bridges in particular
3b	DDC: 725.98 (D2)	27 documents about bridges, not about cable-stayed bridges in particular
3b	DDC: 388.132 (D2)	1 document, not about cable-stayed bridges but about a different kind of bridge
4	Title keyword: Kabelbrücke resp. title keyword: Kabelbrücke* (option: combine keyword search also with DDC search)	1 potentially relevant document when searching with truncation
5a	DDC: 624.23* (D3)	3 potentially relevant documents, e.g. about the Brooklyn Bridge (DDC: 624.23097471)
5b	DDC: 725.98* (D2)	countless documents, relevance not scrutinized
5b	DDC: 388.132* (D2)	countless documents, relevance not scrutinized
6	SWD heading: "Sevilla / Puente del Alamillo" (NT of Kabelbrücke)	1 potentially relevant document
	The whole process (as executed for ranking numbers 1-5) could be repeated for all Narrower and Related Terms	*Source: SWB Union OPAC*[4] *(accessed on July 15, 2010)*

Table 1: Exemplary ranking scenario for searches using CrissCross-mapped data

Another possible application would be the retrieval of documents indexed only with SWD headings via mapped DDC numbers, but this reverse use of the mappings could retrieve documents that are not necessarily matching

4 SWB Online Katalog. Available at: http://pollux.bsz-bw.de/DB=2.1.

the scope of the DDC class, because SWD headings usually are not tied to a certain discipline/aspect in the way DDC classes are.

2.3 *Conceptual Exploration*

Explorative search applications can assist the user in specifying his search query by giving an overview of the neighboring concepts of an initial keyword. In the beginning of a search the user is often still looking for a more precise term or he wants to be inspired by other subjects or subject categories that build the broader contextual frame of his initial keyword.

This section gives a closer look at some of the future possibilities given by the linkages of the CrissCross mappings and the links that already exist within the both knowledge organization systems DDC and the German subject headings authority file SWD.

An initial keyword may be the German word "Erfolg" (success), which is a concept treated in many different disciplines like economics, psychology, or occultism. The German topical heading "Erfolg" is assigned to four DDC classes, namely `650.1 Personal success in business` with D3, `302.14 Social participation` with D3, `158 Applied psychology` with D2, and `131 Parapsychological and occult methods for achieving well-being, happiness, success` with D1.

One thing that could be interesting for the user is to look at other headings mapped to the DDC classes that have been assigned to the German topical heading. Such a list of terms can help getting a first idea of the subjects treated within a discipline, and provides a basis for classic combination of search terms. The keyword "success" could then be easily combined with one like "self-management" or, searching in the field of social psychology, with one like "social recognition" (see Figure 7).

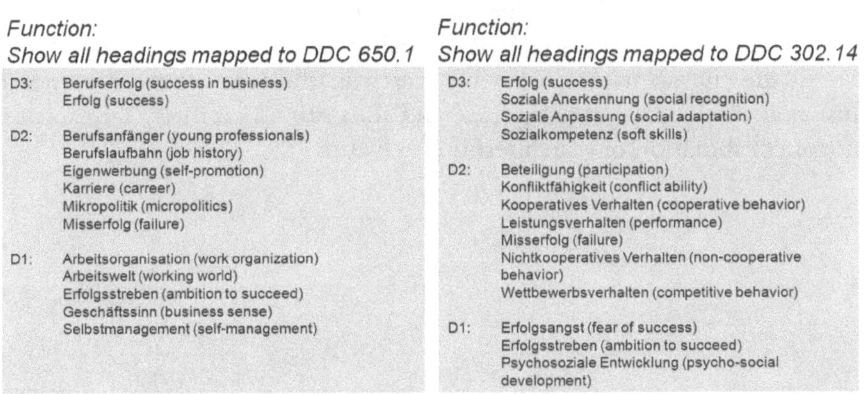

Function:
Show all headings mapped to DDC 650.1

D3: Berufserfolg (success in business)
Erfolg (success)

D2: Berufsanfänger (young professionals)
Berufslaufbahn (job history)
Eigenwerbung (self-promotion)
Karriere (carreer)
Mikropolitik (micropolitics)
Misserfolg (failure)

D1: Arbeitsorganisation (work organization)
Arbeitswelt (working world)
Erfolgsstreben (ambition to succeed)
Geschäftssinn (business sense)
Selbstmanagement (self-management)

Function:
Show all headings mapped to DDC 302.14

D3: Erfolg (success)
Soziale Anerkennung (social recognition)
Soziale Anpassung (social adaptation)
Sozialkompetenz (soft skills)

D2: Beteiligung (participation)
Konfliktfähigkeit (conflict ability)
Kooperatives Verhalten (cooperative behavior)
Leistungsverhalten (performance)
Misserfolg (failure)
Nichtkooperatives Verhalten (non-cooperative behavior)
Wettbewerbsverhalten (competitive behavior)

D1: Erfolgsangst (fear of success)
Erfolgsstreben (ambition to succeed)
Psychosoziale Entwicklung (psycho-social development)

Figure 7: Mappings sorted by Degrees of Determinacy showing class-associated terminology that could help the user orienting in the field of interest. The terms could be picked and combined to allow for more specific Boolean searches

In the German classification tool MelvilClass the sorted display of mapped topical headings in the DDC class has already been realized: The linked topical headings are listed according to their Degree of Determinacy and serve not only as additional access points when searching DDC contents, but also they extend the functionality of the German subject headings authority file to a better support of cognitive exploration within the authority-file itself.[5]

In addition to the utilization of the linkages established in CrissCross, the conceptual relations already existing within the both interlinked KOS can be used in various ways to allow for explorative searches. As previously mentioned in this paper, the headings in the SWD are structured likely to other thesauri, i.e., by broader, narrower, related and synonymous terms. Regarding the example "Erfolg", there are four narrower terms (Berufserfolg, Führungserfolg, Unternehmenserfolg, Werbeerfolg) and one related term (Misserfolg) linked to the top term.

In the DDC all these relations are existing as well, but as DDC classes are more complex, i.e., a single class consisting of DDC number, class heading, notes specifying the class contents or leading to related topics in other classes, the four basic relations can be defined in greater detail, for instance, the hierarchical relationship can be subdivided in notational hierarchy, structural hierarchy and polyhierarchical relationship. Not least, the Relative Index terms function as essential hub to DDC class contents naming the main topics, and often side-topics, too, as well as the discipline where the topic is treated. Following the path of the example "Erfolg", the DDC class `302.14` named "Social Participation" features notational hierarchy, the polyhierarchical relationship to the same subject treated in the class-here note in class `650.1`, equivalence and associative relationship as well as several Relative Index terms (see Figure 8).

As a first step on the way to a fully semantic search, the extraction of all terms that are interlinked either by the CrissCross mappings or by the a priori conceptual relations of both indexing instruments could support the user in the run-up to or during his search in the form of word clouds or clusters listed by subject categories, and thus provide for easy term picking and/or combination of search terms (see Figure 9).

[5] Hubrich 2011.

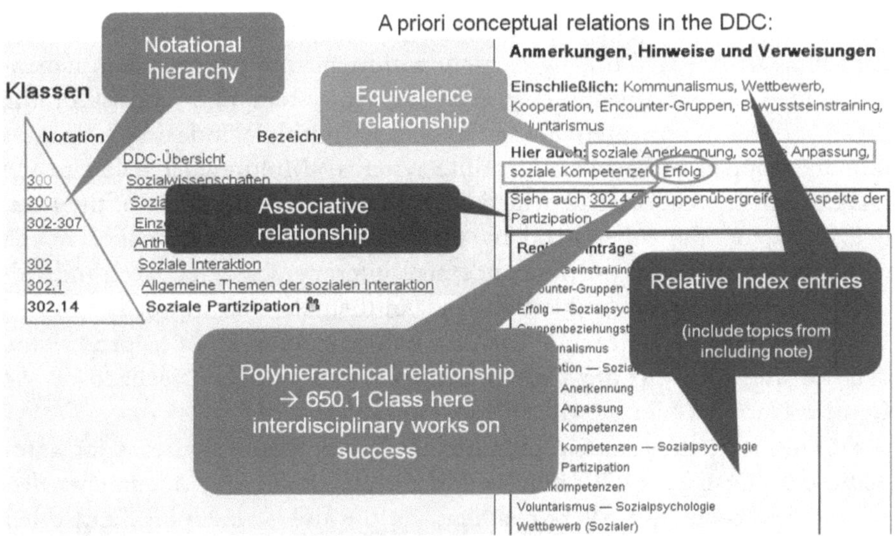

Figure 8: A priori conceptual relations in the DDC

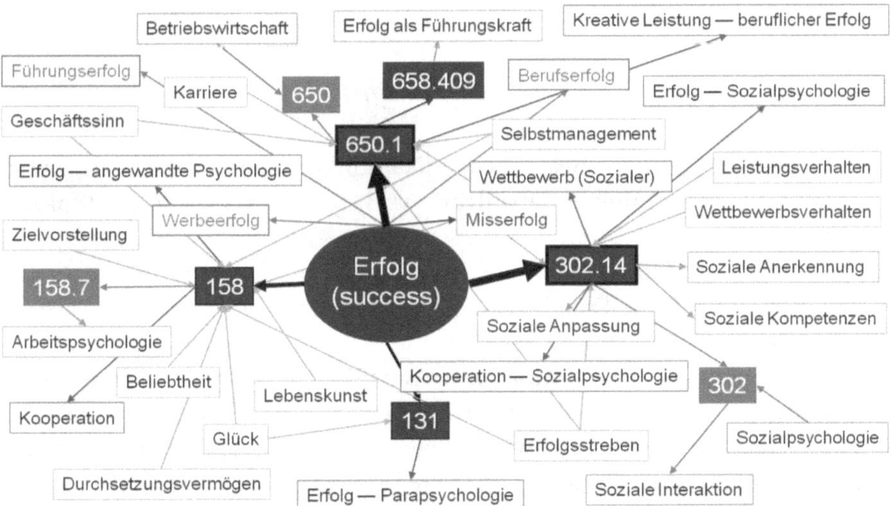

Figure 9: Extraction of terms that are interlinked either by the CrissCross mappings or by the a priori conceptual relations of both SWD and DDC representing the semantic neighborhood of the term "Erfolg"

3. *Perspectives*

This article has pointed out the varied possibilities the CrissCross mappings provide for improving search efficiency in heterogeneous information spaces by supporting verbal searches based on German SWD headings and at the same time automatically support queries for documents indexed by DDC.

Viewed in a more global context, the CrissCross approach is also able to constitute an essential linking element within an international comprehensive knowledge organization system. Such a system may consist of the DDC serving as an international spine and multiple indexing languages that are mapped to it as local satellite systems.[6] Multilingual access to the DDC is on the one hand provided by the multiple translations of the Relative Index, on the other hand by the satellites. The functionality of the whole system is based on the conceptual interoperability between individual systems designed to support all kinds of thematic search processes.

The definition of relation types of the interlinked entities to prepare the data for uses in the context of the semantic web has been realized by the German National Library with its Linked Data Service.[7]

Furthermore, the CrissCross mappings could support systems for automatic classification. DDC numbers could be assigned to documents that are indexed only with SWD headings via the use of mappings and other methods of automatic or semi-automatic classification.

References

Web documents were accessed on December 13, 2010.

Deutsche Nationalbibliothek. (2010). Der Linked Data Service der Deutschen Nationalbibliothek. Available at: http://files.d-nb.de/pdf/linked_data.pdf.

Gödert, Winfried. (2002). "Die Welt ist groß – Wir bringen Ordnung in diese Welt": Das DFG-Projekt DDC Deutsch. In: Information – Wissenschaft & Praxis Nfd 53 : 395–400.

Gödert, Winfried. (2008). Ontological Spine, Localization and Multilingual Access. Some Reflections and a Proposal. In: Knull-Schlomann, Kristina et al. (eds.). New Perspectives on Subject Indexing and Classification. Essays in Honour of Magda Heiner-Freiling. Leipzig-Frankfurt M.-Berlin: Deutsche Nationalbibliothek. 233–240.

Hubrich, Jessica et al. (2008). Improving Subject Access in Global Information Spaces. Reflections upon Internationalization and Localization of Knowledge Organization Systems (KOS). In: Knull-Schlomann, Kristina et al. (eds.). New Perspectives on Subject Indexing and Classification. Essays in Honour of Magda Heiner-Freiling. Leipzig-Frankfurt M.-Berlin: Deutsche Nationalbibliothek. 261–267.

---

6 Gödert 2008; Hubrich 2008.

7 Deutsche Nationalbibliothek 2010.

Jahns, Yvonne. (2009). 20 years SWD: German Subject Authority Data Prepared for the Future. Available at: http://www.ifla2009satelliteflorence.it/meeting2/program/assets/Jahns.pdf.

OCLC (Online Computer Library Center). (2009). DDC Translations. Available at: www.oclc.org/us/en/dewey/about/translations/default.htm.

Translingual Retrieval: Moving between Vocabularies – MACS 2010

Yvonne Jahns, Helga Karg

Abstract: Within the multilingual framework of the CrissCross project, MACS (Multilingual Access to Subjects) has continued its work. MACS has developed a prototype of mappings between three vocabularies: the LCSH (Library of Congress Subject Headings), RAMEAU (Répertoire d'autorité-matière encyclopédique et alphabétique unifié) and the SWD (Schlagwortnormdatei). A database with a Link Management System (LMI), which allows for an easy linking between English, French and German subject headings, was created. The database started working with headings from the disciplines sports and theatre, but by now headings from all other fields of knowledge have been included as well. In 2008–2010, equivalencies between English and French headings which had been produced by the Bibliothèque nationale de France have been completed with the most important German SWD topical terms. Thus, more than 50.000 trilingual links are now available and can be used in different retrieval scenarios. It is planned to use them in The European Library (TEL) in order to support multilingual searches over all European National Library collections. The article informs about the project workflow, methodology of mapping and future applications of MACS links.

1. *Introduction – history and partners of the MACS project*

In 2010 the idea behind the MACS project, namely to generate a multilingual search based on the mapping of those European indexing languages which are used predominantly, was taken a big step forward. Within the German DFG-funded CrissCross project, the mapping process between the topical headings of the LCSH (Library of Congress Subject Headings), RAMEAU (Répertoire d'autorité-matière encyclopédique et alphabétique unifié) and SWD (Schlagwortnormdatei) was continued. In consequence, the topical headings of the SWD were linked to DDC notations and to their English and French equivalents in LCSH and RAMEAU at the same time. The idea to link the three indexing languages SWD, LCSH and RAMEAU was developed several years before in the European MACS project.

MACS (*Multilingual Access to Subjects*) was initiated by the Conference of European National Librarians (CENL) in 1997/1998, with the objective to create a multilingual gateway (not a multilingual thesaurus) that allows subject access to library catalogues in order to overcome linguistic barriers. A working group consisting of four libraries was set up: the British Library

(BL), the Bibliothèque nationale de France (BnF), the Swiss National Library (SNB) and the German National Library (DNB). Between 1997 and 1999 the project's proposal was worked out. A feasibility study, focusing on a subset of headings from the fields of sports and theatre, was realized. It showed a great promise for enlarging the projected scope. Different mapping methods were explored and in 2000/2001 a prototype of a web linking tool was created. Between 2002 and 2004, due to positive previous test results, the Link Management Interface (LMI) was upgraded in order to become a production database. In the following year (2005) a large number of LCSH-RAMEAU mappings provided by the BnF were uploaded and the German National Library began integrating SWD-LCSH-RAMEAU mapping into the CrissCross project scope.

In 2007, the Swiss National Library started editing links over all subject fields. Mapping became part of the operational tasks of the indexing section of the SNB. Following this, Swiss and German colleagues organized a cooperative work process in the LMI. In the meantime the headings were updated and an update routine was installed. This technical work was supported by an intellectual survey and, due to the implemented double check functionality, heading lists are now always up to date.

However it became increasingly clear that it was not practicable to do the linking from the SWD to both DDC and LCSH/RAMEAU in one step as it was planned at the beginning of the CrissCross project. Since the team in Cologne was working to its full capacity mapping SWD to DDC[1], both on the practical and the theoretical level, the German National Library decided to hire twelve free lancers to do the intellectual linking within one year. This team consisted of professional translators. They started the mapping process in 2009. As a result, since 2007, the impressive number of 58,900 SWD-LCSH-RAMEAU links were created with the help of the translators and the Swiss colleagues.

The first use of the links was tested by their integration in a multilingual search interface in the TEL project[2] in 2009.

2. *Project scope*

The starting basis was 70,000 already mapped RAMEAU–LCSH pairs from the Bibliothèque nationale de France. Then, 150,000 potentially equivalent SWD topical headings were added. The German National Library decided to focus on a pool of 50,000 SWD headings to be linked, which had already

---

1 Cf. Jacobs, Mengel & Müller 2011.

2 Cf. http://search.theeuropeanlibrary.org/portal/en/index.html.

been extracted for a preferred linking with DDC notations. The selection was made due to relevance, which refers to the number of titles indexed by the German National Library. These approx. 50,000 headings were divided into 14 work packages made up of neighbouring disciplines (cf. Table 1).

Disciplines	Number of SWD topical headings
Agriculture	1122
Earth sciences, Geology	1144
Sciences, Mathematics, Physics, Astronomy	4457
Technology, Engineering	7112
Computer science	1033
Sociology, Education	2060
Law, Public Administration, Political & Military Science	2386
Economics, Ecology, Transportation	3203
Psychology, Medicine I	3274
Medicine II, Biology	4457
Chemistry	3590
Arts, Cultural Studies, Anthropology	1652
History, Philosophy, Religion	1905
Language & Literature	1249

Table 1: Number of mapped SWD topical headings according to disciplines

3. *MACS working area LMI*

The major software application related to the MACS project is the Link Management Interface (LMI). It can be used to maintain the links between subject headings of various authorities. The LMI is a web-based application and is therefore independent of any partner library system. It is a database with a link management front-end, complemented by an XML based search engine, designed and maintained by Jeroen Hoppenbrouwers, an information science researcher. According to his appraisal the LMI can handle a million links between up to fifty indexing languages.[3] It proved to be very powerful and stable during the project work. The LMI provides many useful features. It is especially thanks to the Swiss colleagues that many of these improvements have been realized within the last years.

3 Hoppenbrouwers 2009.

In the LMI, the editor can search for subject headings in all three vocabularies and get lists of them. With the user interface the editors always get the information whether complete or incomplete links exist in the system. Figures 1 – 3 give an impression of the MACS working area.

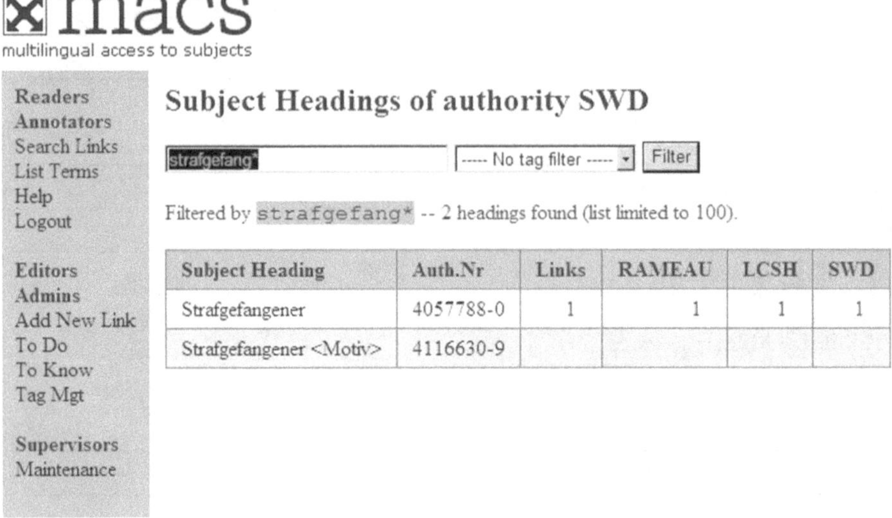

Figure 1: Brief data display of subject headings list and indicated links

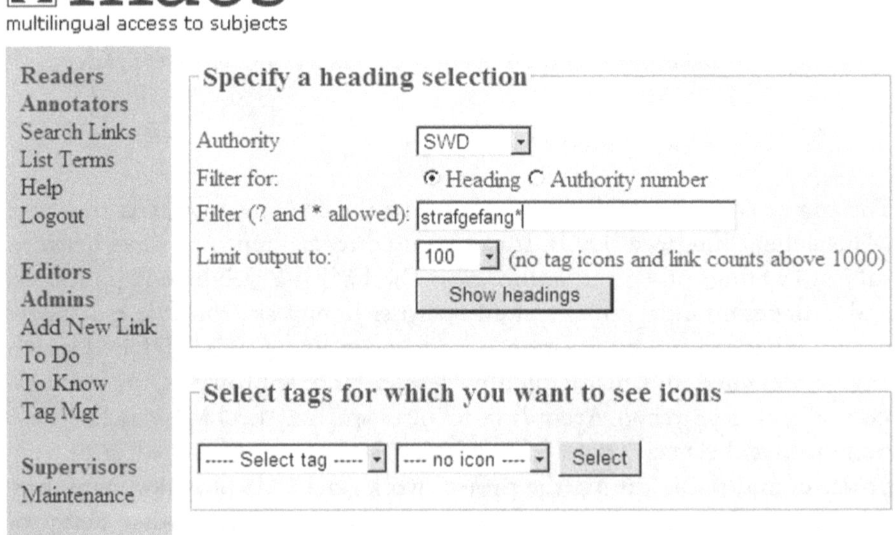

Figure 2: Entry mask for verbal link search

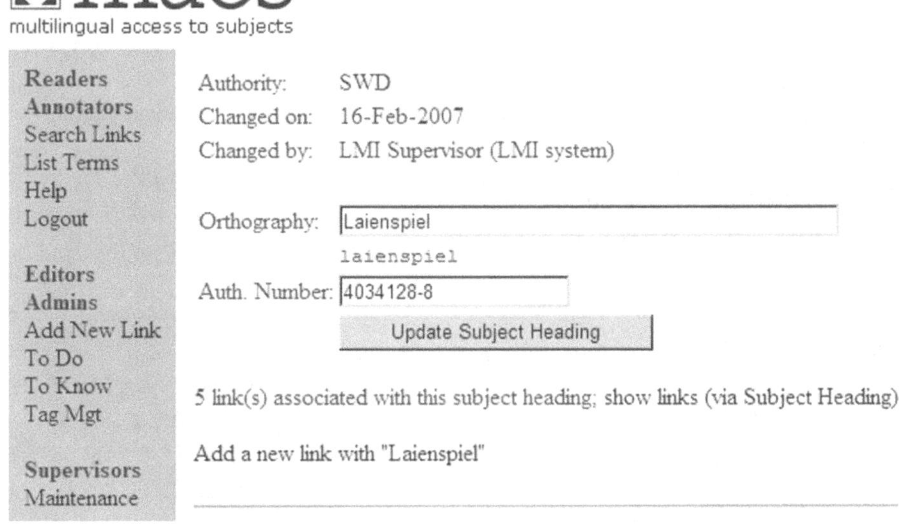

Figure 3: Subject heading information for intellectual update

Headings are synchronised automatically every week respectively monthly with their master authority files, thus ensuring that editors can always work with the latest version. Furthermore, all headings have identifiers to facilitate processing and to avoid doubling. It is also possible to update a heading manually during the mapping process, if the editor recognizes that something has to be changed.

The editor can also search directly for links with headings. A truncated search results in an alphabetical link list in which the editor can then navigate back and forth (cf. Figure 4).

RAMEAU	LCSH	SWD	Domains	MACS Link
Science AND Brasage	Brewing AND Science	Brauwissenschaft	620	MACS0142250
Sciences	Science	Wissenschaft	500	MACS0035543
Sciences -- Aspect politique	Science AND Political aspects	--	999	MACS0083357
Sciences -- Abréviations	Science -- Abbreviations	--	999	MACS0049021
Sciences antiques	Science, Ancient	--	500	MACS0003498

Figure 4: Alphabetical link list

Not only every subject heading but also every MACS link has its identifier which can be used for further cooperative maintenance. The main features are editing functionalities. The editor can complete and change (correct) links or add new links. The data masks for creating a new link respectively editing an existing link are displayed in Figures 5 and 6.

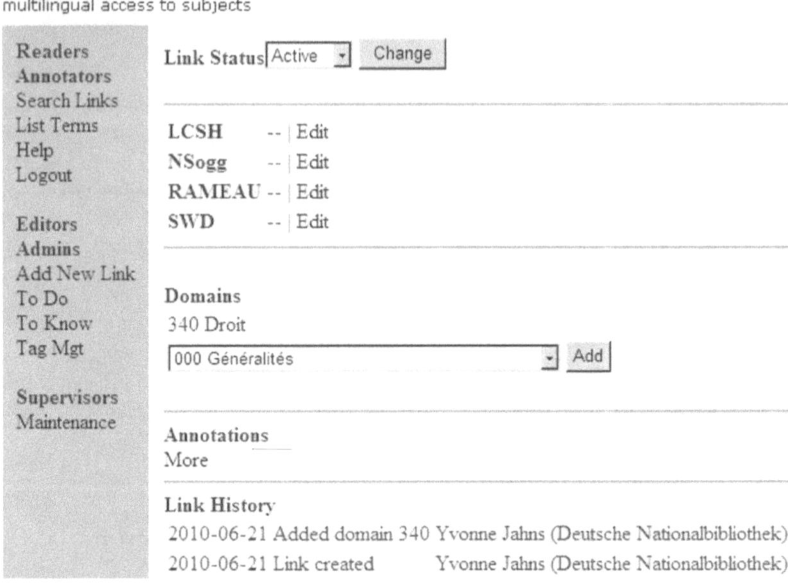

Figure 5: Data mask to create a new link

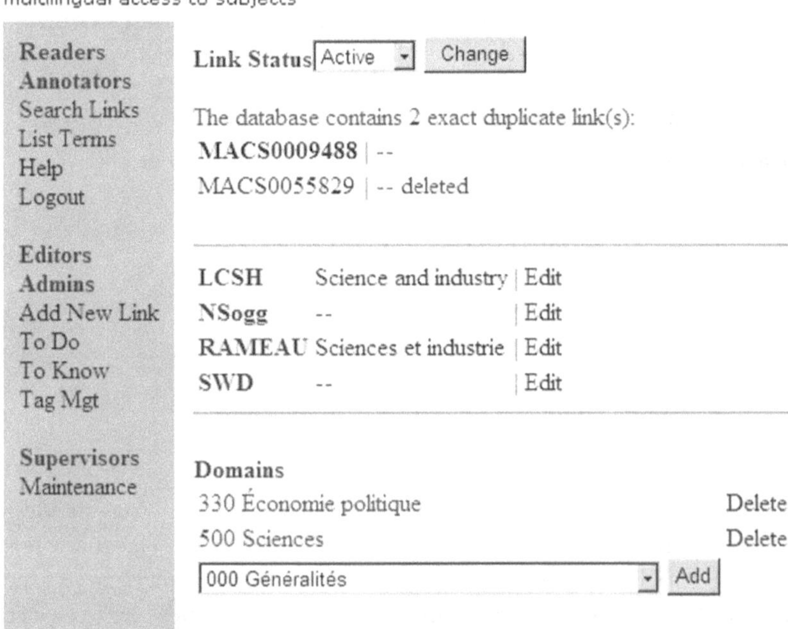

Figure 6: Data mask to edit an existing link

Each MACS link has at least one broad DDC domain. This subject domain number was developed and is used by the Bibliothèque nationale de France. The domains are based on the top hierarchical levels of the DDC (the hundred divisions). This is very similar to how the German, Austrian and Swiss National bibliographies have been structured since 2004[4]. About 60 domains can be used for specifying work areas or filtering subsets (cf. Figure 7).

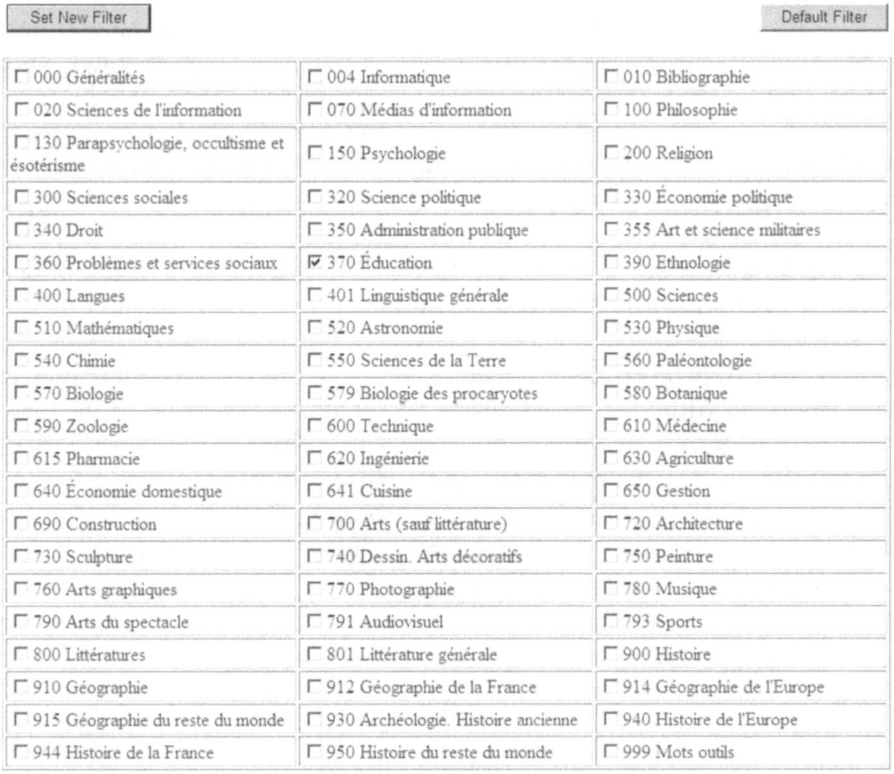

Set New Filter | Default Filter

☐ 000 Généralités	☐ 004 Informatique	☐ 010 Bibliographie
☐ 020 Sciences de l'information	☐ 070 Médias d'information	☐ 100 Philosophie
☐ 130 Parapsychologie, occultisme et ésotérisme	☐ 150 Psychologie	☐ 200 Religion
☐ 300 Sciences sociales	☐ 320 Science politique	☐ 330 Économie politique
☐ 340 Droit	☐ 350 Administration publique	☐ 355 Art et science militaires
☐ 360 Problèmes et services sociaux	☑ 370 Éducation	☐ 390 Ethnologie
☐ 400 Langues	☐ 401 Linguistique générale	☐ 500 Sciences
☐ 510 Mathématiques	☐ 520 Astronomie	☐ 530 Physique
☐ 540 Chimie	☐ 550 Sciences de la Terre	☐ 560 Paléontologie
☐ 570 Biologie	☐ 579 Biologie des procaryotes	☐ 580 Botanique
☐ 590 Zoologie	☐ 600 Technique	☐ 610 Médecine
☐ 615 Pharmacie	☐ 620 Ingénierie	☐ 630 Agriculture
☐ 640 Économie domestique	☐ 641 Cuisine	☐ 650 Gestion
☐ 690 Construction	☐ 700 Arts (sauf littérature)	☐ 720 Architecture
☐ 730 Sculpture	☐ 740 Dessin. Arts décoratifs	☐ 750 Peinture
☐ 760 Arts graphiques	☐ 770 Photographie	☐ 780 Musique
☐ 790 Arts du spectacle	☐ 791 Audiovisuel	☐ 793 Sports
☐ 800 Littératures	☐ 801 Littérature générale	☐ 900 Histoire
☐ 910 Géographie	☐ 912 Géographie de la France	☐ 914 Géographie de l'Europe
☐ 915 Géographie du reste du monde	☐ 930 Archéologie. Histoire ancienne	☐ 940 Histoire de l'Europe
☐ 944 Histoire de la France	☐ 950 Histoire du reste du monde	☐ 999 Mots outils

Figure 7: MACS domains

There are other helpful features as for instance annotation fields, which allow for communication with editing partners directly at the link-level or for a selection of to-do-lists.

In 2009, some aspects of the workflow were reorganized because the LMI tested data export for the TEL interface (see below). Today, the LMI is developing more and more from being a mere tool for link creation to being a dynamic device for authority maintenance. Several Web 2.0 features have been integrated additionally.[5]

4 Cf. http://www.d-nb.de/eng/service/zd/gliederung_dnb.htm.

5 Hoppenbrouwers 2009.

4. *Methodology*

The main accord for the methodological approach is that no language is used as a pivot in the linking process. The headings are not simply translated. The MACS linking methodology establishes links based on an analysis at both the terminological and the semantic level. That means editors not only looked on concepts and the authority record with its relations, but also at the syntactic level and last but not least at the indexed publications. The mapped concepts, represented by the different subject headings, have to be truly close equivalents to provide successful multilingual subject retrieval. The quality of linking is based on the retrieval of consistent sets of bibliographic records from the different catalogues. Recall and precision of the established relations had to be checked in the associated databases.

The Swiss colleagues developed a practical guide which was refined during the work. Its rules are based on the theoretical framework of the British Standard BS 8723 Part 4[6], the IFLA Guidelines for Multilingual Thesauri 2005[7] and a paper written by Landry entitled "MACS Linking Approach in a Federated Networked Environment"[8]. Anyway, the 2009 mapping project was laborious. Although the editors had a very good knowledge of the three languages because they were all professional translators, it was still a challenge for them to use the LMI, to search within three catalogues, to search for the scope of all subject headings in three indexing languages, to look at intra-thesaurus relations and scope notes and to consult dictionaries and encyclopaedias to understand the concepts.

4.1 *Indexing language differences*

The three indexing vocabularies LCSH, RAMEAU, and SWD have very similar underlying principles, following international standards, but different levels of specificity.

Similar structures of authority records are available for all of them. This helps in comparing their scope and their semantic relations. All three are very comprehensive vocabularies, very specific and deeply developed in nearly all disciplines. LCSH is the oldest indexing language, going back to the 19th century. RAMEAU goes back to the Canadian RVM – the Repertoire de vedettes-matière, a French translation of LCSH from the 1950s. SWD is the youngest indexing language created in the 1980s in German speaking countries. Despite their similarities there are some fundamental differences. One

---

6 British Standard BS 8723- 4 2007.

7 Working Group on Guidelines for Multilingual Thesauri 2009.

8 Landry 2005.

of the main differences is that LCSH and RAMEAU terms are represented in the plural whereas SWD terms are represented in the singular form. The most important aspect, which is essential regarding the mapping methodology, is the different syntactical construction. Whereas LCSH and RAMEAU prefer pre-coordinated subject strings, often with qualifying subdivisions, SWD is more post-coordinated. That means complex topics are represented by a combination of headings. Quite interestingly, the concepts of pre- and post-coordination have recently been under discussion in the U.S. Some U.S. colleagues think about transforming the LCSH into a tool that provides more flexible means to create and modify subject authority data.[9]

Another difference is caused by natural language differences that allow e.g. more pre-combined headings in German (cf. Table 2).

4.2 *Types of links*

The MACS approach allows only equivalent relations, based on the idea that correlated indexing languages should produce equivalent retrieval results across systems. Equivalence means identity, synonymy or quasi-synonymy. An exception is the Null (0) relation, which means that a term could not be mapped to other terms. There was no relevance rating made in order to adjust the quality of the relations. A term of one indexing language could be mapped to several terms of the other languages (1:n).

RAMEAU	SWD	LCSH
Theologie	Theologie	Theology
Athlétisme AND Entraîneurs	Leichtathletiktrainer	Track and field coaches
Traducteurs	Übersetzer	Translators
Traducteurs	Dolmetscher	Translators
0	Erdalkalichloride	Alkaline earth chlorides

Table 2: MACS linkages

There is no starting or target language. All equivalence expressions can be read symmetrically. However, we allowed mapping combinations of subject headings if necessary – AND relations (cf. Table 2). This use of Boolean compound cannot be easily interpreted in the opposite direction and causes problems by using the mapping bi-directionally.[10]

9 Cf. Wiesenmüller 2009; Chan 2008.
10 Doerr 2001.

4.3 *Degrees of equivalence*

Following usual mapping frameworks, we distinguish between three degrees of equivalence: exact, overlapping and partial.[11]

Exact equivalence means, that the scope of all three headings is really congruent. Overlapping equivalence means that the headings are not congruent but concepts are overlapping in such a way that a link will help getting relevant retrieval results. For example, the exact German translation and equivalent of English *imperialism* is *Imperialismus*. Additionally, also the German *Neokolonialismus* is part of the French and English heading scope of *imperialism*.

Following British Standard BS 8723 Part 4, partial equivalent links are created to ensure that relevant publications are linked to preserve recall, as an "inexactly or partially equivalent concept may be accepted as equivalent if this will provide acceptable retrieval results in most cases."[12] For example, French *cas (linguist.)* is the broader term of *dative* but RAMEAU treats (the subset) *dative* as a "used for"-relation to *cas*. At the indexing level there is exact correspondence, but on the semantic level there is only partial congruency. This "synonymy principle" was followed in all the indexing languages and thus provided a valid basis for allowing one-to-two links in some instances. If a concept of one indexing language has no exact equivalence to any other concept, then a broader or narrower equivalent to some appropriate concept is accepted. Further examples are shown in Table 3.

RAMEAU	SWD	LCSH
Ètudiants japonais	Japanischer Student	Japanese students
Impérialisme	Neokolonialismus	Imperialism
Cas (linguistique)	Dativ	0

Table 3: Examples for types of equivalence in MACS

4.4 *Mapping problems*

The editors' manual could not answer all questions which came up during the mapping process. Some problems of finding appropriate equivalents should be illustrated here.

Sometimes editors were confronted with different scopes of meaning which occurred due to different linguistic developments. One indexing lan-

[11] Cf. Dextre Clarke 2011.

[12] British Standard BS 8723 Part 4: Chapter 8.2.

guage may develop a topic in far more detail than the others as we have already seen in the example of *dativ*. Sometimes they have different semantics. For example, *cider*, *cidre*, and *Apfelwein* are obviously not the same sort of sparkling wine made of apples. In fact, in the U.S. the term *cider* is even used for a non-alcoholic beverage. Although the production and especially the fermentation processes are regionally different, editors decided that this is an equivalent *on the indexing level*, because users will get adequate publications with all three headings.

After checking the concept represented by the subject heading and consulting the scope notes, editors have to decide whether this is a congruent concept or whether it is an equivalent relationship that leads to consistent retrieval results in different catalogues due to the mapping.

Sometimes relations seemed to be quite evident, but at second view they turned out to be rather different. This indicates how mapping results depend on excellent language skills. For example, the SWD distinguishes between *Altertum* and *Antike*. At first view German *Antike* seems to be equivalent to French *civilisation antique* but German *Antike* is equivalent to *civilisation classique* in French, because the German heading *Antike* is restricted to classical antiquity, the classical period in the Mediterranean region.

Finally, the semantics of the mappings were reviewed by terminology experts of the German National Library, and randomized samples were empirically tested for document recall and precision. Compared to cross-concordances of other projects, we can agree that it is a cost-intensive and time-consuming effort to generate such terminology networks.[13] But we are convinced that it is a good investment and that the data created can be used as a training database for automatic systems.

5. *Use and application of MACS links*

5.1 *Mapped terms in LMI*

To benefit from the MACS work, links have to be made available to cataloguers, end-users and researchers. The links should be further developed and we hope to get some more input in order to overcome the aforementioned mapping problems. At present, the mapped terms are freely accessible via LMI to interested parties. Links can be downloaded from the LMI-database as XMLfile and converted to other formats. The German National Library has published the mappings as Linked Data and has planned to integrate them in its own portal to offer its users a multilingual search across various collections.

13 Mayr & Petras 2009.

5.2 Linked Data

Linked Data has become the de facto standard for publishing and exchanging data on the internet. Many providers (mostly non-profit organizations, universities or public institutions) are already offering their data in a form which is Semantic Web compatible. Developments in the area of the Semantic Web are aimed at improving the usability and accessibility of data. The idea of the Semantic Web also allows for links to be created between data from heterogeneous sources, leading in turn to the establishment of new services. In this context our library data, that has been generated and maintained by trained professionals, can play a major role. In the long term the German National Library is planning to offer a linked data service which will permit the Semantic Web community to use the entire stock of its national bibliographic data, including all authority data. The German National Library has been making parts of its knowledge base available via interfaces (OIA, SRU) for some time now. As part of its Linked Data activities, the German National Library is also aiming at providing RDF data via these interfaces. Initially, however, we are only offering HTTP resolving via the German National Library' web portal and an FTP download of the data.[14]

As of May 2010 the German National Library published 37,547 links from SWD to LCSH and 28,249 links from SWD to RAMEAU as part of its Linked Data Service. Furthermore, the links from SWD to DDC (based on results of the CrissCross project) are included in the service. With this step into the web community it is intended to reach more collaboration partners and customers like research institutions, cultural heritage organizations, internet companies and online communities.

5.3 Copy Cataloguing

One of the desired project aims was to support copy cataloguing processes by using (transforming) multilingual mappings.

The German cataloguer who has to index foreign language documents can use the mapped data to identify the relevant LCSH and is led to the German subject headings by the MACS link. That is, foreign indexing results can be used because they can be transformed into SWD subject heading strings. Even an automatic generation of such a string of index terms based on the links is conceivable.

Figure 8 shows an English title, already indexed with LCSH. The MACS link leads to the equivalent SWD headings that are used for this concept.

---

14 Cf. Deutsche Nationalbibliothek 2011.

Thus the cataloguer in the German National Library can build the string of subject headings shown in Table 4.

!135814987!Lammi-Keefe, Carol J. **Handbook of nutrition and pregnancy** [[Elektronische Ressource]] / ed. by Carol J. Lammi-Keefe ... Totowa, NY : Springer [Heidelberg] : Springer Online-Ressource *HTTP*=q PDF=u http://www.springerlink.com/content/t37575=x H Nutrition and health LCSH headings: Pregnancy --Nutritional aspects ---Handbooks, manuals, etc. Mothers --Nutrition$vHandbooks, manuals, etc. Infants --Nutrition

Figure 8: English title already indexed with LCSH

LCSH	SWD	Domains
Pregnancy -- Nutritional aspects	Schwangerschaft AND Ernährung	610

Table 4: MACS link between LCSH and SWD

The example shows the potential of the multilingual link, namely that it supports indexing foreign language documents and allows to profit from foreign results that preserves manpower and avoids double work. The intellectually generated links can be extremely useful in terms of the improvement of an automatic generation of a string of index terms.

For this benefit it is necessary that the complete authority record (with the thesaurus structure) is easily accessible for the cataloguer in his own database.

5.4 Meta-Searching

5.4.1 Searching heterogeneously indexed catalogues – Query expansion

MACS links are also useful for end-users. Because of the MACS links they do not need to translate search terms or wonder about the right terms cataloguers would have used. The mapping allows them to search with their native language.

The mapping will improve retrieval performance in such a way as to enable the user to access foreign-language titles. Later on it will be perhaps possible to expand the query to foreign catalogues or databases. Furthermore the links can be used for ranking mechanisms or reducing query results.

The present situation can be illustrated by an example from the catalogue of the German National Library. If a user performs an unspecified „all words" query in English without the MACS mappings he only gets documents where the term is part of the title or the document itself. With MACS he will also get titles indexed with SWD headings that do not contain the search term. Because of the SWD-DDC mapping an additional set of titles of documents exclusively classified with the DDC will be available too. A subject search with an English term will be successful with the help of the MACS mapping: The user can access SWD-indexed publications. The mapping can also provide a specification of query results. For example, documents that have been indexed intellectually can be ranked highest.

Some examples from the catalogue of the German National Library can visualize the effectiveness of MACS mappings. A search for documents with the SWD heading *Erneuerbare Energien* can be expanded using the mapping yielding English titles which are not indexed with SWD subject headings (Figure 9).

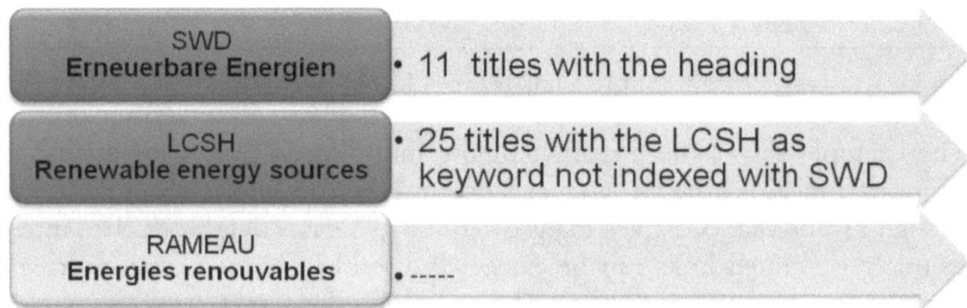

Figure 9: Searching procedure for documents about *Erneuerbare Energien* and the MACS benefit

In Figure 10 the effect is much more apparent. The enhancement of about 800 titles is enormous and relevant.

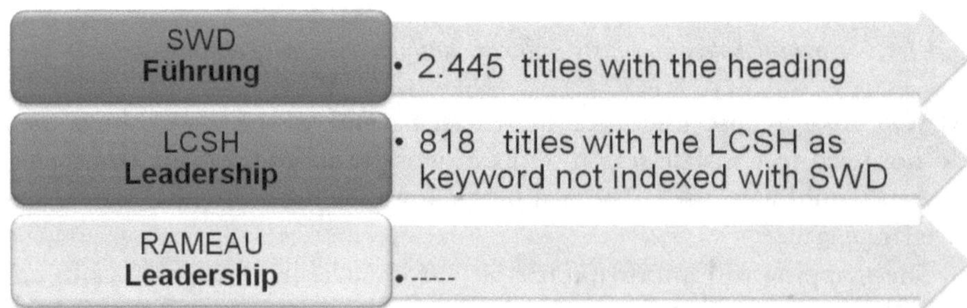

Figure 10: Searching procedure for documents about *Führung* and the MACS benefit

The importance of English as publication language is continuously growing in nearly every knowledge field. As a consequence, the mapping process is getting more and more important for all libraries.

Figure 11 shows how users benefit if they expand their search from their own library catalogue to others world wide. The German search term *Ärztlicher Behandlungsfehler* leads to the subject authority heading *Ärztlicher Kunstfehler* which is connected with the LCSH *medical errors* and the RAMEAU heading *erreurs medicales.* In the catalogue of the German National Library a user gets 196 bibliographic records. In the catalogues of the Bibliothèque nationale de France (BnF) and the Library of Congress (LoC) there are about another hundred titles indexed with the equivalent subject headings (49 BnF, 62 LoC).

This potential has to be transformed into suitable instruments for retrieval and user navigation.

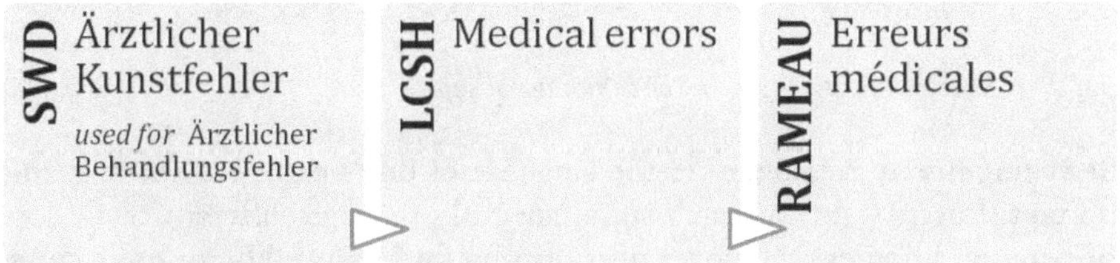

Figure 11: The SWD term *Ärztlicher Kunstfehler* and its MACS linkages

5.4.2 *Meta-Searching European Collections*

Figure 12: Multilingual interface of the TEL-MACS prototype

As a first step, MACS mappings were integrated in a meta-search in the TELplus project in 2008. TELplus is part of the EU eContentplus programme which aims at making digital content in Europe more accessible, usable and exploitable.

European collections which are indexed with LCSH, RAMEAU and SWD can be searched by using the MACS mappings. Therefore a prototype tool was developed that uses mapping sets and provides subject-based trilingual searching.[15] That was done by the TEL office together with MACS partners and the VU University of Amsterdam. The prototype not only uses the manually made MACS mappings but also automatically produced mappings, that were created based on a statistical analysis of dually indexed books. This is a method which was already successfully used within the VIAF project for name authority files.

In this way at least the collections of the National Libraries of Germany, Austria, France, Great Britain, and Switzerland will be available, thus enabling users, researchers and educational workers to search Europe's national libraries simultaneously – efficiently and in a time-saving way.

TEL partners also see advantages for the libraries themselves: Improving access to Europe's cultural heritage can be a marketing strategy for libraries, leading to a better image. It is also a good starting point for cooperation projects between libraries across Europe.

5.4.3 Searching catalogues in the language of choice

Searching library catalogues in the language of one's choice is not only important if users want to search simultaneously through different catalogues of national libraries. Moreover, it is also useful because library users come from different nations and cultures. In multicultural societies more and more libraries are frequented by users, who do not speak the respective national language. For example, 12% of university students in Germany come from abroad[16] and use the university libraries. People who do not speak German very well frequent public libraries in Germany every day. English or French search entries can help them to find relevant resources. Often our web sites have English and French navigation menus, help screens and displays, but to find content is rather challenging if you are not familiar with the German language. Multilingual mapping, though not a translation tool, can nevertheless work as a translation tool. It is a valid approach in case the user is able to understand documents in a foreign language but has difficulties in providing search terms. These are only some examples of possible applications. We are convinced that many libraries or other institutions are interested in controlled vocabularies and translation mechanisms to improve searching quality of their search engines.

---

15 Isaac & Chambers 2010.

16 Cf. data report about facts and figures on the international nature of studies and research in Germany. Available at: http://www.wissenschaft-weltoffen.de/daten/2009/.

Until now MACS has been an intellectual mapping project. Semantic technology, i.e. machine learning, has not been integrated yet. Maybe automated mappings will increase the performance in the future.[17]

References

Web documents were accessed on November 19, 2010.

British Standard BS 8723-4:2007. (2007). Structured Vocabularies for Information Retrieval – Guide – Interoperability between Vocabularies. London: British Standards Institution.

Chan, Lois Mai. (2008). The Future of LCSH: A Response. In: Cataloguing and Classification Quarterly, 46 (4): 433–436.

Clavel-Merrin, Genevieve. (2003). National Libraries as Access Points: The Role of TEL and MACS. Available at: http://www.theeuropeanlibrary.org/portal/organisation/cooperation_old/archive/telproject_archive/pdf/tel_scnl_clavel_eng.pdf.

Dextre Clarke, Stella. (2011). In Pursuit of Cross-Vocabulary Interoperability: Can We Standardize Mapping Types? In this volume.

Deutsche Nationalbibliothek. (2011). The Linked Data Service of the German National Library. Version 3.1. April 21st , 2011. Available at: http://files.d-nb.de/pdf/linked_data_e.pdf.

Doerr, Martin. (2001). Semantic Problems of Thesaurus Mapping. In: Journal of Digital Information 1 (8). Available at: http://journals.tdl.org/jodi/article/viewArticle/31/32.

Hoppenbrouwers, Jeroen. (2009). MACS Project Enters Third Life. Available at: http://www.hoppie.nl/pub/node/89.

Isaac, Antoine; Chambers, Sally. (2010). Prototype Integrating MACS Initial Data and New Alignments into TEL Framework. Available at: http://www.theeuropeanlibrary.org/portal/organisation/cooperation/telplus/documents/TELplus_D3.4_04012010.pdf.

Jacobs, Jan-Helge; Mengel, Tina; Müller, Katrin. (2011). Insights and Outlooks: A Retrospective View on the CrissCross Project. In this volume.

Landry, Patrice. (2003): MACS Update: Moving toward a Link Management Production Database. Available at: http://www.elag2003.ch/papers/MACS-ELAG-article.pdf.

[17] News can be followed up at the MACS community platform at http://macs.cenl.org/.

Landry, Patrice. (2009). Providing Multilingual Subject Access through Linking of Subject Heading Languages: The MACS approach. Available at: http://www.cacaoproject.eu/fileadmin/media/AT4DL/paper-09.pdf.

MacEwan, Andrew. (2000). Crossing Language Barriers in Europe: Linking LCSH to Other Subject Heading Languages. In: Cataloguing and Classification Quarterly 29 (1) : 199–207.

Mayr, Philip; Petras, Vivien. (2009). Cross-Concordances: Terminology Mapping and Its Effectiveness for Information Retrieval. In: ICBC 38 (3). Available at: http://www.ifla.org/IV/ifla74/papers/129-Mayr_Petras-en.pdf.

Wiesenmüller, Heidrun. (2009). LCSH goes RSWK. In: Bibliotheksdienst 43 (7) : 716–747. Available at: http://www.zlb.de/aktivitaeten/bd_neu/heftinhalte2009/Erschliessung010709BD.pdf.

Working Group on Guidelines for Multilingual Thesauri. (2009). Guidelines for Multilingual Thesauri. (IfLA Professional reports 115). Available at: http://archive.ifla.org/VII/s29/pubs/Profrep115.pdf.

Intersystem Relations: Characteristics and Functionalities

Jessica Hubrich

Abstract: Within the frame of the methodological support of the CrissCross project and the research conducted in the Reseda project, a tiered model of semantic interoperability was developed. This correlates methods of establishing semantic interoperability and types of intersystem relations to search functionalities in retrieval scenarios. In this article the model is outlined and exemplified with reference to respective selective alignment projects.

1. *Introduction*

Intersystem relations enhance access to knowledge modelled in knowledge organization systems by building bridges between concepts of different indexing languages. They may also enhance access to information resources as the connected concepts are used to describe the content of documents. In recent years, many mapping efforts were undertaken which all aimed at improving *recall* as well as *precision* of topical queries in heterogeneously indexed information spaces. The applied methods, however, partly differed significantly from each other, resulting in a different quality and functionality of the established intersystem relations. The CrissCross project for example united two cognitive linking strategies: On the one hand subject headings of the German subject headings authority file *Schlagwortnormdatei (SWD)* were unidirectionally linked to notations of the *Dewey Decimal Classification (DDC)* in order to provide an enhanced access to DDC classes and to DDC-indexed information resources via SWD headings.[1] On the other hand – as contribution to the project *Multilingual Access to Subjects (MACS)* – SWD headings were connected to their equivalents in the *Library of Congress Subject Headings (LCSH)* and the *Répertoire d'autorité-matière encyclopédique et alphabétique unifié (RAMEAU)* in order to additionally support multilingual retrieval.[2]

Within the frame of the methodological support of the CrissCross project and the research conducted in the Reseda project[3] a tiered model of semantic interoperability was developed. This characterizes intersystem rela-

1 Cf. Jacobs, Mengel & Müller 2011 and 2010.

2 Cf. Karg & Jahns 2011; Landry 2009; Landry 2006.

3 Cf. Boteram 2010 and Boteram 2011.

tions in respect to search functionalities they may adequately support in heterogeneous information spaces.[4] This article describes the model, correlating levels of retrieval paradigms to levels of semantic interoperability with reference to respective examples from selective mapping projects. As an outlook that goes beyond mere linking activities, it sketches structural models for semantic interoperability and their potential to support cross-cultural exploration in addition to cross-institutional retrieval.

2. *Retrieval paradigms*

Four retrieval paradigms can be distinguished based on (1) the type of access points used in query formulation and (2) the requirements that specific retrieval features place on the modelling of indexing languages and on indexing methods:

- word-based query
- conceptual query
- conceptual exploration
- topical exploration.[5]

Word-based query refers to a basic retrieval feature that is typical for conventional web search engines like Google. It is easy to implement and neither requires an indexing language nor an indexing method at all. The character strings the information seekers use in their query formulation are matched against the character strings used to describe an information resource. The retrieval results lack precision. Subject authority data are only considered in form of subject indexing data if at all. This means that the character strings of the query are matched against the character strings of the main representation of a concept (i.e. preferred label or notation) which is assigned to an information resource to describe its topic. If information seekers are not familiar with the characteristics of the indexing languages and have a complex information need, it is unlikely that they by chance express it adequately in terms of the individual indexing language. However, word-based queries may guide information seekers towards controlled vocabularies and hence towards concept-based search features.

In *conceptual queries*, concepts modelled in indexing languages are used in query formulation. This requires that information seekers know the corresponding knowledge organization systems well. The retrieval results are

---

4 A preliminary version of this model was described in the proceedings of the 11th international ISKO conference in Rome. See Boteram, Gödert & Hubrich 2010.

5 This description should be understood supplemental to other common information retrieval models.

characterized by a good precision. Information retrieval systems that support conceptual queries integrate concept schemes. Not only do they offer the preferred term or notation as a possible access point to information resources but also provide additional access points in form of synonyms and quasi-synonyms.

Word-based as well as concept-based queries mainly correspond to the query-response paradigm; they influence the retrieval process in respect to recall and precision. More sophisticated search methods like explorative search processes aim at clarifying and specifying the information need. They may also help modifying retrieval results. If indexing languages consist of a mere list of terms that represent individual concepts, information seekers are not assisted in exploratory processes. They have to rely on the structural characteristics of the individual language and their own cognitive and associative ability in order to find additional information; they have to use Boolean operators, apply techniques like truncation and possibly go through different word variations in different search processes. As a consequence, exploratory processes are time-consuming and lack efficiency.

Processes of *conceptual exploration* can be supported by integrating a knowledge organization system with a consistent and gapless structure of document-independent a priori relations into an information retrieval system. The expressivity of these relations influences the functionalities they can support. Ambitious approaches require the usage of a differentiated inventory of typed inter-concept relations with assigned logical characteristics that go beyond hierarchical and associative relations commonly modelled in thesauri and classifications. Logical properties of relations like transitivity allow machine-assisted reasoning and automatic query-expansion. The semantic content of typed relations like agent-process relations assist information seekers in cognitive explorative processes. The relations may be used as filters for selective modifications of queries[6] as illustrated in Figures 1 and 2.

6 See also Tudhope, Alani & Jones 2001.

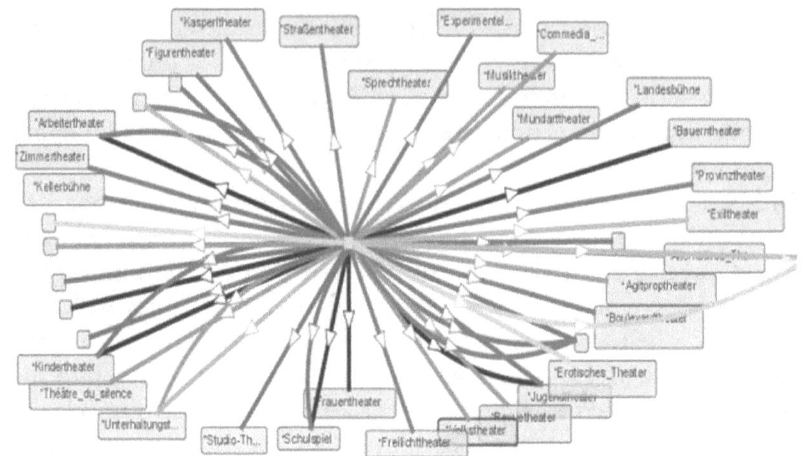

Figure 1: The concept "Theater" (theatre) with typed relations to other concepts[7]

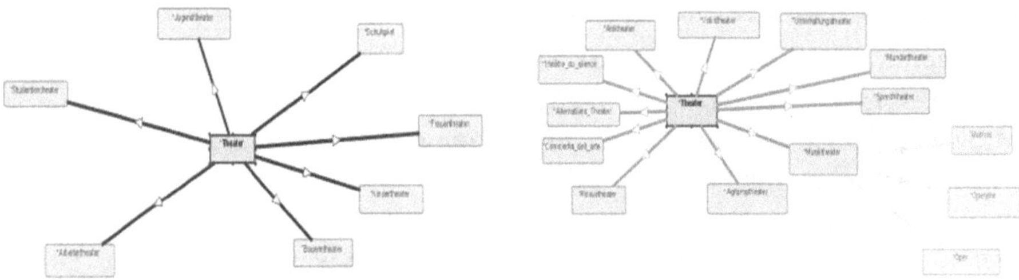

Figure 2: The concept "Theater" (theatre) with all relations that correspond to the genre (left figure) and those that correspond to the agents (right figure)[8]

Conceptual exploration uses a priori relations between individual concepts modelled in knowledge organization systems. In contrast, processes of *topical exploration* focus on a posteriori relations between topics of information resources. These topics are document-specific and may be represented by one or many concepts of an individual indexing language. Complex topics are composed of two or more concepts. Their meaning cannot merely be understood as the sum of the meanings of the individual concepts as in the specific context individual concepts may take over certain roles and functions, only some of their aspects or elements may be addressed and their meaning may be modified. A priori relations that hold between individual concepts do not necessarily also hold between the complex topics that contain these concepts. To assist information seekers in topical explorative processes that include complex topics, sophisticated indexing methods are required that also display document-specific a posteriori relations. Ideally,

7 Figure from Boteram 2008: 75.
8 Figure from Boteram 2008: 76.

these are not only cognitive interpretable but also machine-readable and machine-understandable. This retrieval paradigm is currently rather a desirable vision for the future than reality.

3. *Levels of semantic interoperability*

Heterogeneous catalogues provide access to documents from different countries and institutions that are indexed with linguistically, structurally and typologically different concept schemes. In such an information space the outlined retrieval features lack effectiveness: Language-specific queries only access data subsets and lead to unsatisfactory recall; information seekers have to conduct several queries to retrieve all relevant information. Information retrieval gets more time-consuming. The efficiency of retrieval processes can be improved if concepts of widely used indexing languages are connected. In order to establish semantic interoperability between indexing languages, different methods may be adopted that entail specific characteristics of the created intersystem relations. Up to now three levels of semantic interoperability can be distinguished with regard to the applied linking strategies and the implication(s) these have for the support of specific retrieval features:

- word-based interoperability
- conceptual interoperability
- differentiated interoperability.[9]

All levels have in common that their data can be used for automatic or cognitive expansion of initially conceptual queries and hence for improving recall. The precision of automatically expanded queries, however, in principle differs with respect to the specific interoperability level and may also depend on the directionality of linkages. Thus linkages that are unidirectionally established between a source and a target language may result in a significant loss of precision and functionality when used the other way round. Within the frame of *Semantic Web* and *Linked Data* activities, linkages are commonly created reciprocal and bidirectional to enable a wider range of possible usage. To what extent intersystem relations contribute to processes of knowledge exploration, depends on their expressivity and on the characteristics of the corresponding individual knowledge organization systems.

---

9 These levels refer to direct linking activities in which two concept schemes are involved. Models for semantic interoperability that utilize indirect linkages and structural models like the backbone model are not considered. An overview of methodologies for establishing semantic interoperability that also includes mapping processes between metadata element sets is given by Zeng & Chan (2010). For structural models of semantic interoperability see also section 4.

3.1 *Word-based interoperability*

The most basic method for establishing semantic interoperability uses techniques of automatic pattern matching. These are relatively easy to implement and rather cost-effective. Similarity between concepts of different indexing languages is assessed by comparing the character strings. Strings of preferred labels, notations and class headings are more often taken into account than synonyms or quasi-synonyms as these are sometimes considered less reliable[10] although they are expressions of the same concept. Similarity parameters either rely on the information inherent in the individual indexing languages (scheme level) or on subject indexing data (application level).

The easiest technique to connect concept schemes based on the same natural language (i.e. English) is *lexical alignment* which computes similarity of strings according to "language-agnostic heuristics like string distance"[11]. In the automatic subject alignment experiments conducted in the Stitch project and the Telplus project, this technique was enhanced by including external knowledge organization systems like dictionaries.[12] More sophisticated approaches also consider contextual information such as relational structures. However, these approaches are rarely adopted in the librarian community as many indexing languages – due to their historic development – lack a sufficiently developed relational structure and – due to pragmatic deliberations – do not provide relations with defined logical characteristics. In addition, indexing languages may be typological and structural different and hence not properly comparable in this respect.

The most common technique to connect concept schemes based on different natural languages is *co-occurrence mapping*[13] which is sometimes also referred to as *extensional alignment* or *instance-based matching*[14]. Two concepts are considered as similar if they are assigned to the same information resource, regardless of the peculiarities of the respective subject indexing method. This technique requires a critical mass of indexed data to be effective.

All automatic linking techniques lead to a word-based interoperability that is characterized by rather unspecified and usually non-directional one-to-one linkages. Connected concepts may differ in meaning. As a result, conceptual queries remain confined to individual indexing languages. The intersystem relations nevertheless provide useful additional access points and may assist in-

10 Isaac 2010: 33.
11 Ibid.: 32.
12 Cf. Angjeli & Isaac 2008; Wang et al. 2009; Isaac 2010.
13 Cf. Zeng & Chan 2004: 384; Zeng & Chan 2010: 4655.
14 Cf. Isaac et al. 2007; Isaac 2010.

formation seekers in cognitive processes of query expansion. If these relations are used for an automatic query expansion to improve recall, initial conceptual queries are in principle expanded by word-based queries with controlled terms (or notations). As the linked terms may differ considerably in meaning, the expansion may lead to a significantly decreased precision of the additional result set. Due to their semantic inaccuracy, intersystem relation created on the basis of the comparison of strings cannot adequately assist information seekers in processes of knowledge exploration.

3.2 *Conceptual interoperability*

In contrast to word-based interoperability, concept-based interoperability can improve the recall of initial conceptual queries. Information seekers can also obtain a good precision when the query is automatically expanded using the established intersystem relations. Additional precise access points are provided, making conceptual queries no longer limited to a single indexing language. This is achieved by adopting a cognitive linking method in which the best-possible connection between concepts is created. On the basis of all relevant information stored within the corresponding concept schemes, the document-independent and therefore system-specific meaning of the concepts is determined and compared. Semantic interoperability is defined by identity or significant congruence in the meaning of concepts. Missing definitions and a lack of modelled semantic relations often make high demands on the expertise of the persons creating the linkages.

Intersystem relations may be modelled uni- or bidirectionally, depending on the characteristics of the indexing languages and the envisioned application of the data. In general, modelling directionality is combined with a differentiated description of the characteristics of the intersystem relations and requires the definition of a source and a target language. When bidirectional linkages are established, concept schemes are used as both: as source and as target language. As a result, precise enhanced access points in both directions are provided. Unidirectional linkages are established exclusively from one source vocabulary to one target vocabulary. In information retrieval, their functionalities can only be exploited to the full if a query is expanded in respect to the concepts of the target language.[15]

One concept of one scheme can be connected with one or more concepts in another scheme. As a result, one-to-one, one-to-many, many-to-one or many-to-many linkages may occur in the end. Simple one-to-one mappings can be used for automatic query expansion; they may support interchange-

---

[15] Cf. section 3.3.

ability of concepts in processes of information retrieval. Yet, significant structural, typological and linguistic differences as well as differences in scope and depth of concept schemes often require a one-to-many mapping approach. One-to-many mappings are often associated with a specific directionality though this is not always modelled explicitly. The more concepts in a target language are connected with one particular concept in the source language, the less suitable the created intersystem relations are for automatic query expansion. Still, one-to-many linkages enhance access to schemes and information resources considerably; they should be in any case presented to information seekers for processes of cognitive query expansion.

There are two subtypes of one-to-many mappings that hitherto are not sufficiently distinguished in the terminology. One refers to a linking strategy in which one concept of one source language is linked to and represented by many concepts of the target language. The SWD-DDC mapping in the CrissCross project follows this principle.[16] The other describes a mapping method where one concept in one scheme is connected to and represented by a combination of concepts of the target language. A new compound concept is constituted that is not integral part of either of the original indexing languages though it is composed of elements of one. A kind of auxiliary concept is created whose benefit and limitations especially in connection with various indexing and retrieval strategies have not been fully explored yet.

Commonly, compound equivalent concepts[17] are a combination of concepts of a single target language. In the linking approaches adopted by the MACS project[18] and the KoMoHe project[19] Boolean operators or similar elements are used to create such equivalences. The Linked Data Service of the German National Library pursues another approach in order to provide a bidirectional linkage between SWD subject headings and DDC notations based on the unidirectional mappings of the CrissCross project. The compound concept established for this purpose is called *coordinated concept*. It was automatically created based on the CrissCross data and the DDC subject groups[20] that are used by the German National Library for structuring the different series of the German National Bibliography and the German New Release Service[21]. It consists of a combination of an SWD heading

---

16 Cf. Jacobs, Mengel & Müller 2010: 237.

17 See also Dextre Clarke 2011.

18 Cf. Jahns & Karg 2011.

19 Cf. Mayr & Petras 2008: 178.

20 The DDC subject goups are based for the most part on the uppermost two levels resp. the Second Summary or the Hundred Divisions of the DDC (cf. http://www.oclc.org/dewey/resources/summaries/#hun). For the three top DDC levels see also http://dewey.info/.

21 Cf. http://www.d-nb.de/eng/service/zd/gliederung_dnb.htm.

and a DDC subject group, thus combining elements of the two indexing languages.[22] As a huge amount of such compound concepts were produced, this may as well be described as the creation of an additional intermediate language that is characterized by following elements:

a) It lacks any relational structure.
b) Its concepts are compound SWD-DDC concepts which as such are not used for subject indexing. Yet, particularly in those cases where a DDC group and a SWD heading are both assigned to an information resource, these compounds can be used to improve retrieval.

As a nice side effect, conceptual intersystem relations may also provide enhanced support for processes of knowledge exploration confined to a single indexing language, irrespective of the applied linking method. This may especially occur if a concept scheme with a multitude of very specific concepts and an incomplete relational structure is connected to an indexing language with less specific concepts. The SWD for instance has subject headings that are partly not integrated into the relational structure and that are by far more specific than the DDC classes. In the CrissCross project the SWD headings were linked to the DDC classes with the result that often many SWD headings have been connected to the same DDC notation. Clusters of SWD headings occur that are characterized by their reference to a specific DDC class (cf. Figure 3). This may be utilized to facilitate the retrievability of otherwise stand-alone concepts within assisted processes of knowledge exploration or for processes of search expansion. It may also help closing gaps in the relational structure of the SWD and can be used for modelling more specific intrasystem relations improving the functionality of the SWD.[23]

Figure 3: Clustering of SWD headings via CrissCross linkages

22 Deutsche Nationalbibliothek 2010: 27.
23 Cf. Hubrich et. al. 2008: 294.

Not only do the CrissCross SWD-DDC linkages expand the relational structure of the SWD but they also indirectly differentiate existing intra-system relations. Hence new possibilities for structuring and presenting concepts or clusters of concepts are provided. The SWD – like many thesauri – only models hierarchical and associative relations without any further differentiation. Consequently, some concepts are related to numerous other concepts by just one relation type. The SWD heading *Jagd* (hunting) for instance has many narrower terms which can only be displayed in an alphabetical or unsorted list (cf. Figure 4). For information seekers not all of these may be relevant. To find and select the relevant terms, they have to scroll a potentially long list which may be very exhausting.

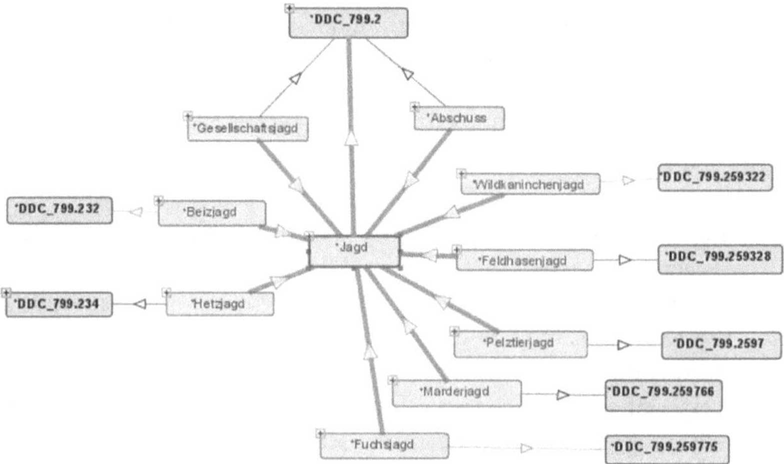

Figure 4: Narrower terms of the SWD heading *Jagd*

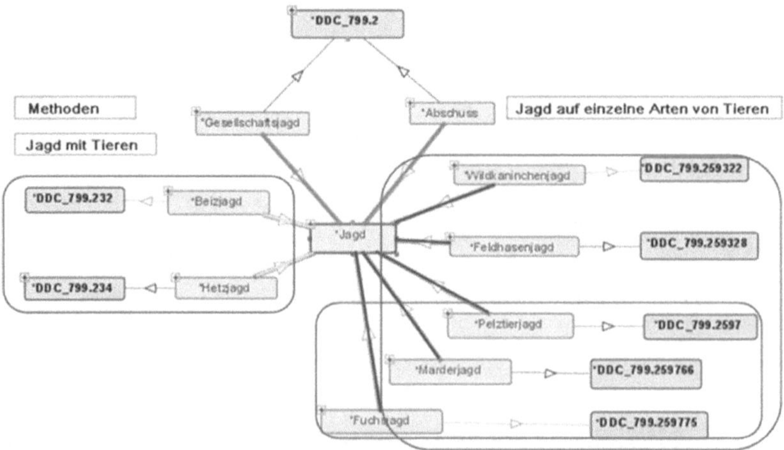

Figure 5: Differentiation of the narrower terms of the SWD heading *Jagd* via CrissCross linkages

Using the connected expressive DDC notations, the narrower terms may be divided into additional clusters of concepts that have – according to the DDC – common characteristics. Based on this, the relations may be further specified. In the case of the SWD heading *Jagd* (hunting), the DDC class headings may be used as an auxiliary to describe the concept clusters and their relation to the broader term more closely. Thus some narrower terms refer to hunting with the aid of animals, others to hunting specific kinds of animals. The latter may even further be differentiated according to the animal species (cf. Figure 5). Grouping the narrower terms in topical clusters, ideally with describing the clusters in natural language, allows information seekers to determine more rapidly the relevance of these SWD headings. Search and exploration processes become more efficient. Specific assistance for cross-language exploration is not provided.

3.3 *Differentiated interoperability*

In this article, differentiated interoperability is understood as a special type of conceptual interoperability. As such it does not only share the same understanding of semantic interoperability as the basic type of conceptual interoperability outlined beforehand but also the fundamental functionalities that are associated with it. It goes beyond the basic type by exposing characteristics of the established linkages and representing them in a way that they are cognitively and/or machine interpretable. Refined or even additional applications are possible. Differentiated intersystem relations may allow additional regulations of the recall of enhanced conceptual queries. They may also foster ranking mechanisms in respect to information resources that are retrieved subsequently to an automatically expanded query. If their semantic content is adequately described, information seekers may quicker recognize differences in meaning and viewpoint. The connected concepts can be used more efficiently in query expansion and in processes of cognitive knowledge exploration. If valid logical attributes are provided, inferences can be drawn on behalf of the machine, preparing the ground for more sophisticated processes of information retrieval in heterogeneous information spaces.[24]

---

[24] An overview of inventories of relations used in mapping projects is given in McCulloch & McGregor 2008: 73ff.

```
800 |s|Kreuzgang
808 |a|M
808 |d|Beispiel in RSWK 3. Aufl.
809 |x|hu *erl
810 31.3a;3.5a
816 726.69#3# [2007-01-01]
816 726.796#3# {2010-06-16}
818 726.79#2# [2007-01-01] {2010-06-16}
```

Figure 6: Example of a CrissCross mapping in the SWD data file

The intersystem relations between SWD and DDC produced in the CrissCross project are characterized by two types of specification; both are stored in conjunction with the respective SWD heading and the corresponding DDC notation/s in the SWD data file (Figure 6). On the one hand a time stamp provides information about the period of validity of the created intersystem relation/s. On the other hand four *degrees of determinacy* make statements about the level of contentual congruence of the connected concepts in the form of numbers. The time stamp takes into account the fact that the meaning of concepts may change in future and guarantees precise transition from SWD to DDC over time. The degrees of determinacy consider the typological and conceptual differences between SWD and DDC as well as the unidirectional one-to-many mapping approach. They are adjusted to the peculiarities of the target language, i.e. the DDC, and allow to structure DDC-related information resources or to regulate the recall of retrieved DDC-indexed documents.[25] When used the other way round, they lack similar functionalities due to the irreconcilable dissimilarities of SWD and DDC. Thus the SWD partly resembles a thesaurus and does not model concepts as classes like the DDC. Truncation as a means to enhance query results cannot be applied in the same way as the SWD indexing data is less expressive than the DDC notations. Whereas DDC concepts are mainly pre-combined and discipline-focused, many SWD headings do not exhibit a specific (a priori) context. Such a context is only constituted a posteriori in the act of subject indexing when several SWD headings are combined to represent a document's topic, following post-coordination rules. Even then the disciplinary context may still not be recognized by machines and may become only obvious after cognitive interpretation. Differentiated query expansion in respect to SWD-indexed information resources requires new, SWD-related criteria for the description of intersystem linkages.

The recommendation of the *Simple Knowledge Organization System (SKOS)* provides a set of five intersystem relations to represent bidirectional link-

25 Cf. Jacobs, Mengel & Müller 2010: 238f.

ages[26] between concepts of distinct indexing languages: *skos:exactMatch*, *skos:closeMatch*, *skos:narrowMatch*, *skos:broadMatch* and *skos:relatedMatch*.[27,28] A closer look at these reveals that only two of them may be adopted to adequately describe the intersystem relations that are in the focus of this article. *Skos:narrowMatch* and *skos:broadMatch* are defined as sub-properties of the common interconcept relations *skos:narrower* and *skos:broader* and display a hierarchical relation. This contrasts with the idea of equivalency that underlies the discussed conceptual and differentiated interoperability. The same applies to the relation type *skos:relatedMatch*. As a sub-property of the interconcept relation *skos:related* it refers to an associative symmetric relation:

> using the SKOS semantic relation properties (*skos:broader, skos:narrower, skos:related*) to link concepts in **different** concept schemes is also **consistent** with the SKOS data model [....] The mapping properties *skos:broadMatch, skos:narrowMatch* and *skos:related-Match* are provided as convenience, for situations where the provenance of the data is known, and it is useful to be able to tell at a glance the difference between internal links within a concept scheme and mapping links between concept schemes.[29]

The remaining two mapping types, i.e. *skos:exactMatch* and *skos:closeMatch*, are quite suitable for expressing equivalent relationships between concepts of distinct indexing languages. According to SKOS they refer to linkages between two concepts that are sufficiently similar to be used interchangeably in a lot of or at least in some information retrieval systems. *Skos:exactMatch* is defined as sub-property of *skos:closeMatch* and differs from the latter by the logical property of transitivity, thus allowing to draw inferences.[30] Such a logical property, however, requires concept schemes which exhibit a gapless relational structure with logical properties. This structure should be taken into account when intersystem relations are established. Otherwise false inferences or none at all may be drawn. Unfortunately, many indexing languages lack a consistent and gapless relational structure due to their historic development.

A more detailed inventory of intersystem relations was developed by Chaplan based on intellectually created linkages between the *Laborline The-*

---

26 Unidirectional linkages have not been in the focus of the SKOS community so far although with the differentiated mapping approach of the CrissCross project a significant case study is available.

27 W3C 2009a and W3C 2009b.

28 SKOS does not distinguish between word-based and conceptual intersystem relations so that the provided intersystem relations may be equally used for representing both though the functionalities of word-based and conceptual intersystem relations differ in retrieval scenarios (cf. section 3.1 and 3.2). In this context they are viewed as a possibility for representing conceptual intersystem relations.

29 W3C 2009b.

30 Ibid.

saurus and the *Library of Congress Subject Headings (LCSH)*.[31] Chaplan distinguishes between 19 match types (see Table 1) which mostly refer to differences in the linguistic form rather than on minor deviations in the meaning of the concepts. As a consequence, they may preferably be adopted for linkages between knowledge system that are similar in language, viewpoint, concept modelling and application. Within the framework of the HILT project[32], Chaplan's match types were examined with the result that 9 out of 19 could be verified for the DDC-spine based terminology server.[33]

Match code	Match type	Examples Laborline Thesaurus	Examples LCSH
1	Exact match	Industrial relations	Industrial relations
2	Exact cross-reference match	Child labor	USE Children–employment
3	Exact match, but with intervening characters	Research management	Research–management
4	Plurals	Displaced worker	Displaced workers
5	Subordination, in the form of a species-genus relationship	Industrywide bargaining	Collective bargaining
6	Superordination, in the form of genus-species relationship	Motor vehicle industry	Automobile industry and trade
7	Part-of-speech difference	Employment interview	Employment interviewing
8	Word-order variation	Illegal alien	Aliens, illegal
9	Further specification	Absenteeism	Absenteeism (labor)
10	Spelling variation	No strike clause	No-strike clause
11	Suffix variation	Quality of working life	Quality of work life
12	Abbreviation or acronym	Alta.	Alberta
13	Subdivision (Represents term that was used only as a subdivision in LCSH)	Measurement	Measurement
14	Concept match	Performance appraisal	Employees–Rating of
15	Homograph	Millinery [referring to hat industry]	Millinery [referring to costume hats]

31 Chaplan 1995.

32 Cf. Dunsire and Nicholson 2011.

33 McCulloch & McGregor 2008.

Match code	Match type	Examples Laborline Thesaurus	Examples LCSH
16	Translation	Precedent	Stare decisis
17	Date or numerical variation	1935	Nineteen thirty-five
18	No match	Boulwarism	deskilling
19	Opposite or negative	Desegregation	Segregation

Table 1: Chaplan's match types[34]

First approaches towards specifying the semantic content of intersystem relations between concepts of knowledge systems that significantly differ in structure, typology, viewpoint, specificity and application were conducted within the scope of the research of the Reseda project with reference to the experiences and observations made in the CrissCross project.[35] A final inventory of specified mapping relations that is general in coverage and specific in depth and that moreover is adjusted to different types of knowledge organization systems have not been developed yet and will remain a task for future research. The intellectual effort which it takes to develop and apply such an inventory, however, is only justified if the relational structure of the individual knowledge systems is likewise improved. Intersystem relations cannot be understood independently from semantic intrasystem relations but have to complement these to a certain extent. Expressive intersystem relations should go along with expressive intrasystem relations.

4. *Structural models of semantic interoperability*

The transition from one knowledge system to another may be eased if the established conceptual intersystem relations are specified. Yet, even differentiated interoperability may not provide additional support for processes of cognitive exploration that go beyond a single knowledge organization system. Significant differences in structure, typology and viewpoint remain a difficulty for the effective simultaneous usage of several knowledge systems, especially if several concept schemes are involved. Processes of assisted cross-exploration, that use established intersystem relations as well intrasystem relations, require an adequate structural model of semantic interoperability. This should not only focus on the intersystem relations but also take into account the relational structure of the corresponding indexing languages.

Many traditional cross-concordances like MACS follow either strictly or at least as far as possible the *non-equivalent pairs model* that aims at establish-

34 Cf. Chaplan 1995: 45–47.
35 Cf. Boteram and Hubrich 2010.

ing direct linkages between concepts of all indexing languages (Figure 7, left). This is very useful for processes of query expansion: regardless which language is used in query formulation, precise enhanced access points can be provided. However, it does not solve the problem of structural differences and distinct viewpoints. The more structural dissimilar concept schemes from different countries are involved in cross-explorative processes, the more difficult it is for information seekers to get familiar with the cultural viewpoints that are reflected in the schemes, especially if concept schemes lack a relational structure.

The *backbone, spine* or *(cross-)switching model* pursued for example in Renardus[36] or Hilt[37] aims at keeping the efforts that come along with establishing and maintaining intersystem relations to a minimum. One indexing language is designated as backbone to which all other vocabularies are linked (Figure 7, right). In retrieval scenarios, the core vocabulary functions as switching language. Precise enhanced access points that may also be used for automatic processes of query expansion are primarily provided for those concepts that are directly linked to the core language. Indirect linkages from one knowledge system through the core system to another knowledge system might cause a loss of precision.[38] Nevertheless, such indirect linkages may be utilized to support cognitive query expansion. With the definition of a core system, a basic orientation and reference point for exploratory processes is given.

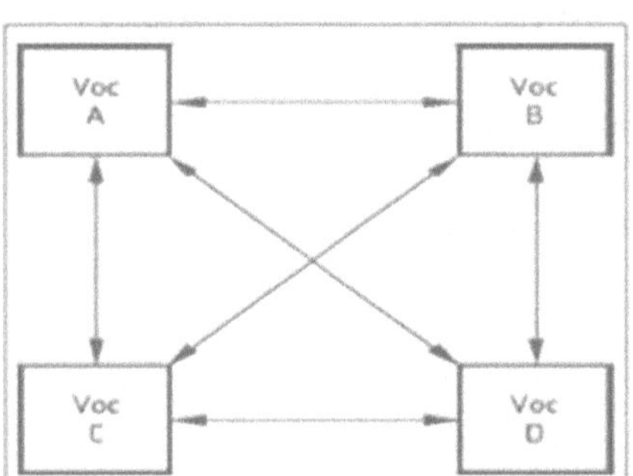

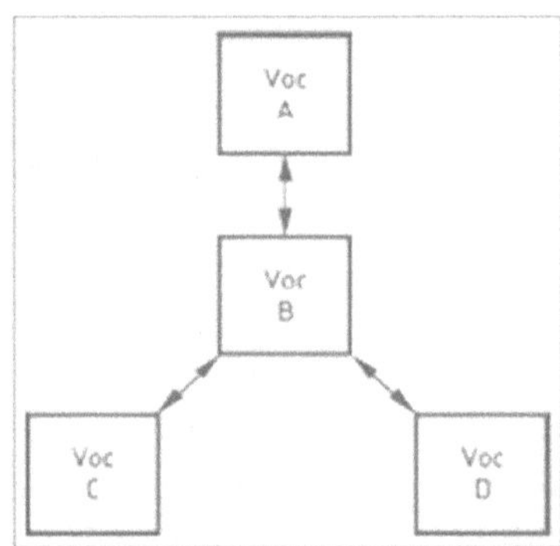

Figure 7: Non-equivalent pairs model, as applied to four vocabularies (left) and backbone model, as applied to four vocabularies (right)[39]

A sophisticated model for structural interoperability, that may further ease cross-explorative processes, is proposed by Gödert.[40] In contrast to other

36 Cf. Day, Koch and Neuroth 2005; Koch, Neuroth & Day 2001.
37 Cf. Dunsire and Nicholson 2011.
38 See also Si, O'Brien & Probets 2009.
39 Figures from Dextre Clarke 2007: 443.

approaches, Gödert does not solely focus on the status quo and on possible linking strategies, but also takes into account desirable developments that would improve the functionality of the indexing languages in homogeneous as well as in heterogeneous information spaces. Following the backbone model, Gödert suggests the development of a de-localized knowledge organization system out of an existing indexing language, most preferably a classification. This may further on take over the role of a switching language that mediates between a multitude of localized semantic networks. The localized semantic networks are also developed out of common indexing languages. They exhibit a gapless and consistent relational structure with logical valid relations that reflect local needs and viewpoints. Spine and satellites are connected by specified intersystem relations adjusted to the peculiarities of the systems (Figure 8).

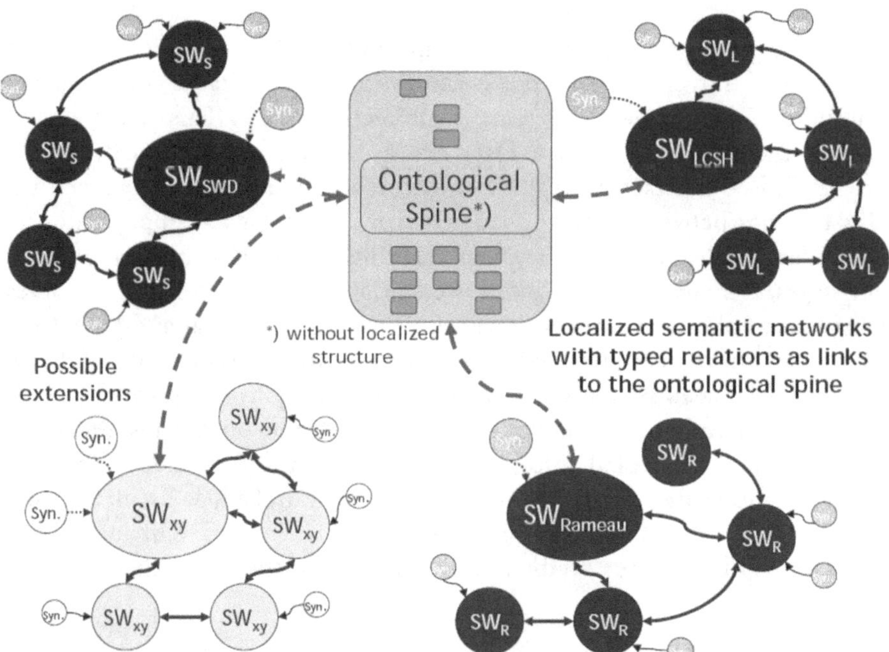

Figure 8: Model of a delocalized core system with linked localized indexing languages[41]

Such a knowledge space could be constructed with the means of *internationalization* and *localization*. In this context *internationalization* can be understood as a process of generalizing an indexing language in respect to the representation of concepts and their semantic relations so that in the end it

40 Gödert 2008.

41 The figure is taken from Gödert 2008: 239.

can handle multiple languages and viewpoints. This does not necessarily mean that the concepts and relations need to be universal or global in an ontological sense. It is absolutely sufficient if they can be commonly agreed on in an international context. *Localization* in turn describes a process of modifying knowledge systems in regard to local information needs. It involves the adequate translation of the internationalized concepts into the specific languages as well as the enhancement and elaboration of local or national concepts and especially of semantic intrasystem relations.[42] *Internationalizing* and *localizing* of existing concept schemes may take a great effort like the specification of intersystem relations but it may come out worthwhile in the end for the information seekers.

5. *Conclusion*

In the course of recent Semantic Web and Linked Data activities, the vision of a kind of universal knowledge organization system that is constituted of a multitude of knowledge systems is indirectly pursuit. This is visually expressed by the Linking Open Data cloud diagram maintained by R. Cyganiak and A. Jentzsch[43]. In this context, semantic relations in general but also linkages between indexing languages in particular are important. This article has focussed on intersystem relations between common indexing languages. Different types of intersystem relations as well as their characteristics and implications for processes of information retrieval and knowledge exploration have been outlined and structural models for semantic interoperability have been presented. Which type of linkage is adequate in specific use cases depends on the envisaged application and on the resources that are available. In a global information space like the Semantic Web many different knowledge systems, that are differently linked, will finally come together. How to take maximum benefit of all these different intersystem relations will be without doubt a central task for further research.

References

Web documents were accessed on May 31, 2011.

Angjeli, Anila; Isaac, Antoine. (2008). Semantic Web and Vocabularies Interoperability: An Experiment with Illuminations Collections. In: World

---

[42] Cf. Hubrich et. al. 2008.

[43] The Linking Data cloud diagram is available at http://richard.cyganiak.de/2007/10/lod/.

Library and Information Congress: 74th IFLA General Conference and Council. 10–14 August 2008, Québec, Canada. Available at: http://archive.ifla.org/IV/ifla74/papers/129-Angjeli_Isaac-trans-en.pdf.

Boteram, Felix. (2008). Semantische Relationen in Dokumentationssprachen – vom Thesaurus zum semantischen Netz. Fachhochschule Köln. (Schriftenreihe der Fachhochschule Köln; 54). Available at: http://www.fbi.fh-koeln.de/institut/papers/kabi/volltexte/band054.pdf.

Boteram, Felix. (2010). "Content architecture": Semantic Interoperability in an International Comprehensive Knowledge Organisation System. In: Aslib Proceedings 62 (4/5) : 406–414.

Boteram, Felix. (2011): Integrating Interoperability into FRSAD. In this volume.

Boteram, Felix.; Hubrich, Jessica; Gödert, Winfried. (2010). Semantic Interoperability and Retrieval Paradigms. In: Gnoli, Claudio; Mazzocchi, Fulvio (eds.). Paradigms and Conceptual Systems in Knowledge Organization. Proceedings of the Eleventh International ISKO Conference 23-26 February Rome, Italy. Würzburg: Ergon. 180–187.

Boteram, Felix; Hubrich, Jessica. (2010). Specifying Intersystem Relations: Requirements, Strategies, Issues. In: Knowledge Organization 37 (3) : 216–222.

Chaplan, Margaret A. (1995). Mapping Laborline Thesaurus Terms to Library of Congress Subject Headings: Implications for Vocabulary Switching. In: Library quarterly 56 : 39–61.

Day, Michael; Koch, Traugott; Neuroth, Heike. (2005). Searching and Browsing Multiple Subject Gateways in the Renardus Service. In: Cor van Dijkum; Jörg Blasius; Durand, C. (eds.). Recent Developments and Applications in Social Research Methodology. Proceedings of the Rc33 Sixth International Conference on Social Science Methodology, Amsterdam. Opladen: Budrich Verlag. [CD-ROM]
The preprint is available at: http://www.ukoln.ac.uk/metadata/publications/rc33-2004/renardus-paper-v2.pdf.

Deutsche Nationalbibliothek. (2011). The Linked Data Service of the German National Library. Version 3.1. April 21st, 2011. Available at: http://files.d-nb.de/pdf/linked_data_e.pdf.

Dextre Clarke, Stella. (2007). Evolution towards ISO 25964: An International Standard with Guidelines for Thesauri and Other Types of Controlled Vocabulary. In: Information – Wissenschaft & Praxis 58 (8) : 441–444.

Dextre Clarke, Stella. (2011). In Pursuit of Interoperability: Can We Standardize Mapping Types? In this volume.

Dunsire, Gordon; Nicholson, D. (2010). Signposting the Crossroads: Terminology Web Services and Classification-Based Interoperability. In: Knowledge Organization 37 (4) : 280–286.

Gödert, Winfried. (2008). Ontological Spine, Localization and Multilingual Access: Some Reflections and a Proposal. In: Knull-Schlomann, Kristina et al. (eds.). New Perspectives on Subject Indexing and Classification. Essays in Honour of Magda Heiner-Freiling. Leipzig et al.: Deutsche Nationalbibliothek. 233–240.

Hubrich, Jessica et al. (2008). Improving Subject Access in Global Information Spaces – Reflections upon Internationalization and Localization of Knowledge Organization Systems (KOS). In: Knull-Schlomann, Kristina et al. (eds.). New Perspectives on Subject Indexing and Classification. Essays in Honour of Magda Heiner-Freiling. Leipzig et al.: Deutsche Nationalbibliothek. 261–267.

Isaac, Antoine et al. (2007). An Empirical Study of Instance-Based Ontology Matching. In: Aberer, Karl et al. (eds.). The Semantic Web. Proceedings of the 6th international Semantic Web Conference, 2nd Asian Conference on Asian Semantic Web Conference, ISWC 2007 + AWSC 2007, Busan, Korea, November 11–15, 2007. Berlin and Heidelberg: Springer. 253–266. Available at: http://www.few.vu.nl/~swang/papers/wang_iswc07.pdf.

Isaac, Antoine (ed.). (2010). EPC-2006-DILI-510003 TELplus: Automatic subject alignment experiments. Available at: http://www.theeuropeanlibrary.org/portal/organisation/cooperation/telplus/documents/TELplus_D3.5_04012010.pdf.

Jacobs, Jan-Helge; Mengel, Tina; Müller, Katrin. (2010). Benefits of the CrissCross Project for Conceptual Interoperability and Retrieval. In: Gnoli, Claudio; Mazzocchi, Fulvio (eds.). Paradigms and Conceptual Systems in Knowledge Organization. Proceedings of the Eleventh International ISKO Conference 23-26 February Rome, Italy. Würzburg: Ergon. 236–241.

Jacobs, Jan-Helge; Mengel, Tina; Müller, Katrin. (2011). Insights and Outlooks: A Retrospective View on the CrissCross Project. In this volume.

Karg, Helga; Jahns, Yvonne. (2011). Translingual Retrieval: Moving between Vocabularies – MACS 2010. In this volume.

Koch, Traugott; Neuroth, Heike; Day, Michael. (2001). DDC Mapping Report: Renardus D7.4. Available at: http://homes.ukoln.ac.uk/~tk213/Mappingreport-d74.htm.

Landry, Patrice. (2006). Multilingual Subject Access: The Linking Approach of MACS. In: Cataloging & Classification Quarterly 37 (3/4) : 177–191.

Landry, Patrice. (2009). Providing Multilingual Subject Access through Linking of Subject Heading Languages: The MACS approach. In: Bernardi, Raffaella; Chambers, Sally; Gottfried, Björn (eds.). Proceedings of the Workshop on Advanced Technologies for Digital Libraries 2009. At4DL 2009. 8th September 2009 Trento, Italy. Bozen: Bolzano University Press. 34–37. Available at: http://www.unibz.it/en/public/university press/publications/all/Documents/9788860460301.pdf.

Mayr, Philipp; Petras, Vivien. (2008). Building a Terminology Network for Search: The KoMoHe Project. In: Greenberg, Jane; Klaas, Wolfgang (eds.). Metadata for Semantic and Social Applications. Proceedings of the International Conference on Dublin Core and Metadata Applications, Berlin 22 -26 September 2008. Göttingen; Univ-Verl. 177–182. Available at: http://edoc.hu-berlin.de/conferences/dc-2008/mayr-philipp-177/PDF/mayr.pdf.

McCulloch, Emma; Macgregor, George. (2008). Analysis of Equivalence Mapping for Terminology Services. In: Journal of Information Science 34 (1) : 70–92. Available at: http://strathprints.strath.ac.uk/3173/1/strath prints003173.pdf.

Si, Eric Libo; O'Brien, Ann; Probens, Steve. (2010). Integration of Distributed Terminology Resources to Facilitate Subject Cross-browsing for Library Portal Systems. In: Aslib Proceedings 62 (4/5) : 415–427.

Tudhope, Douglas; Alani, Harith; Jones, Christopher. (2001). Augmenting Thesaurus Relationships: Possibilities for Retrieval. In: Journal of Digital Information 1 (8). Available at: http://eprints.ecs.soton.ac.uk/4484/.

W3C. (2009a). SKOS Simple Knowledge Organization System Primer. W3C Working Group Note 18 August 2009. Available at: http://www.w3.org/TR/skos-primer/.

W3C. (2009b). SKOS Simple Knowledge Organization System Reference. W3C Recommendation 18 August 2009. Available at: http://www.w3.org/TR/skos-reference/.

Wang, Shenghui et al. (2010). Matching Multi-lingual Subject Vocabularies. In: Agosti, Maristella et al. (eds.). Research and Advanced Technology for Digital Libraries. 13th European Conference. ECDL 2009, Corfu, Greece, September 27 - October 2, 2009. Berlin & Heidelberg: Springer. 125–137.

Zeng, Marcia Lei; Chan, Lois Mai. (2004). Trends and Issues in Establishing Interoperability Among Knowledge Organization Systems. In: Journal of the American Society for Information Science and Technology 55 : 377–95.

Zeng, Marcia Lei; Chan, Lois Mai. (2010). Semantic Interoperability. In: Encyclopaedia of Library and Information Sciences. 3rd edition. Taylor & Francis. 4645–4662.

In Pursuit of Interoperability: Can We Standardize Mapping Types?

Stella G Dextre Clarke

Abstract: In the last few years projects such as DESIRE, MACS, CrissCross and KoMoHe have demonstrated the benefits as well as the challenges of mapping between controlled vocabularies. Each project has taken a slightly different approach to the definition and implementation of appropriate types of mapping. The mapping types supported by SKOS are slightly different again. In an ideal world, all major databases would be interconnected; all widely used thesauri, classification schemes and subject heading schemes would map to each other; and all of us would use the same basic types of mapping to enable universal interoperability. Or would we? This paper will discuss the feasibility and desirability of agreeing and implementing standardized mapping types.

1. Introduction

The development of today's immense communications networks has from the start been dependent on establishment and adoption of standards. Notably the Internet has been underpinned by TCP/IP (Transmission CommunicationProtocol/Internet Protocol), with its five-layer model of contributory standards and protocols for different aspects of data communication. Development of the World Wide Web came with widespread adoption of HTTP (HyperText Transfer Protocol). The more recent emergence of the Semantic Web has been largely reliant on RDF (Resource Description Framework). Without adherence to a bedrock of underlying standards, the networks would fail, and/or deliver gibberish.

Now that the Semantic Web is taking shape, the opportunity arises to gain access to vast stores of knowledge in multiple databases and other networked resources. The role of many standards is to negotiate the interfaces between the different resources and simplify access to many of them at one pass. But despite all the existing standards, there is still a vocabulary problem to overcome. The resources have been written in a multiplicity of languages, and indexed or classified with a large number of different thesauri, classification schemes, etc. It is tempting to suppose that the problem could be overcome by providing semantic mapping between these different vocabularies. The hope is that standardization of the mappings would enable and enhance exploitation of heterogeneous resources by the computer networks.

This paper explores the feasibility of standardization of the types of mapping used at all stages of information retrieval, and introduces ISO 25964, a forthcoming international standard to address this challenge.

2. *Mapping types in current use*

2.1 *Some well publicized projects*

Successful standards rely on consensus among the potential users, and so the first step in design is often to review existing practice. While a comprehensive review is outside the scope of this paper, we shall briefly examine practice in some recent influential projects. For purposes of comparison Tables 1-4 pick out some key features of mappings in the projects MACS; CrissCross; KoMoHe; and Renardus.[1] To add to these four projects, Table 5 summarises the corresponding features recommended in *Semantic Problems of Thesaurus Mapping* by Doerr[2], which draws on experience of mapping between the Art & Architecture Thesaurus (AAT), Mérimée Thesaurus and English Heritage Thesaurus.

Project	MACS (Multilingual ACcess to Subjects)
Context	Enabling multilingual access to collections indexed with different vocabularies in different languages (English, French and German)
Vocabulary type(s)	All are subject heading schemes (LCSH, RAMEAU, SWD)
Mapping types	Equivalence mappings only: either simple or compound. Compound equivalence subdivides into two types: – Heading A = Heading B OR Heading C – Heading A = Heading B AND Heading C Equivalences may be exact, inexact or partial.
Direction of mappings	One-way mappings are prepared, from source to target vocabulary (but source and target vocabularies may be reversed for some project participants and so mappings in the reverse direction are sometimes available.)
Other features to note	Inexact and partial equivalence mappings are established only where they yield acceptable retrieval results in the resource collections of the project partners.

Table 1: Key features of mappings in MACS Project

1 More comprehensive descriptions of the context and mapping methodology may be found in: Landry 2004; MACS linking manual 2010; Jacobs, Mengel & Müller 2011; Mayr & Petras 2008; Koch, Neuroth & Day 2001. See also the website of CrissCross: Mapping of German subject headings to the Dewey Decimal Classification which is available at http://linux2.fbi.fh-koeln.de/crisscross/index_en.html.

2 Doerr 2000.

Project	CrissCross
Context	Improving access to vocabularies and heterogeneously indexed collections (in one natural language)
Vocabulary type(s)	From a subject headings authority file (SWD) to a classification scheme (DDC)
Mapping types	"Degrees of Determinacy" – D1, D2, D3, D4- rather than distinct mapping types . However, D4 corresponds to exact equivalence, while D1 is applied where the conceptual overlap is small, and D2 and D3 are intermediate levels.
Direction of mappings	One-way
Other features to note	From one keyword, many mappings are allowed

Table 2: Key features of mappings in CrissCross Project

Project	KoMoHe (Competence Centre Modelling and Treatment of Semantic Heterogeneity)
Context	Distributed search across systems using 25 different vocabularies
Vocabulary type(s)	Some thesauri and some classification schemes
Mapping types	Three basic mapping types: – Equivalence – Hierarchical – Associative Also there is an explicit "null relationship", for use when no mapping is possible
Direction of mappings	One-way, but typically mappings have been prepared separately in both directions
Other features to note	Any mapping can be one-to-one or one-to-many Every mapping can have a "relevance rating" of high, medium or low (but in practice this capability has not yet received much use).

Table 3: Key features of mappings in KoMoHe Project

Project	Renardus: Cross-browsing European subject gateways via a common classification system (DDC)
Context	Search/browse across gateways using different classification schemes
Vocabulary type(s)	All are classification schemes
Mapping types	Five mapping types: – fully equivalent – broader or narrower equivalent – major or minor overlap
Direction of mappings	One-way, from DDC (Dewey Decimal Classification) to local schemes

Table 4: Key features of mappings in Renardus Project

Project	Doerr's paper on Semantic problems of thesaurus mapping[3]
Context	Query transformation is assumed to be the main application of mappings
Vocabulary type(s)	All are thesauri, applied to documents and/or museum collections
Mapping types	Basic types of mapping are: – exact equivalence – inexact equivalence – broader equivalence – narrower equivalence Exact, broader and narrower equivalence can be simple or compound Compound equivalence means a Boolean expression of target terms using AND, OR or NOT (but in practice no examples are given using NOT)
Direction of mappings	Assumed to operate reciprocally, except that "Boolean compounds can not be easily interpreted in the opposite direction".

Table 5: Key features of mappings in Doerr's paper

Each of these projects has a different context, and different selection of vocabularies to be mapped. Perhaps for these reasons, the approach to mapping is slightly different in each case. This creates a small impediment to any hopes of exploiting all the project results in one extended search system. Each time a search crosses a boundary where the definition of the mapping changes, there is a risk of semantic distortion. Nonetheless, a significant amount of commonality among the mapping types is evident, which is a good omen for any future standardization initiatives. For those projects which involve thesauri, it comes fairly naturally to develop mapping types which emulate the internal relationship types that have long been recommended in national and international standards[4] for thesauri, namely equivalence, hierarchical and associative.

2.2 Existing standards for mapping between vocabularies

In the first decade of the twenty-first century, two standards have already been issued which address the challenge of inter-vocabulary mapping, at least in part. They are:

3 Doerr 2000.
4 International Organization for Standardization 1985 and 1986.

- The British standard BS 8723 *Structured vocabularies for information retrieval – Guide*, of which Part 4[5] deals specifically with interoperability between vocabularies, and
- *SKOS (Simple Knowledge Organization System) Reference*[6], a W3C Recommendation for sharing and linking knowledge organization systems via the Web.

Tables 6 and 7 show key features of the approach to mapping taken by these two standards. The two were developed in parallel, with good communication between the drafting teams, so they have much in common and should not be seen as rivals. However, there is some difference in emphasis and context, and both of them leave something to be desired as our understanding advances and the technological opportunities develop. Hence improvements can be expected in future standards and/or extensions of these ones.

Standard	BS 8723-4 (Structured vocabularies for information retrieval – Guide. Part 4: Interoperability between vocabularies)
Context	Provides for mapping of thesaurus terms for all retrieval contexts, whether used as index terms or as search terms.
Vocabulary type(s)	The emphasis is on thesauri, although other vocabulary types are taken into account
Mapping types	Basic mapping types are: equivalence; hierarchical, associative – Hierarchical mappings are expressed either as"broader" or as "narrower" – Equivalence subdivides into simple/compound
Direction of mappings	Warns that a set of mappings commonly works well in only one direction, and advises that a mapping from Vocabulary A to Vocabulary B should not be used from B to A, without checking its validity in the latter direction.
Other features to note	Degrees of equivalence (such as exact, inexact, partial) are discussed but not formalised as distinct types other than those described above.

Table 6: Key features of mappings in BS 8723-4

5 British Standards Institution 2007.
6 Miles & Bechhofer 2009.

Standard	SKOS (Simple Knowledge Organization System) Reference
Context	Sharing/linking KOSs via the Web
Vocabulary type(s)	SKOS development focused initially on thesauri, but has subsequently extended to classification schemes, subject heading schemes, etc.
Mapping types	Basic mapping "properties" (skos:mappingRelation): – skos:closeMatch (symmetric) – skos:exactMatch (symmetric, transitive) – skos:relatedMatch (symmetric) – skos:broadMatch (inverse of narrowMatch) – skos:narrowMatch (inverse of broadMatch)
Direction of mappings	Mappings in the reverse direction are provided by symmetry or the availability of an inverse mapping
Other features to note	No provision for compound mappings

Table 7: Key features of mappings in the SKOS data model

3. *Introducing ISO 25964-2*

ISO 25964 *Information and documentation – Thesauri and interoperability with other vocabularies*[7] will be a two-part standard, intended to update, revise and replace both ISO 2788[8] and ISO 5964[9] (the current international standards for monolingual and multilingual thesauri respectively) as well as BS 8723. The drafting of ISO 25964 is undertaken by a working group with members from 16 countries, a chairman from the UK and a Secretariat based in the USA. Part 1 of ISO 25964 deals only with thesauri (monolingual and multilingual) and is expected to be published in 2011. This Part does not deal with mapping. Part 2 covers interoperability with other vocabularies, and much of it is taken up with guidelines for mapping.

ISO 25964-2 (as Part 2 is known) sets out the principles and many practical examples of mapping between one thesaurus and another. It also deals with mapping between thesauri and other vocabulary types such as classification schemes, subject heading schemes and name authority lists. As well as describing mapping types in detail, it discusses structural models for mapping across vocabularies, deals with the extra complications of handling precoordination among vocabulary concepts, and has some advice on data management. Drafting is very actively under way, so at the time of this presentation inputs from all interested parties are very much welcomed. During

---

7 International Organization for Standardization 2011a and b.
8 International Organization for Standardization 1986.
9 International Organization for Standardization 1985.

2011 it is hoped that a draft will be circulated within the ISO system (coordinated by ISO SC46/SC9) and will be made available for public comment.

4. *Mapping types in ISO 25964-2*

4.1 *Basic mapping types*

Most of the projects mentioned earlier are built round a context in which mappings are designed either for the conversion of terms in search queries, or for the conversion of terms embedded in document metadata, but rarely both. In ISO 25964-2, however, the treatment of mappings aims to be sufficiently general that it can be applied to either of these situations.

A "mapping" is defined in the latest draft[10] of ISO 25964-2 as a "relationship between a concept in one vocabulary and one or more concepts in another". Table 8 shows the three basic mapping types recommended, coinciding with those in BS 8723-4.

Mapping type	Tag	Example
Equivalence	EQ	laptop computers EQ notebook computers
Hierarchical	NM BM	roads NM streets streets BM roads
Associative	RM	journals RM magazines

Table 8: Basic mapping types in ISO 25964-2, with examples

The second column in Table 8 indicates the tag that should be used in mapping statements. Each of these tags has a parallel in the tags traditionally used for internal relationships, as recommended in ISO 2788, ISO 5964 and ISO 25964-1. Thus NM, BM and RM, standing for "Narrower Mapping", "Broader Mapping" and "Related Mapping" respectively, correspond to the traditional tags NT, BT and RT. The tag EQ stands for Equivalence, and it corresponds to the traditional USE/UF tags used between preferred and non-preferred terms in a monolingual thesaurus.

There is a subtle difference between EQ on the one hand, and USE/UF on the other. EQ marks a mapping between equivalent *concepts* in different vocabularies; whereas USE and UF mark relationships between equivalent *terms* in the same vocabulary. When two or more terms in the same vocabulary are deemed equivalent, one of them is given "preferred" status and the others are non-preferred, hence we use the tag USE to show an equivalence

10 Committee draft, restricted circulation.

relationship in the direction from non-preferred to preferred, while UF marks the direction from preferred to non-preferred. In the context of a mapping between concepts in two vocabularies, however, both concepts have equal status and only one tag is applicable, in either direction.

Despite the simple brevity of Table 8, ISO25964-2 accompanies these basic mapping types with additional recommendations that allow greater semantic specificity, for optional use. According to the draft standard, different degrees of equivalence can be specified, the equivalence mapping can be simple or compound, and it is possible to differentiate between three subtypes of hierarchical mapping. The various options for differentiation will now be described, and will be summarized at the end in Table 9.

4.2 *Compound equivalence*

Equivalence is the mapping type most commonly found in existing mapping projects, but it is far from straightforward. Very often a concept in one vocabulary has no exact equivalent in another, and the best way to represent the concept in the alternative vocabulary can be to use a combination of two or more concepts. This is known as "compound equivalence" or "one-to-many equivalence" (see Tables 1, 4 and 5).

Unlike SKOS, both BS 8723-4 and ISO 25964-2 provide for compound equivalence, and ISO 25964-2 discusses two subtypes known as "Intersecting compound equivalence" and "Cumulative compound equivalence". These are illustrated in Figures 1 and 2.

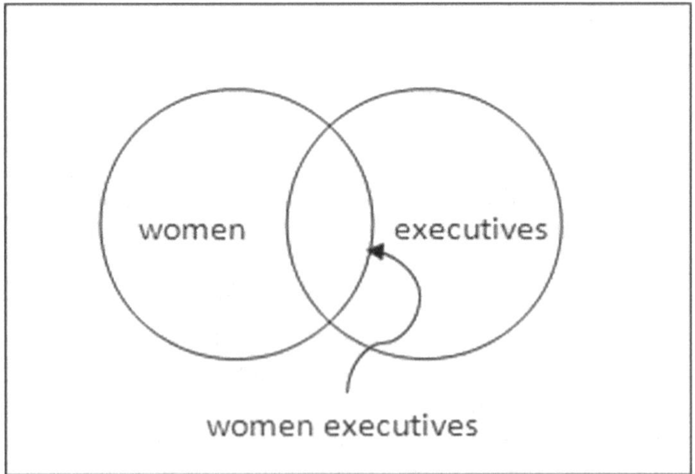

Figure 1: Example of intersecting compound equivalence

Figure 1 illustrates the solution when the concept of "women executives" in one thesaurus can only be represented by the combination of "women" and "executives" in another. The corresponding mapping statement is written:

women executives EQ women + executives

In Figure 2, the concept of "inland waterways" in one thesaurus can only be represented by the combination of "rivers" and "canals" in another. But the situation is quite different from that in Figure 1, and the corresponding mapping statement is written:

inland waterways EQ rivers | canals

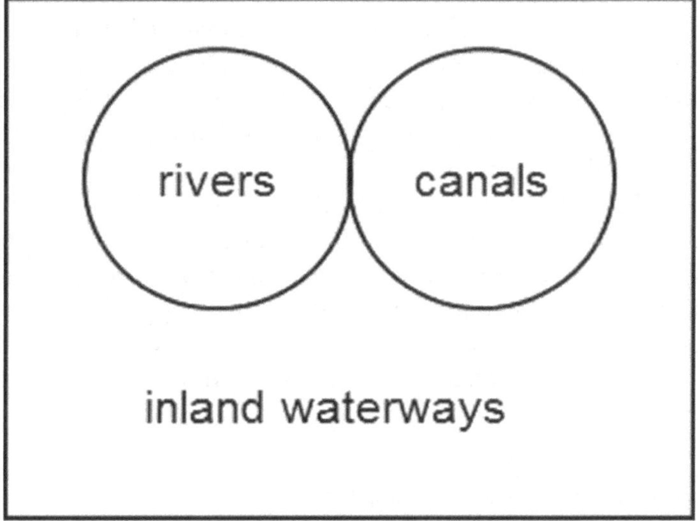

Figure 2: Example of cumulative compound equivalence

Both types of compound equivalence are commonly needed, as was found in MACS, KoMoHe and the projects reported by Doerr. It is therefore to be hoped that one day SKOS will be extended to provide for such mappings.

4.3 Degrees of equivalence

Several of the projects mentioned above distinguish between degrees of equivalence such as exact, inexact or partial. ISO 25964-2 acknowledges that it can be useful to differentiate between equivalences that are exact and those that are inexact. It recommends marking them with the symbols "=" and "~" respectively (cf. example in Table 9).

Exact equivalence	mad cow disease =EQ bovine spongiform encephalopathy guinea pigs =EQ guineapigs
Inexact equivalence	lawns ~EQ turf horticulture ~EQ gardening

Table 9: Examples showing how to mark different degrees of equivalence

Consideration was also given to "partial equivalence", in which the only difference between closely matching concepts in different vocabularies is that one is slightly broader than the other. ISO 25964 does not propose a marker for partial equivalence, but recommends making a choice between the options already available:

a) Establishing a hierarchical mapping e.g., "monarchs NM kings".
b) Establishing an equivalence mapping, marking it as inexact if that distinction is being used, e.g., "container plants ~EQ potted plants".
c) Establishing a cumulative compound equivalence mapping. This can be done when the target vocabulary also contains concept(s) comprising the missing part of the concept in the source vocabulary. For example, the concept of "aircraft" in one thesaurus might not be found in another, where the nearest concept is the somewhat narrower "aeroplanes". But if the second thesaurus also contains "helicopters", it can be argued that in many contexts a combination of this concept and "aeroplanes" adds up to "aircraft". Hence the mapping "aircraft EQ aeroplanes | helicopters".

4.4 *Specialization of hierarchical mapping*

ISO 2788 and ISO 25964-1 make provision for three semantically defined subcategories of hierarchical relationships, namely generic, instantial and partitive. Such relationships are specified using the tags BTG/NTG, BTI/NTI and BTP/NTP respectively. In practice these specialized types of hierarchical relationship have rarely been explicitly used. However, Semantic Web applications are becoming more popular, and if thesauri are to be exploited in this context, more precise semantic relationships will be needed.

In view of the trend towards more precise semantic information, the latest draft[11] of ISO 25964-2 incorporates a similar provision for specialization of hierarchical mappings. Generic, instantial and partitive hierarchical mappings may be identified using the tags BMG/NMG, BMI/NMI and

[11] The inclusion of specialized hierarchical relationships was decided subsequently to the Interoperability Conference held in Cologne; hence the specialized hierarchical relationships were not mentioned on that occasion.

BMP/NMP respectively (cf. Table 10). It should be noted that the partitive hierarchical mapping is recommended only in the limited range of situations familiar to users of ISO 2788, the main ones being for geographical locations, parts of the body, societal structures or fields of study.

Subcategory	Mapping statement example	Reciprocal example
Generic	rats BMG rodents	rodents NMG rats
Instantial	Paris BMI capital cities	capital cities NMI Paris
Partitive	fingers BMP hands	hands NMP fingers

Table 10: Examples of hierarchical mappings

4.5 *Major/minor overlap*

Among the projects mentioned above, the only one to use mappings called "major overlap" and "minor overlap" is Renardus. However, it can be argued that although the definitions differ slightly, "major overlap" is rather similar to Degree of Determinacy 3 in the CrissCross project, and "minor overlap" could correspond to Degree of Determinacy 1.

When concepts in different vocabularies have overlapping scopes, the appropriate mapping type in ISO 25964-2 is inexact equivalence. No particular way of indicating the extent of overlap is prescribed in the standard, but it is acknowledged that in some applications, it may be found useful to characterize inexact equivalence as "major overlap" or "minor overlap". An alternative approach, however, could be to establish inexact equivalence in cases of major overlap, and an associative mapping in the case of minor overlap. This would be consistent with the definitions of the mapping types in ISO 25964-2.

At the time of writing, rather few project results have been published which test the efficacy of these different approaches to expressing the extent of overlap of mapped concepts. Only time will tell which method proves more popular.

4.6 *Summary*

Table 9 shows the options recommended in the latest committee draft of ISO 25964-2, which is still subject to change up until approval of the final version.

Mapping type	Optional differentiation	Examples
Equivalence		laptop computers EQ notebook computers
	Exact	mad cow disease =EQ bovine spongiform encephalopathy
	Inexact	lawns ~EQ turf
	Compound Intersecting Cumulative	 women executives EQ women + executives inland waterways EQ rivers | canals
Hierarchical		roads NM streets; streets BM roads
	Generic	rats BMG rodents; rodents NMG rats
	Instantial	Paris BMI capital cities; capital cities NMI Paris
	Partitive	fingers BPI hands; hands NPI fingers
Associative		journals RM magazines

Table 11: Summary of mapping types in ISO 25964-2, and options for more differentiation

5. *Direction of mappings*

In the four projects examined (see Tables 1-4) mappings were routinely expected to apply in one direction only. Where two-way mappings were needed, an additional project was undertaken to prepare them (or at least check them) in the reverse direction. Similar caution is advised in BS 8723-4. It may seem surprising then, that SKOS routinely expects either symmetry or reciprocity to provide for mappings in the reverse direction.

Probably the main factor behind this apparent disparity is that SKOS does not provide for compound equivalence mappings. This is the type of mapping which causes the greatest difficulty for reversibility.

Since ISO 25964-2 admits compound equivalence as well as other styles of mapping differentiation, it too will advise that mappings prepared for use in one direction need checking before they can be assumed appropriate in the opposite direction.[12]

6. *Prospects for adoption of the standard*

This presentation set out to explore the feasibility of standardization of mapping types, and it has shown that the types of mapping adopted by

12 For more discussion of this issue see Dextre Clarke 2010.

some influential projects are not identical but share a number of similarities. ISO 25964-2 can and will recommend types of mapping that are not very different from these precedents. By describing the mappings in detail and providing multiple examples, it will encourage adoption of a standard approach. However, this standard will only be a "Guide"; there will be no legislation or even regulation compelling anyone to use it. We can only speculate to what extent the user community/ies will actually follow the guidelines in practice.

For standards that are not mandated by any legislation, the following success factors often apply:

1. Keep it simple
2. Address a real need
3. Adopt rules that are already broadly accepted in the user community
4. Keep it within the implementation range of available software
5. Make the standard available easily and free – or at least at a low price
6. Commit to lifelong maintenance

How does ISO 25964-2 measure against these criteria?

6.1 *Keep it simple*

As a consultant serving a diverse mix of clients in both public and private sectors, I have rarely found clients with the capability or ambition to manage mappings more complicated than simple equivalence. The cause is not just the absence of provision for sophisticated mapping capabilities in their existing software, but a Google-dominated mindset among the potential user community. Retrieval techniques that are hard to understand are often dismissed out of hand.

Exceptions to this general rule may be found among some specialists in academia, in the SKOS community and among the managers of the big universal classification schemes, subject heading schemes and widely used thesauri. Even there, however, my guess is that the range of mapping types and associated guidelines in ISO 25964-2 will be perceived as quite complex.

In mitigation, it should be observed that the more sophisticated features, such as compound equivalence, distinguishing degrees of equivalence and use of hierarchical or associative mappings, are optional. For simple applications, simple equivalence may be adequate and implementation need not be a big challenge.

For widespread take-up, it seems vital to present and publicise the standard in such a way that simple equivalence looks very accessible, and the availability of sophisticated optional mapping types does not impede discovery of the basics by non-expert users.

6.2 *Address a real need*

The most evident need today is probably for improving seamless access to many and various legacy collections. One thinks of the large national bibliographic collections, the library catalogues indexed or classified with the DDC (Dewey Decimal Classification), the SWD (Schlagwortnormdatei), RAMEAU or LCSH (Library of Congress Subject Headings), the museum collections catalogued using the AAT (Art & Architecture Thesaurus), and countless other databases.

Providing another incentive is the Semantic Web, promising to unlock additional resources as and when the servers on the networks can cross the semantic barriers strewn across the path.

Less immediately obvious is the potential for streamlining and energizing the management of information flows in all manner of organizations that may not even recognize they are in the information business. In the UK, for example, hundreds of local authorities and other public sector bodies prepare documents for access through their public websites, as well as via their intranets. The same documents very often need to be entered into their records management systems and are sometimes reutilized in applications for other user communities. Commonly, each of these separate systems requires the document to be indexed (or "metatagged") with a slightly different controlled vocabulary. The cost and inefficiency of multiple indexing can often be avoided by the use of mappings between the concepts of the different vocabularies. Good quality mapping is essential to achieve reasonable retrieval performance in each of the systems, but is not always found in practice. In the experience of this consultant, conformance with a standard for good practice in mapping (as well as in the original indexing) has the potential to make a big difference to the effectiveness of information management and the control of budgets.

Arguably, the need for good practice guidance on mapping is greater among the type of organization just described, than among national libraries or the maintenance agencies of the widely used classification schemes and thesauri. The latter typically have specialist staff with a relatively good understanding of controlled vocabularies, who can work out what to do from first principles, whereas the former are much less aware of the opportunities and the pitfalls. So I conclude that the need for the standard is real, and is all around us. ISO 25964-2 will do all it can to satisfy this need, by describing the practice of mapping in simple language, with copious examples. However, this still leaves a challenge to persuade potential users to recognize the usefulness of what they could have.

6.3 *Adopt rules that are already broadly accepted in the user community*

Tables 1-5 show that semantically the mapping types adopted by some high-profile projects are not identical, and the same is true of the underlying definitions of the mapping types.[13] However, the mapping types and their definitions do show similarities, which give some indication of what the community is likely to accept. ISO 25964-2 has built on the common ground as much as possible. Likewise it has retained the positive features of the mapping types in BS 8723-4 and SKOS (see Tables 6 and 7), while enhancing these with some more, optional, capabilities. Another factor favouring acceptance is the strong analogy between the proposed mapping types and the established relationship types for use internally in a thesaurus, as spelt out in ISO 2788.

Not so well established are the proposed syntactic conventions: the tags and symbols to be used in mapping statements. These include EQ, BM, NM, RM, +, |, = and ~.Where possible, the tags and conventions familiar in ISO 2788 have been adopted or adapted by analogy. However, it remains to be seen how widely the user community is prepared to follow the new "standard practice".

In summary, the semantic definitions of the mapping types recommended by the standard present little conflict with existing practice, but the tags and symbols to be used in mapping statements are to some extent novel and the reaction of potential users to this aspect remains to be seen.

6.4 *Keep it within the implementation range of available software*

It is unlikely there will ever be a mass market for tools to build and maintain mappings between controlled vocabularies, for this is a specialist field. At the present early development stage, there are very few off-the-shelf software products for this purpose. Most organizations wanting to prepare and/or use mappings are obliged to build or extend their own software for the purpose. However, some tools are emerging among the SKOS community and we can only hope that availability and capability will spread.

6.5 *Make the standard available easily and free*

One of the biggest impediments to the take-up of ISO 25964 is likely to be the price of obtaining a copy. There was a time, several decades ago, when

---

13 For brevity, these have not been spelt out in the present article, but may be checked in Landry 2004; MACS linking manual 2010; Jacobs; Mengel & Müller 2011; Mayr & Petras 2008; Koch; Neuroth & Day 2001; Doerr 2000.

the costs and hence prices of national and international standards were very effectively subsidized by national governments. Since then the pricing model of the national standards bodies has placed most standards in the information sector beyond the reach of all but the most dedicated followers. An analysis of this problem may be found in *The case for new economic models to support standardization efforts* by Lynch[14].

In the context where increasingly users expect information to be freely accessible via the Internet ("free" in more than one sense of the word) the idea of placing a high price on a standard needed primarily for networked information flows seems absurd. Would-be purchasers may be even more surprised on discovering that the work contributed by the experts who draft this and other standards is unpaid, nor is it subsidized in any way. However, no solution to this problem is in sight. Although the price of ISO 25964 has still to be announced, there is little likelihood it will be small.

6.6 Commit to lifelong maintenance

Without active maintenance, a standard in the rapidly evolving context of the Internet and other information networks is liable to become unfit for purpose and fall into disuse. This will hopefully not be the fate of ISO 25964. ISO and the national standards bodies do provide a maintenance infrastructure. The international committee ISO TC46/SC9/WG8, which has been working on this project for the last three years and has still to complete the drafting, may continue to maintain the standard for the indefinite future. Procedures are already in place for reviewing the standard, on a five-year cycle. Success in this case is likely to depend on the commitment of the international team of experts on the drafting committee.

7. Conclusion

This paper set out to explore the feasibility of achieving standardization of the types of mapping between vocabularies used for information retrieval.

From a purely technical perspective, the project looks feasible enough. The types of mapping described in section 5 above are not radically different from the practice observed in a number of projects that are influential in the community likely to use mappings in the context of searching over the Internet, and particularly the Semantic Web. The project to enshrine these in ISO 25964 is well under way, with good prospects of the standard reaching approval in 2012.

---

14 Lynch 1998.

The degree to which it is taken up in practice remains to be seen. Potential obstacles are the high price of international standards, and the paucity of commercially available software to handle the mappings in all the stages from establishing them through to using them in applications for indexing and/or searching. The potential users who could exploit mapping techniques during indexing applications are probably harder to reach than the community involved in Semantic Web search applications, and this could impede take-up. Another possible barrier is perceived complexity, although this may be overcome if potential users recognize that use of the "complex" features is optional and need not burden simple implementations of equivalence mappings.

Despite the obstacles, there is now a reasonable momentum behind the ISO 25964 project. Much interest has been expressed, and the need for standardization in Semantic Web applications is not disputed. ISO possesses the necessary infrastructure to support maintenance for the foreseeable future.

Post-script

Following the presentation given in Cologne in July 2010, the work of the drafting committee has continued and note has been taken of audience feedback during the presentation. This has led to several small amendments to the recommendations proposed for ISO 25964, which have been incorporated in the text of this paper. Further amendments are possible when the draft is circulated more widely for comment. At the time of writing it is anticipated that a Draft International Standard will become available for public comment later in 2011.

References

Web documents were accessed on March 31, 2011.

British Standards Institution. (2007). BS 8723-4:2007 Structured Vocabularies for Information Retrieval – Guide – Interoperability between Vocabularies. London: British Standards Institution.

Dextre Clarke, Stella. (2010). Types of Mapping Recommended in ISO 25964, and the Question of Reciprocity. In: 9th European NKOS Workshop at the 14th ECDL Conference, Glasgow, Scotland, 9 September 2010. Presentation. Available at: http://www.comp.glam.ac.uk/pages/research/hypermedia/nkos/nkos2010/presentations/dextreclarke.pdf.

Doerr, Martin. (2000). Semantic Problems of Thesaurus Mapping. In: Journal of Digital Information 1 (8). Available at: http://jodi.ecs.soton.ac.uk/Articles/v01/i08/Doerr/.

International Organization for Standardization. (1985). ISO 5964-1985. Documentation -Guidelines for the Establishment and Development of Multilingual Thesauri. Geneva: International Organization for Standardization.

International Organization for Standardization. (1986). ISO 2788-1986. Documentation -Guidelines for the Establishment and Development of Monolingual Thesauri. 2nd ed. Geneva: International Organization for Standardization.

International Organization for Standardization. (2011a). ISO/FDIS 25964-1: Information and Documentation – Thesauri and Interoperability with Other Vocabularies – Part 1: Thesauri for Information Retrieval. Geneva: International Organization for Standardization; Final Draft to be circulated Spring 2011.

International Organization for Standardization. (2011b). ISO DIS 25964-2: Information and Documentation – Thesauri and Interoperability with Other Vocabularies – Part 2: Interoperability with Other Vocabularies. Geneva: International Organization for Standardization; Draft to be circulated for public comment late 2011.

Jacobs, Jan-Helge; Mengel, Tina; Müller, Katrin. (2011). Insights and Outlooks: A Retrospective View on the CrissCross Project. In this volume. Presentation available at: http://linux2.fbi.fh-koeln.de/cisko2010/praesentationen/2010-07-19_jacobs_mueller_mengel.ppt.

Koch, Traugott; Neuroth, Heike; Day, Michael. (2001). Renardus: Crossbrowsing European Subject Gateways via a Common Classification System (DDC). In: McIllwaine, Ia C. (ed.). Subject Retrieval in a Networked Environment. Proceedings of the IFLA Satellite Meeting held in Dublin, OH, 14-16 August 2001 and sponsored by the IFLA Section on Classification and Indexing and the IFLA Section on Information Technology. München: Saur. 25–34.

Landry, Patrice. (2004). Multilingual Subject Access: the Linking Approach of MACS. In: Cataloging & Classification Quarterly 37 (3/4) : 177-191

Lynch, Clifford A. (1998). The Case for New Economic Models to Support Standardization Efforts. [Web Page]. Accessed 2011 Mar 22. Available at: http://www.niso.org/publications/white_papers/wp-lynch/.

MACS linking manual. (2010) [restricted circulation] Swiss National Library in collaboration with the Deutsche Nationalbibliothek.

Mayr, Philipp; Petras, Vivien. (2008). Building a Terminology Network for Search: the KoMoHe Project. In: Greenberg, Jane; Klas, Wolfgang (eds.). Metadata for Semantic and Social Applications. Proceedings of the International Conference on Dublin Core and Metadata Applications; Berlin 22 – 26 September 2008. Göttingen: Univ.-Verl. Göttingen. 177-182. Also available at: http://dc2008.de/programme/papers.

Miles, Alistair; Bechhofer, Sean (eds.). (2009). SKOS Simple Knowledge Organization System Reference. W3C Recommendation [Web Page]. 2009 Aug 18. Available at: http://www.w3.org/TR/skos-reference.

A Science Model Driven Retrieval Prototype

Philipp Mayr, Philipp Schaer, Peter Mutschke

Abstract: This paper is about a better understanding of the structure and dynamics of science and the usage of these insights for compensating the typical problems that arises in metadata-driven Digital Libraries. Three science model driven retrieval services are presented: co-word analysis based query expansion, re-ranking via Bradfordizing and author centrality. The services are evaluated with relevance assessments from which two important implications emerge: (1) precision values of the retrieval services are the same or better than the tf-idf retrieval baseline and (2) each service retrieved a disjoint set of documents. The different services each favor quite other – but still relevant – documents than pure term-frequency based rankings. The proposed models and derived retrieval services therefore open up new viewpoints on the scientific knowledge space and provide an alternative framework to structure scholarly information systems.

1. Introduction

In typical metadata-driven Digital Libraries three major difficulties arise: (1) the vagueness between search and indexing terms, (2) the information overload by the amount of result records obtained by information retrieval (IR) systems, and (3) the problem that pure term frequency based rankings, such as term frequency – inverse document frequency (*tf-idf*), provide results that often do not meet user needs.[1]

We will present an overall approach to use computational science models as enhanced search stratagems[2] within a scholarly IR environment. These computational models can be implemented within scholarly information portals. We assume that a user's search should improve by using these science model driven search tactics when interacting with a scientific information system.

This paper will at first introduce three scientific models: (1) co-word analysis and the derived concept of search term recommendation, (2) coreness of journals and (3) centrality of authors. The basic assumptions and concepts are presented.[3] The section on implementation deals with the set up prototype system that operationalizes the three models. The conducted evaluation and study with 73 students is described in the following section.

1 Mayr et al. 2008.
2 Bates 1990.
3 See in detail Mutschke et al. 2011.

The paper closes with a discussion of the observed results and the conclusion on the presented models.

2. *Models for Information Retrieval Enhancement*

The standard model of IR is the *tf-idf* model which proposes a text-based relevance ranking.[4] As *tf-idf* is text-based it assigns a weight to term *t* in document *d* which is influenced by different occurrences of *t* and *d*. Variations of the basis term weighting process have been proposed, like normalization of document length or by scaling the *tf* values but the basic assumption stays the same.

2.1 *Query Expansion via Search Term Recommendation*

Search Term Recommenders (STR) are an approach to compensate the long known language problem in Information Retrieval[5]: Searching an information system a user has to come up with the "correct" query terms so that they best match the document language to get an appropriate result.

STR are based on statistical co-word analysis and build associations between free terms (i.e. from title or abstract) and controlled terms (i.e. from a thesaurus) which are used during a professional indexation of the documents (see Figure 1). The co-word analysis implies a semantic association between the free and the controlled terms. The more often terms co-occur in the text the more likely it is that they share a semantic relation. These relations can be calculated and operationalized by different algorithms like LSA, PLSA, SVM and many others. In our setup we use STR for automatic query expansion where the original query of the user is enhanced with semantical "near" terms from a controlled vocabulary.

2.2 *Bradfordizing*

Bradfordizing is an alternative mechanism to re-rank result lists according to core journals to bypass the problem of very large and unstructured result sets (see Figure 2). The approach of Bradfordizing is to use characteristic concentration effects (Bradford's law of scattering) that appear typically in journal literature. Bradfordizing defines different zones of documents which are based on the frequency counts in a given document set. Documents in core journals – journals which publish frequently on a topic – are

---

4 Manning et al. 2008.
5 Blair 2003; Petras 2006.

ranked higher than documents which were published in journals from the following zones. In Information Retrieval a positive effect on the search result can be assumed in favor of documents from core journals.[6]

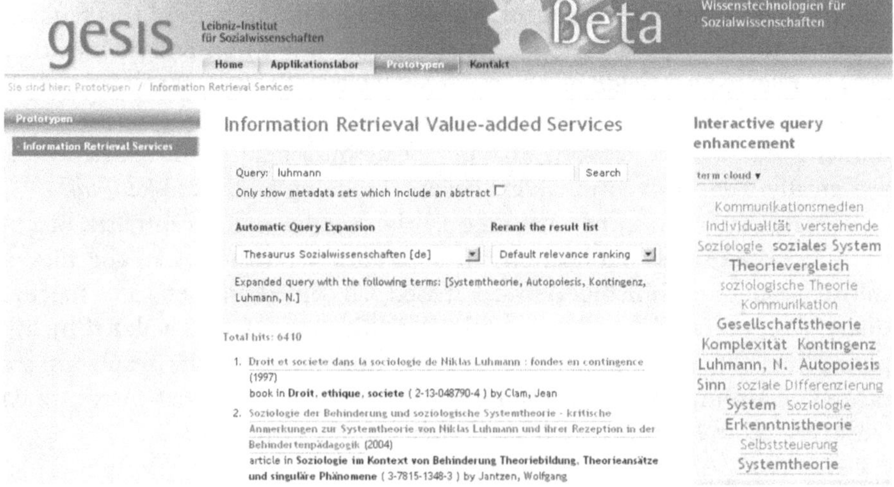

Figure 1: Mapping between user terms and controlled terms in the IRM prototype. Example search term "luhmann" and highly associated controlled terms (controlled context on the right) from a STR build on the Thesaurus Sozialwissenschaften.

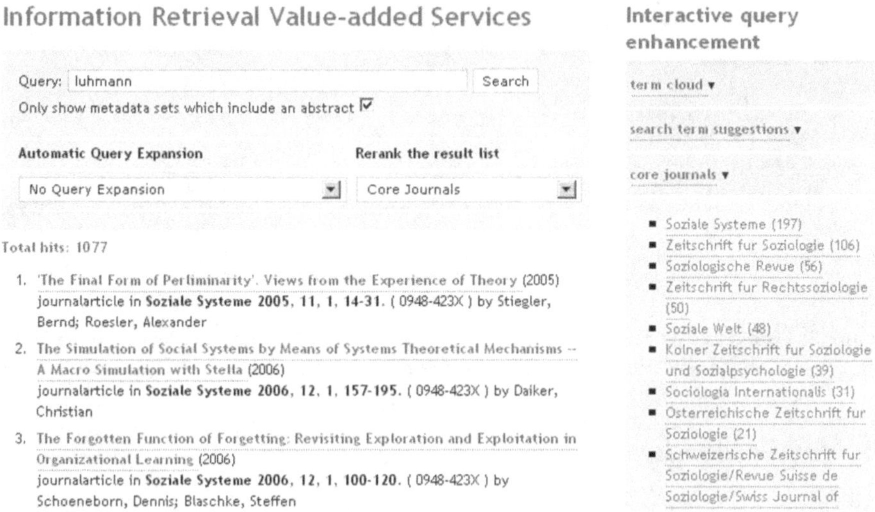

Information Retrieval Value-added Services

Query: luhmann Search

Only show metadata sets which include an abstract

Automatic Query Expansion: No Query Expansion

Rerank the result list: Core Journals

Total hits: 1077

1. 'The Final Form of Perliminarity'. Views from the Experience of Theory (2005) journalarticle in Soziale Systeme 2005, 11, 1, 14-31. (0948-423X) by Stiegler, Bernd; Roesler, Alexander
2. The Simulation of Social Systems by Means of Systems Theoretical Mechanisms -- A Macro Simulation with Stella (2006) journalarticle in Soziale Systeme 2006, 12, 1, 157-195. (0948-423X) by Daiker, Christian
3. The Forgotten Function of Forgetting: Revisiting Exploration and Exploitation in Organizational Learning (2006) journalarticle in Soziale Systeme 2006, 12, 1, 100-120. (0948-423X) by Schoeneborn, Dennis; Blaschke, Steffen

Interactive query enhancement

term cloud

search term suggestions

core journals

- Soziale Systeme (197)
- Zeitschrift fur Soziologie (106)
- Soziologische Revue (56)
- Zeitschrift fur Rechtssoziologie (50)
- Soziale Welt (48)
- Kolner Zeitschrift fur Soziologie und Sozialpsychologie (39)
- Sociologia Internationalis (31)
- Osterreichische Zeitschrift fur Soziologie (21)
- Schweizerische Zeitschrift fur Soziologie/Revue Suisse de Soziologie/Swiss Journal of

Figure 2: Using core journals for re-ranking in the IRM prototype. Search term "luhmann" and core journals (journal context on the right).

6 White 1981; Mayr 2009.

2.3 *Author Centrality*

Author centrality is another way of re-ranking result sets. Here the concept of centrality in a network of authors is an additional approach for the problem of large and unstructured result sets. The intention behind this ranking model is to make use of knowledge about the interaction and cooperation behavior in special fields of research (see Figure 3). The (social) status and strategic position of a person in a scientific community is used too. The model is based on a network analytical view on a field of research and differs greatly from conventional text-oriented ranking methods like *tf-idf*.

A concrete criterion of relevance in this model is the centrality of authors from retrieved publications in a co-authorship network. The model calculates a co-authorship network based on the result set to a specific query. Centrality of each single author in this network is calculated by applying the betweenness measure and the documents in the result set are ranked according to the betweenness of their authors so that publications with very central authors are ranked higher in the result list.[7]

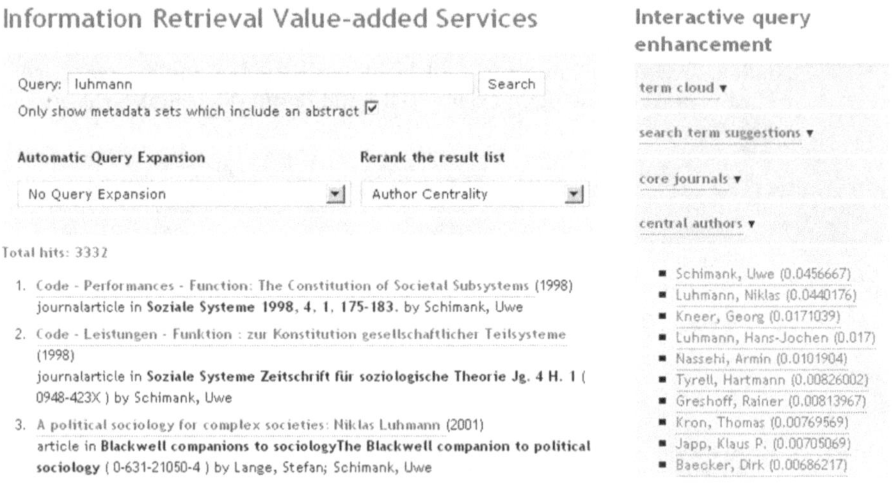

Figure 3: Using author centrality for re-ranking in the IRM prototype. Search term "luhmann" and central authors (author context on the right).

3. *Implementation*

All proposed models are implemented in a live information system using (1) the Solr search engine, (2) Grails Web framework and (3) Recommind Mindserver to demonstrate the general feasibility of the approaches. Solr is

7 Mutschke 2004.

an open source search platform from the Apache Lucene project[8] which uses a *tf-idf* based ranking mechanism[9]. The Mindserver is a commercial text categorization tools which was used to generate the STR. Both Bradfordizing and author centrality as re-rank mechanism are implemented as plugins to the open source web framework Grails. Grails is the glue to combine the different modules and to offer an interactive web-based prototype[10].

These retrieval services can be applied in different query phases. In a typical search scenario a user first formulates his/her query, which can then be enriched by a STR that adds controlled descriptors from the corresponding document language to the query. With this new query a search in a database can be triggered. The search returns a result set which can be re-ranked using either Bradfordizing or author centrality. Since search is an iterative procedure this workflow can be repeated many times till the expected result set is retrieved.

4. *Evaluation*

By measuring the contribution of our services to retrieval performance we expect deeper insights in the structure and the functions of the science system. The evaluation plays the role of a "litmus test" for the adequacy of the science models proposed.

4.1 *Methods*

The standard approach to evaluate Information Retrieval systems is to do relevance assessments. In respect to a defined information need documents are marked as relevant or not relevant. Large standard test collections (like TREC, CLEF etc.) contain pre-assessed documents from domain experts where all containing documents are judged relevant or not relevant. Since modern collections usually are too large to be assessed in total only subsets of the collection are assessed. *Pooling* is used to disguise the origin of the document.[11] In this standard approach subsets of the collections are formed by pooling the top *n* documents returned by the different IR systems to be evaluated. In the next step the assessors have to judge the documents in the subsets without knowing the originating IR systems.

8 Cf. http://lucene.apache.org/Solr/.
9 Cf. http://lucene.apache.org/java/2_4_0/scoring.html.
10 Cf. http://www.gesis.org/beta/prototypen/irm/.
11 Voorhees and Harman 2005.

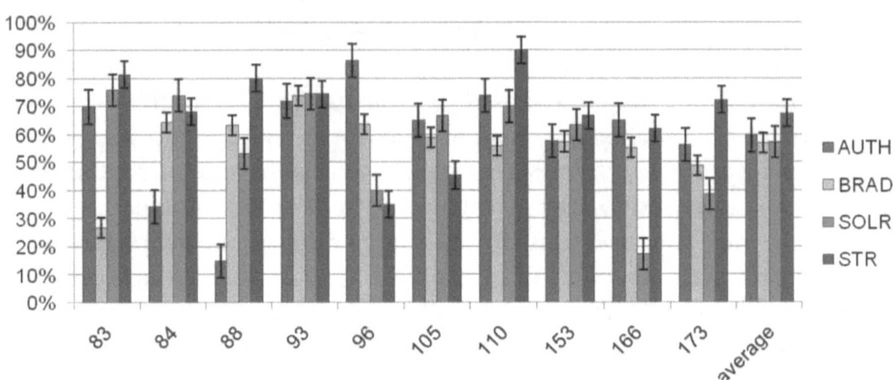

Figure 4: Precision@10 for each topic and service (Relevance assessments per topic / total amount of single assessments), including standard error

4.2 *Assessed Data Set*

We conducted a user assessment with 73 students who used the SOLIS database with 369,397 single documents (including title, abstract, controlled keyword etc.). After a briefing each student had to choose one out of 10 different predefined topics. Topic title and the description were presented to form the information need. The pool was formed out of the top n=10 ranked documents from each service and the initial *tf-idf* ranked result set respectively. Duplicates were removed, so that the size of the sample pools was between 34 and 39 documents each. The assessors could choose to judge relevant or not relevant (binary decision) – in case they didn't assess a document this document is ignored in later calculations.

The assessors did 43.78 assessments in average which sums up to 3,196 single relevance judgments in total. Only 5 participants did not fill in the assessment form completely, but 13 did more than one. Since every assessor could freely choose from the topics the assessments are not distributed evenly. Topic 83 was picked 16 times – topic 96 twice.

5. *Results*

5.1 *Precision*

The precision P of each service was calculated by

$$P = \frac{|r|}{|r + nr|}$$

for each topic, where $|r|$ is the number of all relevant assessed documents and $|r+nr|$ is the number of all assessed documents (relevant and not relevant). All precision values and numbers of relevance assessments can be seen in Table 1. A graph of all precision values including standard error can be seen in Figure 4.

The average precision of the STR was highest (68%) compared to the baseline from the SOLR system (57%). The two alternative ranking methods Bradfordizing (BRAD) and author centrality (AUTH) scored 57% and 60% respectively.

5.2 *Inter-rater agreement*

The assessors in this experiment were not professionals and/or domain experts but mainly library and information science students. However Al-Maskari et al.[12] showed that this evaluation setup can produce relevant data. They compared official TREC with non-TREC assessors. The agreement changed due to the different topics and the actual ranking position of the assessed document and was between 75% and 82%. The agreement rates of these studies can be compared to our assessments where the overall agreement between all topics and all participants was 82%. 124 of 363 cases were perfect matches where all assessors agreed 100% (all relevant and non relevant judgments matched).

To further rate the reliability and consistency of agreement between the different assessments a statistical measure is needed. Fleiss' Kappa is a measure of inter-grader reliability for nominal or binary ratings.[13] It is an extension of Cohen's Kappa for two-grader ratings. It can be interpreted as expressing the extent to which the observed amount of agreement among raters exceeds what would be expected if all raters made their ratings completely randomly.

Kappa scores can range from <0 (less than chance) over 0.0 (chance) to 1.0 (full agreement). Different interpretations of Fleiss's Kappa were proposed.[14] All Kappa scores in our experiment range between 0.20-0.40 (topics 84, 110 and 153) and 0.40-0.52 (rest of topics) respectively. Average score was 0.4 and median score was 0.43 which are fair up to moderate levels of agreement or mainly acceptable in the more conservative interpretations.

12 Al-Maskari et al. 2008.

13 Fleiss 1971.

14 Landis and Koch 1977 or Osman et al. 2010.

	non relevant				relevant				precision (in %)			
id	AUTH	BRAD	SOLR	STR	AUTH	BRAD	SOLR	STR	AUTH	BRAD	SOLR	STR
83	42	104	36	25	98	38	114	109	70,00	26,76	76,00	81,34
84	71	38	27	26	37	69	77	56	34,26	64,49	74,04	68,29
88	51	22	28	12	9	38	32	48	15,00	63,33	53,33	80,00
93	28	26	25	26	72	74	73	76	72,00	74,00	74,49	74,51
96	3	8	12	13	19	14	8	7	86,36	63,64	40,00	35,00
105	15	18	15	24	28	26	30	20	65,12	59,09	66,67	45,45
110	13	22	15	5	37	28	35	45	74,00	56,00	70,00	90,00
153	42	40	36	32	57	54	62	64	57,58	57,45	63,27	66,67
166	30	39	72	33	56	48	15	54	65,12	55,17	17,24	62,07
173	41	48	57	26	53	46	36	68	56,38	48,94	38,71	72,34
avg.									*59,58*	*56,89*	*57,37*	*67,57*

Table 1: Relevance judgments for each topic and service with calculated precision

5.3 Overlap of top document result sets

A comparison of the intersection of the relevant top 10 document result sets between each pair of retrieval service shows that the result sets are nearly disjoint. 400 documents (4 services * 10 per service * 10 topics) only had 36 intersections in total. Thus, there is no or very little overlap between the sets of relevant top ranked documents. The largest, but still very low overlap is among the standard *tf-idf* ranking from SOLR and STR which have 14 common documents.

6. Discussion

The evaluation of the STR enhanced system showed that term suggestions can provide an overview over different areas of discussion by adding new concepts. Additionally the STR can support different domains and perspectives.[15] This is known as a “query drift” in automatic query expansion but in the application of the STR the service retrieves more relevant documents. While the result set of a STR enhanced query grows and broadens (because of the OR-ing of the added terms) the first n=10 hits are more pre-

15 See Petras 2006.

cise and narrowed. This contradiction can be explained with the high descriptive power of the controlled terms that are added to the query and is an indicator for the high quality of the semantic mapping between the language of scientific discourse (free text in title and abstract) and the language of documentation (controlled thesauri terms).

Discussing the results of the two proposed re-ranking methods Bradfordizing and author centrality brings up two central insights: (1) users get new result cutouts with other relevant documents which are not listed in the first section (first n=10 documents) of the original list and (2) Bradfordizing and author centrality can be a helpful information service to positively influence the search process, especially for searchers who are new on a research topic and don't know the main publication sources or the central actors in a research field.

The Bradford approach always runs the risk and critic of disregarding important developments outside the core. It is often criticized to favor majority views and mainstream journals and ignores minority standpoints. This is a serious argument but it has to be seen as a problem of the data set producers because Bradfordizing only works with existing document sets, which are compiled (and prefiltered) by database producers.

The basic assumption of author centrality based ranking is that central authors are strongly associated with the mainstream topics of a research field and that the phenomenon of authors of high betweenness are supposed to be of high community driving relevance for the science system can be utilized. This perception of the strategic role of highly central actors in science might explain the high precision of rankings done by author betweenness: Authors of high betweenness address the key topics of a field.

7. *Conclusion*

Looking at the precision values and the overlap of the result sets two important insights can be noted: (1) precision values of the retrieval services are the same or better than the *tf-idf* retrieval baseline and (2) each service retrieved a disjoint set of documents. The different services each favor quite different – but still relevant – documents than pure term-frequency based rankings. The proposed models and derived services open up new viewpoints on the scientific knowledge space and also provide an alternative framework to structure the science system.

In a next step we plan to evaluate the proposed retrieval services with strictly scientific topics and scientist who are assessing documents in their specific research field.

Acknowledgements

Special thanks go to the students at Humboldt University (guided by Vivien Petras) and University of Applied Science in Darmstadt who took part in our assessment. We thank Hasan Bas who implemented the assessment tool.

This work was funded by DFG, grant no. INST 658/6-1.

References

Al-Maskari, Azzah; Sanderson, Mark; Clough, Paul. (2008). Relevance Judgments between TREC and Non-TREC Assessors. In: Proceedings of the 31st Annual International ACM SIGIR.

Bates, Marcia J. (1990). Where Should the Person Stop and the Information Search Interface Start? In: Information Processing & Management 26 : 575-591.

Blair, David C. (2003). Information Retrieval and the Philosophy of Language. In: Annual Review of Information Science and Technology 37 : 3–50.

Fleiss, Joseph L. (1971). Measuring Nominal Scale Agreement Among Many Raters. In: Psychological Bulletin 76 (5) : 378–382.

Landis, J. Richard; Koch, Gary. G. (1977). The Measurement of Observer Agreement for Categorical Data. In: Biometrics 33 (1) : 159-174.

Manning, Christopher D.; Raghavan, Prabhakar; Schütze, Hinrich. (2008). Introduction to Information Retrieval. Cambridge: Cambridge University Press.

Mayr, Philipp; Mutschke, Peter; Petras, Vivien. (2008). Reducing Semantic Complexity in Distributed Digital Libraries: Treatment of Term Vagueness and Document Re-ranking. In: Library Review 57 (3) : 213-224.

Mayr, Philipp. (2009). Re-Ranking auf Basis von Bradfordizing für die verteilte Suche in Digitalen Bibliotheken. Dissertation. Humboldt-Universität zu Berlin, Berlin.

Mutschke, Peter. (2004): Autorennetzwerke: Netzwerkanalyse als Mehrwertdienst für Informationssysteme. In: Bekavac, Bernard; Herget, Josef; Rittberger, Marc (Hrsg.). Information zwischen Kultur und Marktwirtschaft: Proceedings des 9. Internationalen Symposiums für Informationswissenschaft (ISI 2004), Chur, 6.-8. Oktober 2004. Konstanz: UVK Verl.-Ges. 141–162.

Mutschke, Peter; Mayr, Philipp; Schaer, Philipp; Sure, York. (2011). Science Models as Value-Added Services for Scholarly Information Systems. In: Scientometrics.

Osman, Deanna; Yearwood, John; Vamplew, Peter. (2010). Automated Opinion Detection: Implications of the Level of Agreement between Human Raters. In: Information Processing & Management 46 (3) : 331–342.

Petras, Vivien. (2006). Translating Dialects in Search: Mapping between Specialized Languages of Discourse and Documentary Languages. Dissertation. Berkeley: University of California.

Voorhees, Ellen M.; Harman, Donna K. (Eds.). (2005). TREC: Experiment and Evaluation in Information Retrieval. Cambridge: The MIT Press.

White, Howard D. (1981). 'Bradfordizing' Search Output: How It Would Help Online Users. In: Online Review 5 (1) : 47–54.

Would an Explicit Versioning of the DDC Bring Advantages for Retrieval?

Claudia Effenberger, Julia Hauser

Abstract: The DDC is constantly changing. In order to keep the classification up-to-date with scientific advancement and literary warrant, the editorial process regularly revises specific areas in the tables or schedules and, as a result, particular topics in a class are relocated into other classes or new, subordinate classes are created. In the German National Library, the DDC is the most important system for classification and indexing. Strictly speaking it is necessary to regularly review the correctness of the DDC notations, since their new meaning may not correctly reflect the contents of the bibliographic medium any longer. However, for economic reasons this is not possible with the result that a search for literature on a specific topic may return improper resources, as that topic might not be represented by the used DDC notation anymore. In a small research project, the German National Library is currently investigating if it is possible to solve this problem by giving each version of a DDC class a unique identifier. By doing this it would be possible to explicitly label which version – and thus which topics are contained – of a DDC class was used for the classification of a particular resource. If those identifiers conform to the generic URI syntax, we can model the relations between the bibliographic resources, the subject headings and the different versions of the DDC classes as a semantic network using RDF and then investigate if this approach can improve retrieval in heterogeneously indexed collections. This article presents some preliminary results.

1. *The Dewey Decimal Classification and the German National Library*

In the 1870s, a young librarian named Melville Louis Kossuth Dewey developed a system of classification which revolutionized the library world.[1] The first edition of the Dewey Decimal Classification (DDC) was published in 1876 and, since then, it has become the most widely used classification system in the world. About 200,000 libraries in over 135 countries use it and, in over 60 countries, it is used for the national bibliography.[2]

In Germany, there have been discussions about the use of the DDC for a long time. In 1998 the discussions became more serious and, in October

1 Cf. article "Melvil Dewey" in *Statemaster Encyclopedia*. Available at http://www.statemaster.com/encyclopedia/Melvil-Dewey.

2 Cf. DDC Einleitung 2005: xlviii.

2002, the project "DDC Deutsch" finally started. The goal was a translation of the DDC into German and the development of a German webversion of the DDC. The project ended in August 2005 and in October of the same year the first print-version of the German DDC was available. In the following January, the German webservice, named Melvil, went online.[3] The German National Library began using the DDC in 2006 and currently it is their most important system for classification and indexing. Most publications in the Series A[4], B[5], and H[6] of the National Bibliography have a DDC notation. Furthermore, the national bibliography is structured using a system derived from the top two levels (the 100 divisions) of the DDC.

2. *Revisions in the DDC*

The DDC plays an important role in classification and indexing not only in the German National Library, but also around the world. However, the DDC was developed over 140 years ago and the world has changed a lot during this time. Computer science, terrorism and genetics are only some examples of topics Melvil Dewey did not have to consider when he was working on the DDC. The changing world makes it necessary for the DDC to change constantly, too, in order to keep the classification up-to-date with scientific advancement and literary warrant. On that score, we have revisions in the DDC. The DDC revisions mostly belong to one of the categories *new classes*, *new built numbers* or *the relocation of particular topics*.

Old version	
363.3	Other aspects of public safety
363.32	Control of violence and terrorism

[3] Cf. the history of the DDCdeutsch project sketched on the project website at http://www.ddc-deutsch.de/projekt/historie.htm.

[4] A – Monographs and periodicals from the publishers' booktrade. Books, magazines, non-music recordings, further AV media, microfiches and electronic publications. It includes, starting from the bibliographic year 2004 translations and Germanica which have been issued separately in Series G so far.

[5] B – Monographs and periodicals from outside the publishers' booktrade. Books, magazines, non-music recordings, other AV media, microfiches and electronic publications.

[6] H – University Publications. Dissertations and postdoctoral theses at German universities and dissertations and postdoctoral theses in German language at foreign universities.

New version	
363.3	Other aspects of public safety
363.32	Social conflict
363.321	Aspects of social conflict
363.323	Crowds
363.325	Terrorism

Table 1: Old and new version of `363.32`

Table 1 gives an example for the creation of new classes. As you can see, the class `363.32 Control of violence and terrorism` was very vague. However, it has now changed into `363.32 Social conflict` and there are three new subordinated classes to specify the classification.

612.821	Sleep phenomena
612.821072	Sleep–human physiology–research,...
612.8210833	Sleep–human physiology–preschool children
612.8210835	Sleep–human physiology–adolescents

Table 2: New built numbers of class `612.821`

Table 2 gives an example for new built numbers. In order to cater for particular aspects of a topic for which there is no notation specific enough – in this case `612.821` – the classifier can build a notation.

We now concentrate on an example for the relocation of a particular topic into a new class. The class `726.7 Monastic buildings` (in German „Klosteranlagen") has the subordinated class `726.79 Parts and accessory structures` (in German „Teile und Nebengebäude) which, in turn, has cells, cloisters, refectories in an including note ("einschließlich Klausen, Kreuzgänge, Refektorien"). In this class there has been a change; "cloisters" has been separated out and there is now a new subordinated class `726.796 Cloisters` (in German „Kreuzgänge"). Of course the including note in `726.79 Parts and accessory structures` has also changed and no longer mentions "cloisters".

The revisions of the DDC make it necessary to continously review the correctness of already assigned DDC notations because it is possible that the new meaning of a class may no longer reflect the contents of a title correctly. The title „Mittelalterliche Kreuzgänge in Europa" (in English „Medieval cloisters in Europe") for example was classified with `726.79 Parts and accessory structures` because, at the time of classification in 2008, there was no class for "cloisters". However, "cloisters" are now no longer included in `726.79 Parts and accessory structures` and there is the more appropriate class, the new subordinated class `726.796 Cloisters`. In order to keep the collection up-to-date with the changes in classification, the publication should be re-classified from `726.79 Parts and accessory structures` to `726.796 Cloisters`. However, this is not easily possible without intellectual intervention and libraries generally do not have enough staff to do so.

Old version	
726	Buildings for religious and related purposes
726.7	Monastic buildings
726.79	Parts and accessory structures Including cells, cloisters, refectories
New version	
726	Buildings for religious and related purposes
726.7	Monastic buildings
726.79	Parts and accessory structures Including cells, refectories
726.796	Cloisters Class here comprehensive works on cloisters [formerly 726.69]

Table 3: Old and new versions of class `726.79`

The problem is that we have modifications in the DDC, but these modifications are not transferred to the assigned notations and this can lead to incomplete search results. For example, if you are searching for the class `726.796 Cloisters` in the catalogue of the German National Library you will only find the title: „Die singenden Steine von Moissac – Entschlüsselung der geheimnisvollen Programme in einem der schönsten Kreuzgänge Europas“ (in English: “Singing stones of moissac – decoding of mysterious programs in one of Europe's most beautiful cloisters”). However, if you are searching for the superordinated class and use a truncation, you will find more titles that are relevant:

- Der Kreuzgang der Abtei Altenryf (in English: The cloister of the Altenryf Abbey)
- Mittelalterliche Kreuzgänge in Europa (in English: Medieval cloisters in Europe).

The problem is that these titles were classified before there was the new class for “cloisters” and, because of that, the titles have been classified with `726.79 Parts and accessory structures`. However, even if the titles were not classified with `726.796 Cloisters`, we still want to find them if they deal with the same topic. We need to be more independent of class changes and to be able to find all the relevant titles in spite of modifications in the notations.

In a small research project at the German National Library, we are working on the question "Would an explicit versioning of the DDC bring advantages for retrieval?". In this project, we are evaluating if the problem of the modifications in the DDC classes and the missing modifications in the DDC notations can be solved using Semantic Web technologies. The project is on a conceptual level and this paper presents the preliminary results.

3. *Semantic Web as a solution*

In general, the aim of the Semantic Web is to offer information in a way that is exploitable by computers. The data model of the Semantic Web is quite simple: Statements are expressed with subject, predicate and object in RDF (Resource Description Framework) which has been a W3C recommendation since 2004.[7] You can make any statement about information in the World Wide Web using subjects for resources or rather the thing you want to talk about, predicates for attributes of the subjects and objects for the value of the predicate. RDF intends to represent metadata of Web resources such as the title or author of a resource. You can also describe vocabularies like authority data, thesauri or classifications like the DDC with RDF. In September 2010, the German National Library published the German translation of the DDC as linked data[8] as part of its linked data service.[9] The service offers an RDF representation of the DDC with class names, notations and see-references under a creative commons licence[10]. This is a first step and can be used as the basis to implement the model on the versioning of the DDC.

When representing data in RDF, you need unique identifiers for all entities in the domain of discource in order to make explicit what you are talking about. These identifiers are URIs (Uniform Resource Identifier) which enable us to clearly identify all objects and resources.[11]

SKOS is an RDF vocabulary that describes controlled vocabularies like thesauri, classifications and taxonomies.[12] As you can see below, SKOS

7 W3C 2004.
8 Cf. http://linkeddata.org.
9 Deutsche Nationalbibliothek 2010.
10 Cf. the website of creative commons. Available at http://creativecommons.org/licenses/by-nc-nd/3.0/deed.de.
11 W3C 2008.
12 W3C 2009.

helps us to describe the relations between DDC classes and their subordinated classes and also the CrissCross[13] relations between DDC classes and topical headings of the German Subject Headings Authority File (SWD).

We can use those concepts that come from the Semantic Web context to solve the problem of the changing DDC: Identifiers are created for each version of a DDC class and a semantic network built for searching. We need a unique identifier for each version of a DDC class. In our example, we give the new DDC class `726.796 Cloisters` a URI built from the DDC notation and, in addition to this, a time stamp identifying the date the class was changed. An example could look like this: http://dewey.info/class/726.796/2009/03/30/. In the case of `726.796 Cloisters`, 2009/03/30 is the date when the class was first published. The timestamp in the identifier makes it possible to differentiate between the versions of a DDC class. For the class `726.79 Parts and accessory structures` we have two identifiers: One is for the older version in which "cloisters" was included in the class with the time stamp of 2005: http://dewey.info/class/726.79/2005/11/02. The new version of `726.79 Parts and accessory structures` no longer includes cloisters and gets the timestamp of 2009: http://dewey.info/class/726.79/2009/03/30/. The newly created class `726.796 Cloisters` gets the timestamp of 2009, too: http://dewey.info/class/726.796/2009/03/30/.

If we adopt the versioning, we can identify the actual scope that the DDC class had when a title was classified. For example, the title "Mittelalterliche Kreuzgänge in Europa" (in English: "Medieval cloisters in Europe") deals with cloisters. This book was classified in 2007 when "cloisters" was still contained in an including note of `726.79 Parts and accessory structures` and this is why this title is classified with the DDC notation `726.79`. The title "Infirmarien – Kranken- und Sterbehäuser der Mönche" (in English: "Infirmaries – hospitals and hospices of the monks") is a general title about parts and accessory structures, so was classified with the new version of `726.79 Parts and accessory structures`. The last example is "Die singenden Steine von Moissac " (in English: "Singing stones of Moissac"), a title about cloisters which was classified in March 2010 and consequently got the new DDC class `726.796 Cloisters` which was built in 2009.

Currently, our bibliographic data does not contain any information regarding which version of a DDC class was used when classifying the item. It would be helpful not to lose this useful information. If we saved it in the descriptive entry, there would be no doubt about which version of a DDC

13 Cf. http://www.d-nb.de/wir/projekte/crisscross.htm.

class is meant. The date that identifies the change of the class could be saved in field 5401 of our intern PICA format. This is the field of the base number of the class. The date of validity could be fixed in brackets like this: 726.79[2005-11-02] {2009-03-30}. This example refers to the older version of `726.79`, in which "cloisters" was included. The initial date is written in squared brackets and the changing date is written in curly brackets. In the German subject headings, the time of validity is fixed in the same way. In case of the DDC class `726.796`, there would be no changing date in square brackets for new titles about cloisters as this class is still valid: 726.796[2009-03-30].

Now, if we had the versioning which identifies the real meaning of the versions of a DDC class, we could model the relations between titles, subject headings and the different versions of the DDC classes as a semantic network. Figure 1 shows the search with the semantic network and the versioning.

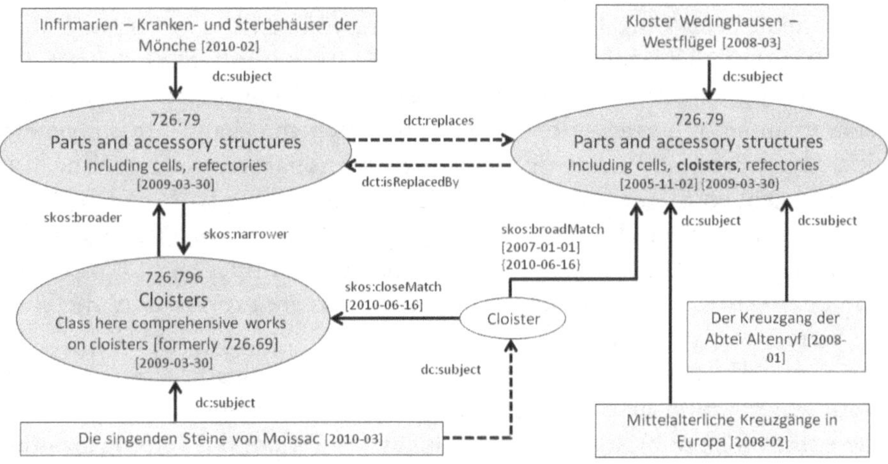

Figure 1: Search with the semantic network and the versioning

In the DDC class `726.79 Parts and accessory structures`, there has been a change; on the left-hand side there is the new version of the class without cloisters. This version replaces the older one on the right-hand side in which "cloisters" was included. We decided to use dct:replaces or rather dct:isReplacedBy to express this relation. These elements are part of the DCMI Metadata Terms[14]. Since the change, `726.796 Cloisters` have been separated out and have become a new subordinated class of `726.79 Parts and accessory structures`. The subordination to

14 DCMI Metadata Terms. Available at http://dublincore.org/documents/dcmi-terms/.

`726.79 Parts and accessory structures` is modeled as a skos:narrower or rather skos:broader relation.

This figure also shows the CrissCross connection between the German subject heading "Kloster" (in English: cloister) and the DDC classes which is modeled with SKOS. Formerly, when "cloisters" was included in `726.79 Parts and accessory structures`, the relation between the subject heading "Kloster" (in English: cloister) and the DDC class `726.79 Parts and accessory structures` was a skos:broadMatch-relation. This connection was valid from 2007 to June 2010. Now, since `726.796 Cloisters` became an own DDC class, there is a skos:closeMatch. This connection is still valid. This can be recognised by there just being one date in squared brackets.

The boxes, which are connected with the older version of `726.79 Parts and accessory structures`, show titles which were classified before the change in the class: at the top is a general title about parts and accessory structures of monastic buildings (in English: „Monastry of Wedinghausen – west wing") and, at the bottom, you can see two titles dealing with cloisters. The title "Infirmarien – Kranken- und Sterbehäuser der Mönche" (in English: "Infirmaries – hospitals and hospices of the monks") is an example of a title which was classified after the change. It is a general title about parts and accessory structures of monastic buildings. The title "Die singenden Steine von Moissac" (in English: "Singing stones of Moissac") is a title about cloisters which has been classified with the new DDC class `726.796 Cloisters`. The relations between titles and DDC classes and between titles and German subject headings are expressed by the Dublin Core Metadata Element dc:subject.[15]

Currently, our data model does not have versioning and a semantic network which would help us to get the real meaning of the DDC classes in the entries (Figure 2), instead we implicitly always use the current meaning of a DDC class:

15 Dublin Core Metadata Element Set. Version 1.1. Available at http://dublincore.org/documents/dces/.

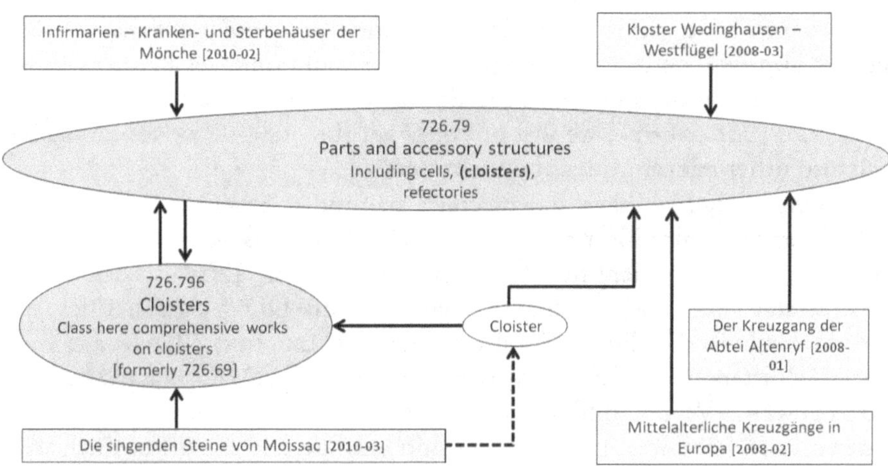

Figure 2: Search without Semantic Network and Versioning

If, in this scenario, we have a request for the DDC notation `726.79 Parts and accessory structures`, you will just get one hit as, since the change, only one single title has been classified. You will not find the titles about cloisters which were classified before "cloisters" became an own DDC class. The system does not know the difference between the class `726.79 Parts and accessory structures` with cloisters or without cloisters. The search could be improved with versioning and semantic network. If you search for the new class `726.796 Cloisters`, you get the title which was classified after the new class was built. In addition to this, you get the titles about cloisters which had been classified previously when "cloisters" was included in the class `726.79 Parts and accessory structures`; the new version of `726.79 Parts and accessory structures` is connected with and replaces the older version. The only problem is that you could get irrelevant documents and information ballast because there will also be results that do not fit your request, i.e. you will get titles about parts and accessory structures in general, too. There are also examples of changes in the DDC where the new class is an absolutely new one and not part of an older class – you will not have this problem with these.

4. *Summary and perspectives*

We started with the problem of modifications in the DDC and no modifications in the notations. We are missing relevant titles due to this which is unsatisfactory because we want to have a complete search result. In our example, we were searching for the notation `726.796 Cloisters` in our online catalogue and we only got one single title "Singing stones of Moissac".

However, if we had a unique identifier and a semantic network we could greatly improve the search results; in fact, we could then get a correct search result in spite of the modifications. So, if we are searching for the notation `726.796 Cloisters`, we will not only get the one title we found before, but also other relevant titles about cloisters.

In conclusion, we have shown you a method to improve the search results in spite of modifications in the DDC. It consists of two steps: In the first step we create identifiers for each version of the DDC classes. In the second step we build a semantic network with DDC classes, titles and German subject headings. Thanks to this, we can find all relevant titles about cloisters if we are now searching for the DDC class `726.796 Cloisters`. We can differentiate the two versions of the class `726.79 Parts and accessory structures` and include the titles which were classified with the old version of this class in our search result.

In our example, we were searching for DDC notations. Of course there are more ways of searching and most users do not search directly with DDC notations. In our next step, we will analyse how this concept can be expanded to a verbal search as this is how users commonly search. We will then include the relative index entries for each DDC class as these are the natural language terms the classifiers use as access points to DDC notations. The German subject headings will also be important. The CrissCross connections between the DDC classes and the German subject headings can be used to improve the search. How effective the enhancements will be is not yet certain, but the previous results are promising indeed.

References

Web documents were accessed on December 13, 2010.

Deutsche Nationalbibliothek. (2010). Linked Data Service der Deutschen Nationalbibliothek. Available at: http://www.d-nb.de/hilfe/service/linked_data_service.htm.

DDC-Einleitung. (2005). Einleitung in die Dewey-Dezimalklassifikation. Available at: http://www.ddc-deutsch.de/publikationen/pdf/ddc_22_deutsch_einleitung.pdf.

W3C. (2004). RDF Primer. W3C Recommendation 10 February 2004. Available at: http://www.w3.org/TR/rdf-primer/.

W3C. (2008). Cool URIs for the Semantic Web. W3C Interest Group Note 03 December 2008. Available at: http://www.w3.org/TR/cooluris/.

W3C. (2009). SKOS Simple Knowledge Organization System Primer. W3C Working Group Note 18 August 2009. Available at: http://www.w3.org/TR/skos-primer/.

Interoperability and Semantics in RDF Representations of FRBR, FRAD and FRSAD

Gordon Dunsire

Abstract: This paper describes recent work on registering Resource Description Framework (RDF) versions of the entities and relationships from the Functional Requirements for Bibliographic Records (FRBR) and Functional Requirements for Authority Data (FRAD) models developed by the International Federation of Library Associations and Institutions (IFLA). FRBR was developed several years before FRAD, and is under-developed in areas which FRAD was expected to cover; FRAD therefore makes significance reference to FRBR. Similarly, FRAD leaves a full treatment of subject authority data to the ongoing development of Functional Requirements for Subject Authority Data (FRSAD) which was finalised during 2010. Although the FRBR Review Group is charged with consolidating all three models in due course, the RDF versions of FRBR, FRAD, and FRSAD are being created in separate namespaces, with a separate Web Ontology Language (OWL) ontology to connect the three models. The paper discusses interoperability issues arising from this work. Such issues include class definitions and sub-classes, reciprocal properties, and disjoint classes and properties. The paper discusses similar work on the International Standard Bibliographic Description (ISBD), also maintained by IFLA, and related issues arising from the RDF representation of the metadata element set of RDA: resource description and access, which is based on the FRBR and FRAD models. The work is ongoing, and the paper updates the original conference presentation to the end of October 2010.

1. *Background*

In September 1997, the International Federation of Library Associations and Institutions (IFLA) produced *Functional requirements for bibliographic records*, the final report of the IFLA Study Group on the Functional Requirements for Bibliographic Records approved by the Standing Committee of the IFLA Section on Cataloguing. FRBR, as the report has come to be known, was published in 1998 by K.G. Saur[1]. The purpose of the study leading to FRBR was "to delineate in clearly defined terms the functions performed by the bibliographic record with respect to various media, various applications, and various user needs [covering] the full range of functions ... that encompasses not only descriptive elements, but access points (name, title, subject, etc.),

1 IFLA Study Group on the Functional Requirements for Bibliographic Records 1998.

other 'organizing' elements (classification, etc.), and annotations."[2] The study used an entity-relationship approach, identifying entities that are of key interest to users, attributes of those entities, and relationships between entities that are the most important in bibliographic resource discovery. The intention of the work was to develop "a conceptual model that would serve as the basis for relating specific attributes and relationships (reflected in the record as discrete data elements) to the various tasks that users perform when consulting bibliographic records."[3] However, the study did "not cover the extended range of attributes and relationships that are normally reflected in authority records" and "recognized that an extended level of analysis would be necessary for a fully developed conceptual model"[4].

Accordingly, the Working Group on Functional Requirements and Numbering of Authority Records (FRANAR) was established in April 1999 by the IFLA Division of Bibliographic Control and the IFLA Universal Bibliographic Control and International MARC Programme (UBCIM). *Functional requirements for authority data: a conceptual model* (known as FRAD), the final report of FRANAR, was approved by the Standing Committees of the IFLA Cataloguing Section and IFLA Classification and Indexing Section in March 2009, and subsequently published by K.G. Saur[5]. There was thus a gap of some 12 years between FRBR and FRAD. Furthermore, FRAD noted that while FRANAR "included some aspects of subject authorities in the authorities model, it has not undertaken the full analysis that the FRBR Study Group envisioned."[6] Instead, that task was assigned to the IFLA Working Group on the Functional Requirements for Subject Authority Records (FRSAR) formed in 2005. FRANAR and FRSAR thus worked in parallel from 2005, with FRSAR releasing a draft report for world-wide review by the time FRAD was published in 2009. *Functional requirements for subject authority data: a conceptual model* (known as FRSAD) was approved by the Standing Committee of the Classification and Indexing Section in June 2010[7].

IFLA's FRBR Review Group took on the task of reviewing and maintaining FRBR, FRAD, and FRSAD as the "FRBR family of models"[8] in 2009,

---

2 Ibid.: 2.
3 Ibid.: 3.
4 Ibid.: 4.
5 IFLA Working Group on Functional Requirements and Numbering of Authority Records (FRANAR) 2009.
6 Ibid.: 1.
7 IFLA Working Group on the Functional Requirements for Subject Authority Records (FRSAR). 2010.
8 Cf. the website of the FRBR Review Group: Functional requirements: the FRBR family of models. Available at: http://www.ifla.org/node/2016.

and in 2010 agreed to develop a consolidated model for the family. This process is now underway, and is being informed by the work of the FRBR Namespace Project.

This project was initiated during the World Library and Information Congress 73rd IFLA General Conference held in Durban, South Africa, in August 2007. The task of the project was "to define appropriate namespaces for FRBR (entity-relationship) in RDF and other appropriate syntaxes"[9]. The creation of the project was stimulated by the Data Model meeting[10] held at the British Library in London on 31 May and 1 April 2007 between representatives of the Joint Steering Committee for Development of RDA (JSC)[11], the Dublin Core Metadata Initiative (DCMI)[12], and various other Semantic Web communities. This meeting had resulted in the creation of the DCMI RDA Task Group[13] to investigate options for representing bibliographic concepts and metadata in Resource Description Framework (RDF)[14], the data model of the Semantic Web. *RDA: resource description and access*[15] provides a set of guidelines and instructions on formulating data to support resource discovery. FRBR and FRAD are the conceptual models underlying RDA, and the FRBR Review Group realized that RDF representations of the models would be required for the work of the DCMI RDA Task Group.

At around the same time, the Material Designation Study Group of IFLA's ISBD Review Group, which was developing a consolidated edition of *International standard bibliographic description* (ISBD), recommended the development of an XML schema for ISBD. This resulted in the creation of the ISBD/XML Study Group[16] in 2008. The Study Group agreed during the World Library and Information Congress 74th IFLA General Conference, held in Québec City, Canada, in August 2008, not to spend time on a general XML schema, but instead create RDF representations of the ISBD elements that could be expressed in RDF/XML.

---

9 Dunsire 2008: 1.

10 Cf. the notes on the website of the British Library. Bibliographic Standards. Data Model Meeting. Available at: http://www.bl.uk/bibliographic/meeting.html.

11 Cf. the website of the Joint Steering Group for Development of RDA. Available at: http://www.rda-jsc.org/rda.html.

12 Cf. the website of Dublin Core Metadata Initiative. Available at: http://dublincore.org/.

13 Cf. the DCMI/RDA Task Group wiki. Available at: http://dublincore.org/dcmirdataskgroup/.

14 Cf. RDF Working Group 2004.

15 Cf. the website of the Joint Steering Group for Development of RDA. Available at: http://www.rda-jsc.org/rda.html.

16 Cf. the website of the ISBD/XML Study Group. Available at: http://www.ifla.org/en/node/1795.

The surge of activity by the IFLA groups and the need for IFLA-controlled namespaces to contain RDF representations led to the formation of the IFLA Namespaces Task Group in late 2009 to identify requirements and propose options for the development, support, and promotion of IFLA standards in the Semantic Web. The Group's report was submitted in May 2010 to IFLA's Professional Committee[17], which accepted a recommendation to create an IFLA Namespaces Technical Group which would carry out work on the other recommendations concerning requirements and options, and report to the new IFLA Bibliographic Standards Program (Core Activity) which was approved at the same time. A paper discussing IFLA's activities in relation to the Semantic Web[18] was presented at the World Library and Information Congress 76th IFLA General Conference, held in Gothenburg, Sweden, in August 2010.

2. *Methodology*

The DCMI RDA Task Group had decided to use the NSDL Metadata Registry, now the Open Metadata Registry (OMR)[19], to create basic RDF representations of RDA elements and vocabularies, including uniform resource identifiers (URIs), labels, definitions and scope notes. This has proved successful, so the FRBR Namespace Project and ISBD/XML Study Group are using the same infrastructure. In addition to the RDA vocabularies[20], the OMR currently contains RDF element sets for the FRAD model, FRBRer model, FRSAD model, and ISBD elements, and RDF vocabularies for FRAD user tasks, FRBRer user tasks, FRSAD user tasks, ISBD content form, ISBD content qualification of dimensionality, ISBD content qualification of motion, ISBD content qualification of sensory specification, ISBD content qualification of type, ISBD media type.

All three of the FR family models are based on entity-relationship analyses which can be readily mapped into the basic RDF entities of class and property.

Each "entity" identified in an FR model becomes an RDF class. For example, the FRBR Group 1 entities (work, expression, manifestation, and item) are represented as the RDF classes Work, Expression, Manifestation,

17 Cf. the website of the IFLA Professional Committee. Available at: http://www.ifla.org/en/professional-committee.

18 Dunsire, Willer 2010.

19 Cf. the website of the Open metadata registry. Available at: http://metadataregistry.org/.

20 Cf. the RDA (resource description and access) vocabularies. Available at: http://metadataregistry.org/rdabrowse.htm.

and Item respectively. Note that class labels are capitalized according to an RDF labelling convention which is reflected in this paper; for example, "work" refers to an entity name and "Work" to a class label.

Attributes assigned to each FR entity become RDF properties. For example, the logical attribute "intended audience" assigned to the FRBR entity work is represented by an RDF property with the label "has intended audience". Relationships between FR entities also become RDF properties. The high-level structural relationship between the FRBR entities work and expression is represented by an RDF property with the label "is realized through".

2.1 Terminology

The terminology used for class and property labels, definitions and scope notes is based as closely as possible on the relevant source documentation; for the FR models this consists of the published reports. Minor adjustments have been made to improve consistency, but otherwise it should be possible to match the RDF representations with the original text. This is intended to make it easier to relate the source documentation to the RDF text and use it for further information about the context and background of the models. A standard approach has been adopted to create human-readable labels for the RDF properties based on attributes: the label consists of the attribute name preceded by the word "has", as shown in the example for the attribute "intended audience" given above. This results in a "verbal" label which can be interpreted in near-natural language when an RDF instance triple based on the property is labelled for human readability. Instance triples consist of three parts: the subject of a metadata statement based on an RDF property; the RDF property itself; and the object or value of the property. The first two parts must be expressed as machine-readable URIs, but the corresponding labels can be substituted to give a human-readable version, for example "this work:has intended audience:adult". The structure of a triple is based on concepts from logic and linguistics. The middle part of a triple, an RDF property, is technically a predicate in descriptive logic, equivalent to a verb phrase in natural language.

Some attributes are assigned to more than one entity. In some cases, the name of the attribute is explicitly distinct in the documentation. For example, "form of expression" is an attribute of the FRBR expression entity and "form of work" is an attribute of the work entity. The corresponding property labels can be created in the standard way and remain distinguishable: "has form of expression" and "has form of work". In other cases, the documented attribute name is not distinct. For example, FRAD assigns the attribute "address" to both the person and corporate body entities. The standard RDF property label for both would be "has address", and a user would have to check the RDF definition to determine which property to use. Identical property labels might also be confusing and misleading, so in these cases the entity name is added to the label to give distinctive labels, for example, "has address (person)" and "has address (corporate body)". This approach has been used throughout the RDF representations, where applicable, to ensure that all property labels are unique within the namespace.

Definitions for the RDF classes are generally derived directly from definitions in the source documentation. Definitions for attribute properties usually consist of the definition in the source documentation preceded by the standard phrase "Relates a ... to" with the name of the class to which the attribute is assigned inserted in the placeholder. For example, the definition of the property "has intended audience" is "Relates a work to the class of user for which the work is intended, as defined by age group, educational level, or other categorization." Definitions for relationship properties similarly start with the phrase "Relates a ... to a ..." followed by a phrase based on the definition of the relationship taken from the documentation, with the names of the related classes inserted in the placeholders. For example, the definition of the relationship property "is realized through" is "Relates a work to an expression that is the realization of the work." The wording of the source documentation may be rearranged to create consistent phrasing in the definition.

Examples embedded in the definition of a property or class in the documentation are removed and used to form a scope note for the property or class, where appropriate. For example, "E.g., sound cassette, videodisc, microfilm cartridge, transparency, etc." is the scope note for the FRBR property labelled "has form of carrier". Explanatory "includes" notes in the documentation are also treated as scope notes. For example "Includes real individuals" is one of several notes attached to the definition of the FRAD entity person. Each class and property has at most one scope note which may concatenate several sets of examples and "includes" notes from the documentation.

2.2 *Related namespaces*

Each of the FR models has been given its own namespace, although classes and properties represented in a prior model are re-used where indicated in the documentation: FRSAD and FRAD use classes and properties from FRBR, where those classes and properties are identical in definition. In some instances a later model redefines an earlier class or property, in which case a new RDF representation is made. For example, FRAD uses the FRBR class Expression and FRBR property "has form of carrier", but redefines the FRBR class Corporate Body by restricting it to a corporate body with a name, resulting in a separate FRAD class for Corporate Body. RDF properties relating such redefined entities will be made available as extensions to the relevant namespaces.

The principle reason for keeping the FR namespaces separate is the length of time between publication of FRBR and FRAD, during which FRBR has been used in applications without reference to FRAD, and the parallel but independent development of FRAD and FRSAD. The separate namespaces ensure that the integrity of any application of one of the models remains intact and self-contained, without being influenced by the others.

Generally, there is no re-use of RDF resources from external community namespaces such as DCMI metadata terms[21], although the use of some FOAF[22] properties for FRAD is under investigation. Again, this ensures that there is no unintended influence on the integrity of the models. Equivalences between the FR (and ISBD) namespaces and appropriate external namespaces are likely to be established after the RDF representations are completed.

2.3 *Inferencing*

An RDF property may be declared with a domain or range. A domain is a class which is intended to be the subject of the property, while a range is intended to be the object or value of the property. This allows inferences to be made when the property is used in an instance triple. For example, if a property has a domain, then it can be inferred that the subject of a corresponding instance triple must be a member of the class given by the domain.

All properties based on FR attributes have a domain but no range. The FR models deliberately avoid specifying what type of value should be assigned to an attribute, to allow any application based on the model to be extended to suit its needs. Thus no inferences about the object value can be made from triples based on FR properties. The domain of the attribute properties is the class to which the attribute is assigned. For example, the FRBR property "has form of carrier" is declared to have the domain of FRBR class Manifestation, because "form of carrier" is an attribute of the entity "manifestation". It can therefore be inferred from the instance triple "this:has form of carrier:DVD" that "this" is a manifestation.

All properties based on an FR entity relationship have both a domain and a range based on the classes representing the related entities. For exam-

21 Cf. the DCMI metadata terms. Available at: http://dublincore.org/documents/dcmi-terms/.

22 Cf. the FOAF vocabulary specification. Version 0.98. Available at: http://xmlns.com/foaf/spec.

ple, the FRBR property "is realized through" has domain FRBR Work and range FRBR Expression. It can be inferred from the instance triple "this:is realized through:that" that "this" is a FRBR work, and "that" is a FRBR expression. Such inferencing is a powerful tool when instance triples are created from legacy bibliographic records which may be duplicates describing the same resource, or incomplete or of otherwise low quality.

3. *Interoperability*

3.1 General issues

It has not always been easy to create consistent RDF labels or definitions based on the source documentation for the FR family. The text of the original reports was written for human consumption, and there is some evidence of deliberate variation in phrasing to make it more readable. For example, the terms "prior", "preceding", and "first" are used in an apparent interchangeable way in FRBR. There are also minor inconsistencies in the use of indefinite articles in relationship phrases. Most include an indefinite article ("a" or "an"), but some do not; for example "has a reproduction" and "has reconfiguration". The appropriate article has been added to the RDF labels to remove inconsistencies, so the label in this example becomes "has a reconfiguration". A comment has been added to the RDF property when such amendments have been made, to alert users to resulting inconsistencies between the RDF representation and the source documentation. Although each report uses a generally consistent layout, there is much less consistency between the reports.

A specific issue was encountered in interpreting the FRBR model. The source documentation for FRBR refers to sub-types of entities, for example "musical work" and "serial". Specific attributes are assigned to these sub-types. For example, "key" is an attribute of "musical work" which is not applicable to other sub-types of the entity work. The first draft of the RDF representation treated these sub-types as sub-classes so, for example, a FRBR class for Musical Work was created and a property added to indicate that it was a sub-class of the FRBR class Work. The documentation does not, however, give formal definitions of these sub-types, and further discussion with the FRBR Review Group showed that there could be significant overlap and mixing of any definition that might to be constructed for the RDF representations; for example a musical work can also be a serial. The Group agreed that the sub-types were not intended to be sub-classes, so they were subsequently removed from the OMR. This leaves it open to applications of FRBR to model the documented sub-types as well as others to suit their needs, if any. The RDF property labels for such attributes contain the sub-type, for example "has key (musical work)", but the property domain is the class for the main entity which in this example is Work.

3.2 *Opaque URIs*

Opaque URIs are used for FR and ISBD classes and properties, for example "http://iflastandards.info/ns/fr/frbr/frbrer/C1001" rather than "http://iflastandards.info/ns/fr/frbr/frbrer/Work". This results in abbreviated references, using XML namespace declarations or qualified names (qnames), such as frbrer:C1001 instead of frbrer:Work. In this syntax, the qname "frbrer" is substituted automatically during machine-processing by the equivalent namespace "http://iflastandards.info/ns/fr/frbr/frbrer/", and the linking colon removed. The computer treats a URI as a text string which uniquely identifies a class or property, and does not parse the string to extract any other "meaning". Such opaque URIs have no human-readable semantic content and must be de-referenced to the corresponding label for presentation to human users. But IFLA operates in a multilingual environment, and the use of such opaque URIs avoids Anglophone or any other natural language bias; an English label may be just as difficult to read for a Russian user as a Russian label for an English user. Multiple RDF labels in different languages can easily be associated with a single opaque URI (using the @language-code syntax), and there are many translations of the FR and ISBD source documents into non-English languages available for such purposes. The URI must be persistent and not change. The de-coupling of label from URI allows subsequent changes to labels without causing confusion. If, for example, indefinite articles were to be removed from the labels in the consolidation of the FR family to shorten their length, there would be no resulting issues such as articles remaining embedded in the URIs.

3.3 *Semantic issues*

Variations in the text of the FR family source documentation beg the question: do differences in documentation reflect real semantic differences? Close examination of the text and detailed discussion with the FRBR Review Group are required to determine this. A minor example is found with the FRBR entity work, which is defined as "A distinct intellectual or artistic creation." However, FRAD claims it uses the FRBR entity "as modified in the ICP Glossary" (that is, *Statement of international cataloguing principles*[23]) and therefore defines it as "A distinct intellectual or artistic creation (i.e.,

---

[23] IFLA 2009. Available at: www.ifla.org/files/cataloguing/icp/icp_2009-en.pdf.

the intellectual or artistic content)." The FRBR Review Group has agreed that there is no real semantic difference between these definitions, so FRAD can safely re-use the FRBR class Work. An explanatory comment is added to the RDF representation.

A major example of variation between FRBR and FRAD is found with the entity person. The FRBR definition is "An individual" while that for FRAD is "An individual or a persona or identity established or adopted by an individual or group." FRAD states that this is also modified from FRBR, but gives no additional information. The FRBR Review Group agrees that the different definitions are sufficiently great to require FRAD to create its own class for Person. The situation is further complicated by the semantic relationship between an object-oriented version of FRBR, known as FRBRoo[24], and the *CIDOC conceptual reference model* (CIDOC CRM)[25] which introduces yet another apparently distinct definition for person. As noted above with reference to the entity corporate body, it is intended to represent the semantic relationships between such different classes using RDF properties; in this case it will be challenging exercise.

3.4 *Ontological issues*

The FR source documentation identifies pairs of inverse relationships. For example, FRBR states that the relationship "is realization of" is the inverse of "is realized through": an expression is a realization of a work, and a work is realized through an expression. These are represented in RDF as inverse properties with the OWL statement "frbrer:P2001 owl:inverseOf frbrer: P2002".

RDF properties based on attributes have no inverses because they have no ranges. When a property is inverted, its domain becomes the range of the inverse property, and the range becomes the domain. Properties with no domains can weaken the integrity of the model and remove the ability to apply inferencing to instance triples. The FR models are ontologically rich; this intrinsic value can be made explicit by using OWL to define relationships between properties and classes in addition to the inverse pairs given in the source documentation. The OWL transitive, asymmetric, and disjoint relationships are particularly important for the FR models, requiring a careful analysis of the source documentation to determine their applicability.

For example, the FRBR property labelled "has an alternate" has the class Manifestation as both its domain and range, and FRBR explicitly gives an

24 International Working Group on FRBR and CIDOC CRM Harmonisation 2008.

25 Cf. the website of the International Council of Museums. The CIDOC conceptual reference model. Available at: http://www.cidoc-crm.org/.

inverse property labelled "is an alternate to", also with domain and range of Manifestation. But any two instances of Manifestation to which the property applies are mutually alternate: they can be swapped as domain and range in the property and its inverse. One of the properties is therefore ontologically redundant, and the model can be represented more elegantly by declaring the remaining property as symmetric. That is, "has an alternate" is symmetric, allowing the inference that "this manifestation:has an alternate:that manifestation" implies "that manifestation:has an alternate:this manifestation", which is identical in meaning to "that manifestation:is an alternate to:this manifestation". The property labelled "is an alternate to" can therefore be dropped from the FRBR namespace, and its explicit reference in the source documentation can be represented as an alternate label to the property labelled "has an alternate". This property is also transitive: "this manifestation:has an alternate:that manifestation" and "that manifestation:has an alternate:another manifestation" implies "this manifestation:has an alternate:another manifestation".

All FRBR classes are mutually disjoint. That is, a value which appears to be both an instance of a Work and an Expression (or Person, or Place, etc.) is inferred to be representing different entities. Similarly, many FRBR properties are disjoint, so the value "1900" appearing as the title of a manifestation and as the date of publication of the same manifestation is inferred to be referring to two distinct things (a title, and a date).

Ontological properties will be used to represent relationships between entities in the separate FR models. For example, the FRAD class Corporate Body is likely to be related to the FRBR class Corporate Body using the rdfs:subClassOf property. Such linking properties may be published as an addendum to the existing FR models, and will have a significant role in informing the development of the consolidated model. The consolidated FR model may also require additional classes and properties, and some classes and properties from the separate models may be deprecated. It is worth noting that redundant classes and properties will not be removed from the separate namespaces; their URIs must be permanent, although their future use will be discouraged.

3.5 RDA

The DCMI RDA Task Group has created its own FRBR classes within the RDA namespace in order to avoid any delays waiting for the FRBR namespace versions to be approved. The original timescale for final approval of the RDA classes and properties was well in advance of that for the FRBR equivalents; as it happened, delays in producing the final draft of RDA and development of the RDA Toolkit have resulted in the FRBR classes and properties being approved first, in September 2010. The RDA equivalents are still in "new-unapproved" status. JSC and the Task Group have yet to determine whether to substitute the FRBR namespace classes in RDA, or declare equivalence with the RDA versions.

There is a potential conflict with FRBR in the RDA database implementation scenarios[26]. In RDA, the Manifestation class is linked to both the Work and Expression classes via the "embodies" relationship, while in FRBR only the Expression class can be linked. While it is possible to create a non-FRBR property for the Manifestation-Work link in RDA, further investigation is required to determine whether this would result in a semantic reasoning collision if the FRBR classes are used instead of the RDA equivalents.

FRBR identifies sets of entities (represented as RDF classes) as Groups 1, 2 and 3, but these were not intended to be interpreted as RDF super-classes. Instead, they simplify the entity-relationship diagrams by collapsing multiple relationships into a single generic relationship between groups. But those relationships are to be interpreted as being between individual entities and not groups, and represented in RDF as a set of multiple properties between classes and not a single property between super-classes, as reflected in the FRBR namespace. For example, there are distinct FRBR properties with the labels "is subject (item) of", "is subject (person) of", "is subject (place) of", etc., instead of a single generic property with the label "is subject of". JSC and the DCMI RDA Task Group are discussing the utility of declaring such super-classes in the RDA namespace to simplify and reduce the corresponding properties. This approach was taken by an earlier RDF representation of FRBR, *Expression of core FRBR concepts in RDF*[27], which was not approved by IFLA.

3.6 ISBD

ISBD is a data model for representing bibliographic metadata records, rather than a conceptual model such as the FR family. ISBD has only one class, Resource, which is implied in the source documentation. Further investigation is required to determine if this is a super-class of FRBR Work, Expression, Manifestation, and Item. If so, it would be equivalent to the concept of FRBR Group 1, even though that is not intended to be a class.

---

26 Cf. notes to the Joint Steering Committee for Development of RDA. RDA database implementation scenarios. 2009. Available at: http://www.rda-jsc.org/docs/5editor2rev.pdf.

27 Cf. Davis, Ian, and Richard Newman. Expression of core FRBR concepts in RDF. Available at: http://vocab.org/frbr/core.html.

There are no relationship properties in ISBD because it only addresses a single Resource. ISBD does not specify any relationships between bibliographic resources or between a resource and associated authority records. All ISBD RDF properties are based on attributes. All properties have a domain of ISBD Resource, but there are no ranges because ISBD does not specify what types of value an attribute can have. As a result, there are no inverse properties in the ISBD namespace. Further work is required to map ISBD properties to FRBR properties; preliminary analysis suggests there is significant overlap.

As such, it has been easier to develop the ISBD namespace than the FR namespaces. The balance of complexity is restored, however, because ISBD specifies a sequence for attributes within a bibliographic record, and indicates whether an attribute is mandatory or repeatable within a record, unlike the FR models which have nothing to say about these qualities. The ISBD/XML Study Group is representing these aspects of ISBD in a Dublin Core application profile (as is the DCMI RDA Task Group with RDA); the interoperability of application profiles remains the subject of intense discussion with Semantic Web communities, as, for example, in a recent meeting at the DC-2010 conference[28].

Like RDA, and unlike the FR family, ISBD specifies some controlled vocabularies for the values of its content and carrier attributes. A draft mapping[29] of ISBD Content form and media type descriptors (assembled from the controlled vocabularies which have been represented in RDF/SKOS in the OMR) to the RDA content and carrier type controlled vocabularies has been created by mapping the ISBD and RDA terms to the RDA/ONIX framework for resource categorization[30], which is intended to act as the hub for interoperability between bibliographic content and carrier terminologies. The draft mapping is under consideration by the ISBD Review Group as part of the development of the final consolidated edition of ISBD.

4. *Conclusion: Improving interoperability*

There are therefore at least 3 namespaces relevant to bibliographic resources in development: FR family (comprising the 3 original models plus the consolidated model), ISBD, and RDA. There is likely to be significant overlap in

---

28 Agenda, notes and related material available at: http://www.w3.org/2001/sw/wiki/JointMeeting2010.

29 Cf. the Draft Minutes by Dunsire, Gordon. Analysis of content and carrier designators in the ISBD consolidated edition with respect to the RDA/ONIX framework. 2010. Available at: http://www.ifla.org/files/cataloguing/isbdrg/area-0-analysis.pdf.

30 RDA/ONIX framework for resource categorization, version 1.0 (ROF). Available at: http://www.loc.gov/marbi/2007/5chair10.pdf.

the semantics of their individual classes and properties, so any interoperability between the namespaces will improve the quality and quantity (through inferencing) of linked-data instance triples based on these properties.

There are several current opportunities for improving interoperability in bibliographic metadata created by libraries.

The Vocabulary Mapping Framework (VMF) matrix[31] is based on an analysis of resource, role and relator terms used in several publisher and library models and encoding schemes, including FRBR, FRAD, ISBD, and RDA. The matrix exhausts a "relational space" for resources and the agents associated with them in various roles, and enables a hub-and-spoke mapping, in RDF, between any pair of models or applications. A class or property URI is declared as equivalent to the nearest VMF node, independently of any relationship it may have to other classes or properties within its own namespace. All nodes are connected within the matrix, so any external URI attached to a node is therefore connected to any external URI attached to another node; the two URIs do not have to belong to the same external namespace. Significant further work is required to compute minimum pathways between nodes within the matrix to produce efficient and effective interoperability, as there will usually be multiple connecting pathways between any two nodes.

The coherent and consistent management environment of IFLA namespaces envisaged in the report of the IFLA Namespaces Task Group will improve interoperability between classes and properties derived from IFLA standards, and encourage interoperability with external communities. One of the activities envisaged is the RDF representation of relationships between classes and properties from different IFLA namespaces, and with appropriate external namespaces such as FOAF.

The deliverables and other outputs of the W3C Library Linked Data Incubator Group[32] should also help to improve interoperability between library namespaces and those of other communities. The Group's mission is "to help increase global interoperability of library data on the Web"[33]. The Group has had extensive discussions about the IFLA models, RDA, and other bibliographic namespaces, most recently at a face-to-face meeting[34] held at the end of the DC-2010 conference in Pittsburgh, USA.

---

31 Cf. the website Vocabulary Mapping Framework (VMF) matrix. Available at: http://cdlr.strath.ac.uk/VMF/documents.htm.

32 Cf. W3C Library Linked Data Incubator Group. Available at: http://www.w3.org/2005/Incubator/lld/.

33 Cf. W3C. Library Linked Data Incubator Group. Charter. Available at: http://www.w3.org/2005/Incubator/lld/charter.

34 Agenda, notes and related material available at: http://www.w3.org/2005/Incubator/lld/wiki/F2F_Pittsburgh.

Interoperability of these models for bibliographic metadata is essential for supporting the interoperability of value vocabularies for subjects in knowledge organization schemes, by supplying context and ontologies for inferencing rules that can be used to determine the appropriate use of such vocabularies in library linked data triples and thus enriching the Semantic Web.

References

Web documents were accessed on October 30, 2010.

Dunsire, Gordon. (2008). Declaring FRBR Entities and Relationships in RDF. Available at: http://www.ifla.org/files/cataloguing/frbrrg/namespace-report.pdf.

Dunsire, Gordon; Willer, Mirna. (2010). Initiatives to Make Standard Library Metadata Models and Structures Available to the Semantic Web. In: World Library and Information Congress: 76th IFLA General Conference and Assembly. Meeting 149. Information Technology, Cataloguing, Classification and Indexing with Knowledge Management "Libraries and the Semantic Web", 10-15 August 2010, Gothenburg, Sweden. Available at: http://www.ifla.org/files/hq/papers/ifla76/149-dunsire-en.pdf.

IFLA (2009). Statement of International Cataloguing Principles. Available at: www.ifla.org/files/cataloguing/icp/icp_2009-en.pdf.

IFLA Study Group on the Functional Requirements for Bibliographic Records (ed.). (1998). Functional Requirements for Bibliographic Records: Final Report. München: K.G. Saur. Version as amended and corrected through February 2009 available at: http://www.ifla.org/files/cataloguing/frbr/frbr_2008.pdf.

IFLA Working Group on the Functional Requirements for Subject Authority Records (FRSAR). (2010). Functional Requirements for Subject Authority Data (FRSAD): A Conceptual Model. Available at: http://www.ifla.org/files/classification-and-indexing/functional-requirements-for-subject-authority-data/frsad-final-report.pdf.

IFLA Working Group on Functional Requirements and Numbering of Authority Records (FRANAR). (2009). Functional Requirements for Authority Data: A Conceptual Model. München: K.G. Saur.

International Working Group on FRBR and CIDOC CRM Harmonisation. (2008). FRBR Object-oriented Definition and Mapping to FRBRer. Version 0.9 Draft. Available at: http://archive.ifla.org/VII/s13/wgfrbr/FRBRoo_V9.1_PR.pdf.

RDF Working Group W3C(2004) Resource description framework(RDF). Available at: http://www.w3.org/RDF/.

FRSAD: Challenges of Modeling the Aboutness

Maja Žumer

Abstract: The Functional Requirements for Subject Authority Records Working Group (FRSAR WG) is the third IFLA Working Group of the FRBR family. It was formed in April 2005 and it was charged with the task of developing a conceptual model of FRBR Group 3 entities within the FRBR framework as they relate to the "aboutness" of works. This paper introduces the Functional Requirements for Subject Authority Data (FRSAD), the model developed by the FRSAR WG, and discusses issues raised during the world-wide review.

1. Background

A third IFLA Working Group of the FRBR family was formed in April 2005 to address subject authority data and investigate the use of subject authority data by different users in different contexts. The role of the working group was defined in the following terms of reference:

- to build a conceptual model of Group 3 entities within the FRBR framework as they relate to the *aboutness* of works,
- to provide a clearly defined, structured frame of reference for relating the data that are recorded in subject authority records to the needs of the users of those records, and
- to assist in an assessment of the potential for international sharing and use of subject authority data both within the library sector and beyond.

The draft of the FRSAD report was submitted for world-wide review in 2009. After a thorough discussion of comments the new version was prepared and discussed within the working group and finally submitted. The report was approved in July 2010.

2. The FRSAD Model

FRBR defines the many-to-many subject relationship between work and entities of Groups 1, 2, and 3 (Figure 1).

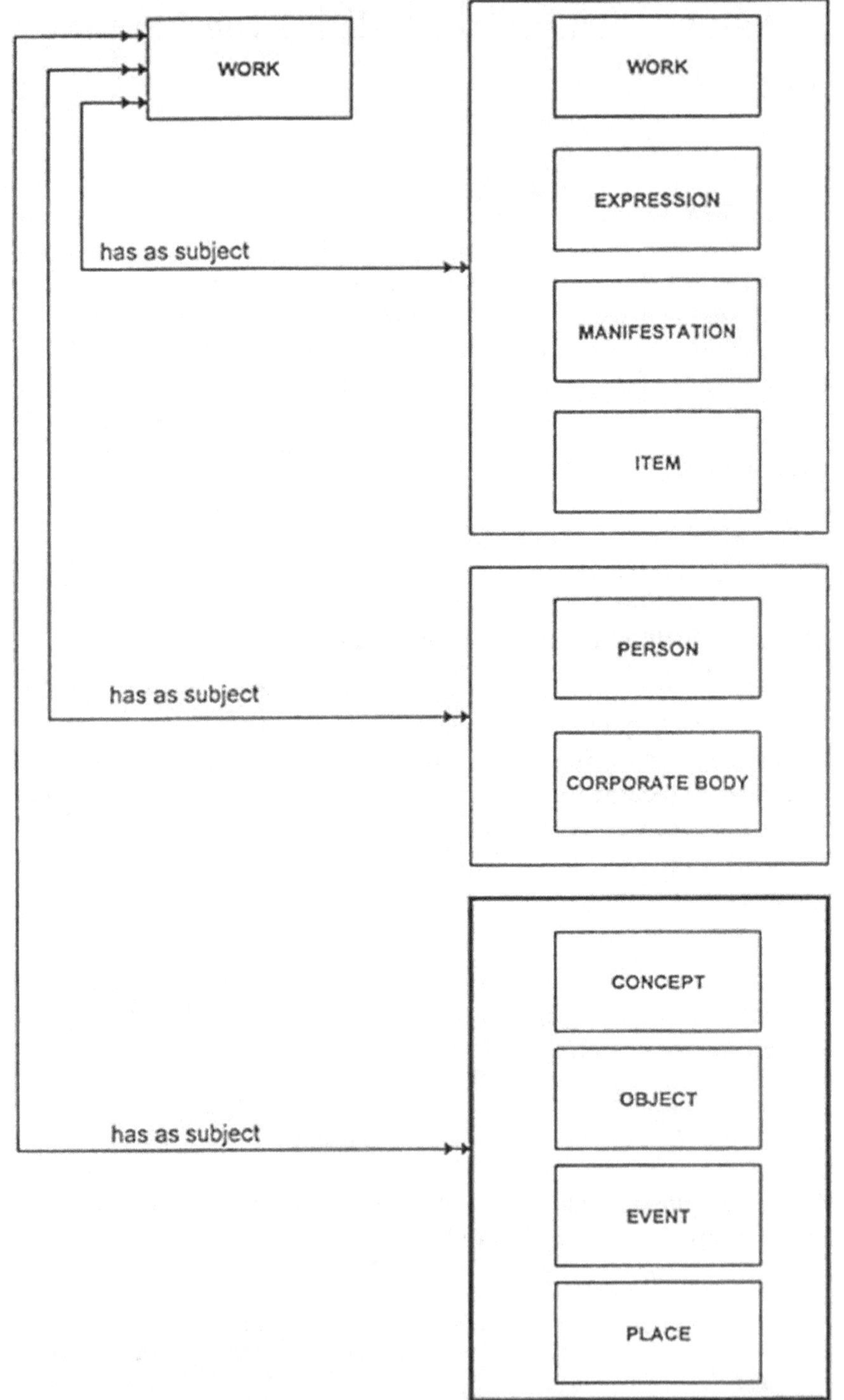

Figure 1: Subject relationship in FRBR

IFLA FRBR Group 3 entities are recognized as the subjects of works (i.e. the results of intellectual or artistic endeavour). They "represent an *additional* set of entities that serve as the *subjects* of works"[1], in addition to Group 1 and 2 entities, which can also be subjects of works. Group 3 includes concept (an abstract notion or idea), object (a material thing), event (an action or occurrence), and place (a location).

From the time the FRSAR Working Group (FRSAR WG) was formed, there seems to have been a general agreement in the FRBR research community that Group 3 entities should be revisited.[2] The working group was considering several scenarios. In addition to enhancing the FRBR model based on Group 3 entities by adding 'time', the approaches of other existing models were discussed, including the <indecs> model[3], Ranganathan's facets[4], and the pragmatic list of entities developed by two Italian researchers, Buizza and Guerrini[5]. These models present solid references for revising the FRBR conceptual model. The working group analyzed and discussed possible solutions based on each of these models, from conservative models making minor amendments of FRBR Group 3 to radical models proposing a completely new model. However, the working group found that none of these models and the ones based on them could be universal enough to reflect the needs of today's subject authority data, considering particularly different domains and subject access tools. By 2007, the working group shifted focus to the development of a more general and abstract model, justified by a pilot user study, which confirmed that there is no universally applicable and useful categorization of subjects.

In this framework, all controlled access points related to all three entity groups, as defined by the FRBR conceptual model, have the potential to be the topic of a *work*. In other words, all of the Group 1, 2 and 3 entities can have an "is-subject-of" relationship with the *work*. The FRSAR Entity Subgroup proposed a more abstract conceptual model and presented it at the IFLA conference in 2007. As presented in Figure 2, the model should be understood with two key points of view:

1. This model confirms one of the basic relationships defined in FRBR: *WORK has as subject THEMA / THEMA is subject of WORK.*
   1.1 *THEMA* is the term used to refer to anything that can be subject of a work. It is defined as "any entity used as subject of a *work*"[6].

---

1 IFLA 1998: 16, emphasis added.
2 Delsey 2005.
3 Rust and Bide 2000.
4 Ranganathan 1962.
5 Buizza and Guerrini 2001.
6 FRSAD 2010: 15.

1.2 *THEMA* includes any FRBR entities -- the existing Group 1 and Group 2 entities and, in addition, all other subjects of works. It can be viewed as a super-entity or super-class of all FRBR entities, enabling us to model relationships and attributes on a more general and abstract level.

2. This model also proposes a new relationship: *THEMA* has appellation *NOMEN*/*NOMEN* is appellation of *THEMA*.

   NOMEN is defined as any sign or sequence of signs (alphanumeric characters, symbols, sound, etc.) by which a thema is known, referred to or addressed, for example, "love", "∞", or "595.733".

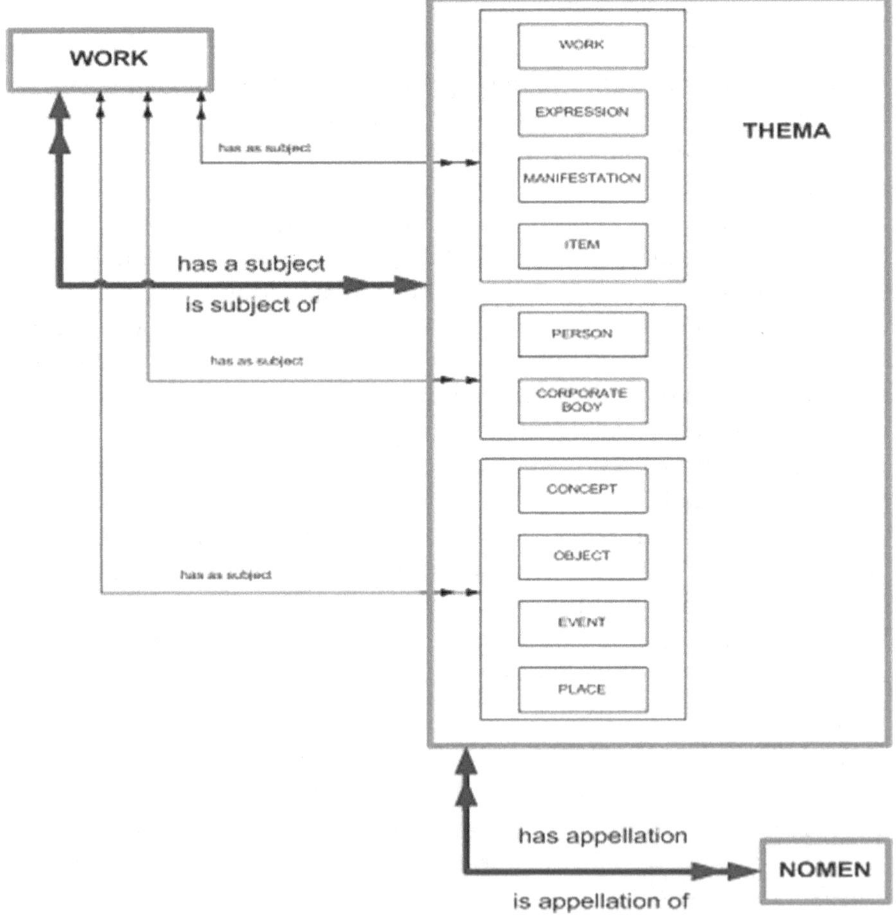

Figure 2: FRSAD's relation to FRBR

To simplify Figure 2, the FRSAD model can be illustrated as in Figure 3.

Figure 3: FRSAD Conceptual Model

Some important characteristics of the model are:

- The "has as subject/is subject of" relationship is a many-to-many relationship. Any *work* can have more than one *thema;* and any *thema* can be the subject of more than one *work.*
- In general (i.e. in natural language or when mapping different vocabularies) the "has-appellation/is appellation of" relationship is also a many-to-many relationship. A *thema* has one or more *nomen* and there may be a *nomen* referring to more than one *thema.*
- It is important to note that, in a given controlled vocabulary and within a domain, though, a *nomen* should be an appellation of only one *thema.*

Attributes of *thema* and *nomen,* and relationships between and among *themas* and *nomens,* and *thema*-to-*nomen* relationships are all discussed in detail in the FRSAD report.[7]

The importance of the *THEMA-NOMEN* model for the subject authority data is to separate *subjects* from what they are known by, referred to, or addressed as. This enables us to define attributes and relationships for the appellation separately.

3. *Some issues raised during the world-wide review*

Among the comments received during the world-wide review, four will be presented and discussed here.

3.1 Terminology

While some comments explicitly praised the choice of Latin terms for the main entities of FRSAD, some expressed concerns about this choice: Latin terminology was labelled as old fashioned, confusing, and presumptuous, but no real alternative was suggested. The choice of Latin terms is explained in the FRSAD document:

> The Working Group chose Latin terms, *thema* (plural *themata* or *themas*) and *nomen* (plural *nomina* or *nomens*), because they have no pre-existing meaning in our con-

7 IFLA 2010.

> text, are culturally neutral and do not require translation. For *thema*, other possible (English) terms include "subject", "topic", and "concept"; however, even discussions within the Working Group proved that there are very different views on granularity (some see "subject" and "topic" as synonyms, while others see "topic" as a component of "subject"). The Working Group needed to distinguish *thema* from the previously defined FRBR entity *concept*. For *nomen*, it is the case that the term "name" is often considered synonymous to proper name. In addition, the Working Group needed to distinguish *nomen* from the FRAD entity *name*.[8]

The problems are similar in other languages and the choice of Latin, which does not have to be translated, has already been tested in translating FRSAD presentations into all official IFLA languages. Translators reported no problems.

3.2 *FRSAD is too general and abstract*

Soon after FRBR was published, Strunck noted that "Some students find it unnecessarily complicated to operate with the abstract entities of the model as you cannot study these entities per se. They find the definition of the entities to be academic and airy." [9] The problem seems to persist with FRSAD.

The library community has no tradition of conceptual models, FRBR being the first of its kind. It is therefore understandable that practicing librarians are often focusing on detailed rules and not on the big picture. Modeling is difficult and cannot be mastered without some education. It would therefore be necessary to include those topics in the curricula of library schools. Not only will that enable the young professionals to understand and contribute to the development of FRBR and related models, it would also help them to conduct a more efficient communication with developers of computer tools.

3.3 *FRSAD is not specific to libraries*

Some have commented that FRSAD does not model closely the current cataloguing practice. While this is true, it is also intentional. A lot of developments in the area of subject access, including the development of different knowledge organisation systems, is currently conducted outside the library domain. In addition, the mission and purpose of a conceptual model is not to blindly model the current practice, but rather to question it and propose improved solutions in order to pave the way for better, more popular and used bibliographic information systems.

---

8 IFLA 2010: 16.
9 Strunck 1999.

3.4 *Complexity is not modelled*

According to some comments, *thema* is too general and does not cover appropriately the difference between simple and complex *themas*. Although everybody intuitively understands that some topics are simpler than others ('cats' vs. 'winter fishing in the Cuyahoga river'), a proper definition of complexity is difficult. It seems that we mostly associate the complexity of a *thema* with the complexity of its *nomen*. The problem is addressed in FRSAD document:

> *Themas* can vary substantially in complexity or simplicity. Depending on the circumstances (the subject authority system, user needs, the nature of the *work*, etc.) the aboutness of a *work* can be expressed as a one-to-one relationship between the *work* and the *thema*; this means that the totality of the aboutness is encompassed in a single *thema*. In other circumstances the relationship is one-to-many, meaning that the aboutness of the *work* is captured in two or more *themas*. It is virtually impossible to define what the universal "atomic" level of a *thema* might be, because any *thema* can be fragmented further. The argument can be reversed: simple *themas* may be combined or aggregated, resulting in more complex *thema(s)*. In each particular implementation the atomic level is specified and rules guide the creation of *nomens* for complex *themas*.[10]

It is therefore up to application profiles, developed to support particular implementations, to deal with complex *themas* by specifying the rules for creation of complex *nomens*. Rules guide the creation of e.g. subject heading strings or faceted classification. This is therefore another area which is language/domain/system specific and should be addressed in application profiles.

4. *Conclusion*

FRSAD is finished and approved. The most important challenge ahead is the harmonisation of the models of the FRBR family. In parallel, application profiles should be developed for and by particular domains to confirm FRSAD in practice.

References

Web documents were accessed on December 13, 2010.

Buizza, Pino; Guerrini, Mauro. (2002). Conceptual Model for the New "Soggettario". Subject Indexing in the Light of FRBR. In: Cataloging & Classification Quarterly 34 (4) : 31–45.

[10] IFLA 2010: 17.

Delsey, Tom. (2005). Modeling Subject Access. Extending the FRBR and FRANAR Conceptual Models. In: Cataloging & Classification Quarterly 39 (3/4) : 49–61.

IFLA. (1998). Functional Requirements for Bibliographic Records. Final Report. München: K.G. Saur.

IFLA. (2010). Functional Requirements for Subject Authority Data (FRSAD). A Conceptual Model. Approved by the Standing Committee of the IFLA Section on Classification and Indexing. Available at: http://www.ifla.org/files/classification-and-indexing/functional-requirements-for-subject-authority-data/frsad-final-report.pdf.

Ranganathan, Shiyali R. (1962). Facet Analysis: Fundamental Categories. In: Ranganathan, Shiyali R.: Elements of Library Classification. 3rd ed. Bombay, New York: Asia Publishing House. 82–89.

Rust, Godfrey; Bide, Mark. (2000). The <indecs> Metadata Framework. Principles, Model and Data Dictionary. Indecs Framework Ltd. Available at: http://www.doi.org/topics/indecs/indecs_framework_2000.pdf .

Strunck, Kirsten. (1999). About the Use of "Functional Requirements for Bibliographic Records" in Teaching Cataloguing. In: 65th IFLA Council and General Conference, Bangkok, Thailand, August 20 – August 28, 1999. Available at: http://ifla.org/IV/ifla65/papers/108-131e.htm.

Two Tales of a Concept: Aligning FRSAD with SKOS

Michael Panzer

Abstract: The FRSAD model provides an abstract analysis of subject authority data. The article tries to assess the compatibility of this conceptual framework with formalisms and practices that have emerged from the Semantic Web community. Through applying SKOS, it becomes apparent that some interpretive decisions necessary to accommodate the rigor of formal knowledge representation languages are not supported by FRSAD itself. Difficulties in clearly aligning the thema entity with either a SKOS or OWL counterpart reveal ambiguities in the FRSAD model regarding the ontological status of thema, which seems to reflect a general uncertainty regarding the aboutness of subject authority data in the library domain.

1. *Introduction*

The conceptual model at the heart of the Functional Requirements for Subject Authority Data (FRSAD) provides an analysis of the FRBR Group 3 entities. Yet, as is to be expected of functional requirements, the model is defined in a fundamentally abstract way. In most cases, in order to use it as basis for vocabulary creation, management, and publishing, the entities, relationships, and attributes defined by the FRSAD model have to be expressed in another model, formalism, or language.

Appendix C of the FRSAD conceptual model already contains some initial assessments regarding mappings to related models and standards, but further concretization is needed. Established models chosen for practical application can often be expected to possess somewhat stricter formal semantics in such ways that an alignment of FRSAD with these formalisms will require concretizations not entirely derivable from the FRSAD model itself.

In the following, I will try to achieve two separate, but complementary goals: As a first step, I will apply the Simple Knowledge Organization System (SKOS) to FRSAD in a more concrete way than the FRSAD conceptual model already attempts to, trying to assess the degree to which FRSAD can be straightforwardly aligned with SKOS. As a second step, an alternative alignment with SKOS will be suggested and then used as an analytic tool to shed a light on some knowledge representation aspects of FRSAD, trying to analyze some of its underlying ontological assumptions.

Recently, models that have emerged from Semantic Web or linked data efforts seem to pose a challenge for domain models (in a very loose sense of the word) originating from the library realm like FRSAD. Semantic Web element vocabularies, with their heritage outside of the realm of classic bibliographic knowledge organization systems, tend to have a somewhat stricter way of knowledge representation combined with a cross-disciplinary focus, but also sometimes a limited understanding of the deep traditions of knowledge organization developed in library and information science communities. Yet, with the library realm starting to redefine its domain with efforts like FRBR, FRSAD, or RDA, there is new opportunity and also obligation to meet the challenge of the Semantic Web, as its tools seem to claim mostly the same territory that has been claimed by library knowledge organization systems in the past.

2. *FRSAD with SKOS*

As its central entity, SKOS provides skos:Concept, an instance of owl:Class. On the surface, the skos:Concept entity seems to be an appropriate match for FRSAD's *thema.* With the help of RDF Schema and the Web Ontology Language (OWL), SKOS provides the means of expressing the two associated attributes of *thema*: type and scope.

It may seem counter-intuitive that the "type" of a *thema* cannot be expressed by just using rdf:type, because this would create an instance of skos:Concept, i.e., an individual skos:Concept or *thema*, not a restricted set of instances with its members belonging both to *thema* and a "type" of *thema* like, e.g., *event.* Instead, the "type" relationship has to be mapped to OWL's fundamental subclass axiom rdfs:subclassOf. Specific "types" of *thema* may then be created as subclasses of skos:Concept, with their members being more specific and having more attributes than skos:Concept itself, while the subclasses still retain all abilities of expressing further relationships that can only be applied at the class level, not at the instance level.

On the other hand, rdf:type can be used appropriately to model the "possible distinction [...] at the *thema* level between **Classes** and **Instances**"[1], for which it is a workable mapping. Following the definitions of the working group, both classes and instances would count as "types" of *thema.* However, it is important that vocabularies make clear distinctions whether a subclass or a class/instance relationship holds between two *themas.* Contrary to library knowledge organization systems, where both types have traditionally been treated as hierarchical relationships, ontology lan-

1 FRSAD 2010: 21.

guages like OWL draw a clear line between hierarchical relationships between sets of individuals (i.e., subclass hierarchies) and relationships between classes and individuals (i.e., class/instance).[2]

"Scope" can be aligned straightforwardly with the SKOS documentation property skos:scopeNote.

Handling the *nomen* entity proves to be a harder problem in SKOS. For associating lexical labels with concepts, SKOS defines the properties skos:prefLabel, skos:altLabel, and skos:hiddenLabel (all are instances of owl:AnnotationProperty and sub-properties of rdfs:label). For non-lexical labels, SKOS provides the skos:notation property (an instance of owl:DatatypeProperty). However, all of these properties are only intended to be used with plain (in case of skos:prefLabel, ...) or typed (in case of skos:notation) RDF literals. A literal is not a good match for a *nomen*, as RDF does not allow literals to be used as subjects of statements (i.e., it is not possible to make assertions about literals). Also, literals cannot have attributes except either language or data type, which seems to preclude the use of SKOS' label and notation properties as a candidate for FRSAD's "has appellation" relationship. It would, in fact, not even be possible to assert that a label *is* a *nomen*.

Fortunately, SKOS defines an optional extension for labels (SKOS-XL), providing "additional support for identifying, describing and linking lexical entities"[3]. In essence, the XL data model defines a class skosxl:Label, which allows for treating labels of concepts as separate resources (with identifiers), opening up a variety of possibilities for relating lexical entities. In conjunction with the newly defined property skosxl:label, SKOS-XL now satisfies all requirements of the "has appellation" relationship and the *nomen* entity. A skosxl:Label can be linked to skos:Concepts and also to other skosxl:Labels, making it structurally possible to express *thema*-to-*nomen* and *nomen*-to-*nomen* relationships in SKOS.

I will not attempt to map all general attributes of *nomen* suggested by the working group to SKOS-XL counterparts; it will suffice to say that most would have to be derived as sub-properties from existing relationships in the XL data model (e.g., skosxl:labelRelation) or newly defined as extensions of SKOS-XL (e.g., for "script of nomen"). Some are already available in the SKOS vocabulary, like skos:inScheme, and can be reused for skosxl:Label. As required in the FRSAD model, this property can be used to assert in which scheme the nomen is established.

---

2 For a discussion of the applicability of OWL to hierarchical relationships in classification systems, see Green & Panzer 2011.

3 SKOS Reference 2009.

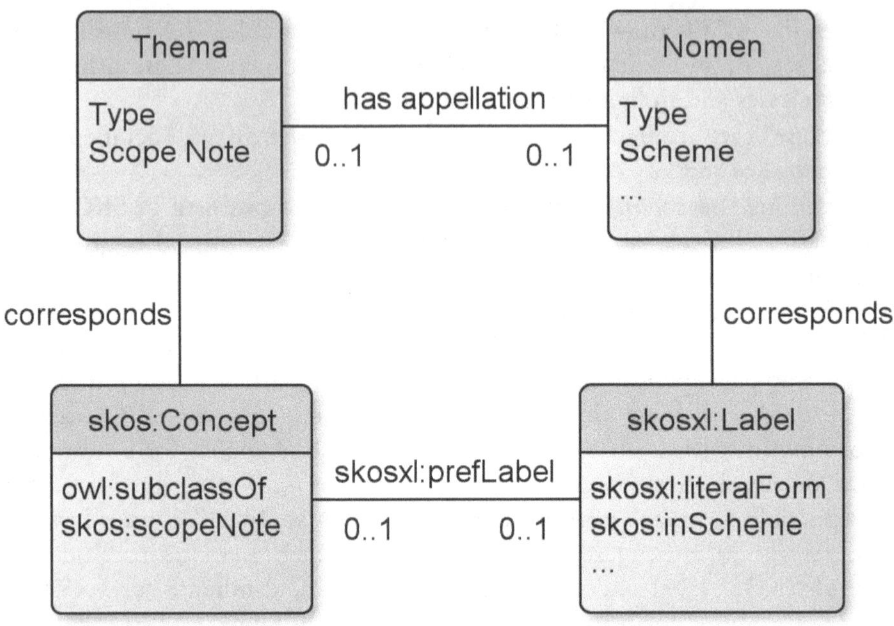

Figure 1: *Thema* viewed as skos:Concept

A closer look at the proposed mapping in Figure 1 reveals possible shortcomings of this alignment. Many properties of *nomen* would have to be newly defined for skosxl:Label, and, more importantly, the skos:inScheme property, a central relationship for controlled vocabularies, is not used for skos:Concept (as *thema*) at all, but exclusively for the *nomen*, which seems to go slightly against the model for concepts and concepts schemes in SKOS. Also, the distribution of attributes vs. relationships between skos:Concept and skosxl:Label seems rather lopsided. FRSAD envisions a *thema* having almost no attributes, including no associated scheme, but having a variety of semantic relationships. On the other hand, the *nomen* has a variety of attributes, but almost no relationships. In RDF Schema, attributes and relationships are both expressed as properties. Attributes can be regarded as properties that correspond to attribute-value pairs, whereas relationships are equivalent to links to other resources.

Therefore, *themas* can be embedded in networks of semantic relationships, but seem to be underspecified otherwise (which is acknowledged in the FRSAD model), whereas *nomen* seem to be very well described, but almost unconnected otherwise. *Thema*, in this regard, looks like not much more than a link-hub for a *nomen*, with important information that would potentially apply to a *thema-nomen* combination confined to the *nomen* level. Combined with the limited expressiveness of the *thema-nomen* relationship (a *nomen* can only be the appellation of a *thema*), there seems to exist a complementarity between *thema* and *nomen*, a latent dependency even. Is it plausible to assume that a specific nomen established in a controlled vocabulary will not also require a complementary *thema* to be established that carries semantically the indented conceptualization? Yet FRSAD does not acknowledge that semantic relationships are really defined at the vocabulary level. For example, the broader term of the *thema* "nucleic acids" may be "biomolecules" in LCSH, in another scheme it may be "biochemistry." FRSAD, with *thema* interpreted as skos:Concept, would assume that these are different *themas* (represented by functionally equivalent *nomens*) just because they have different semantic relationships.

Or could the FRSAD model also be interpreted in a different way by not equating *themas* with concepts of all kinds, but rather with "things" of all kinds? The next section will analyze the requirements and implications of the FRSAD model understood in this broader way.

3. *FRSAD against SKOS*

In the previous section, I almost naïvely assumed a straightforward correspondence between *thema* in FRSAD and skos:Concept in SKOS.

Confining *themas* to instances of skos:Concept requires at least two main assumptions: subjects (and "the whole universe of subject-related entity classes"[4]) exist independently from other objects in the world (that are not subjects). According to this assumption, "Paris" (the city in France) is a different individual than "Paris-as-a-subject;" "nucleic acids" is different from "nucleic-acids-as-a-subject." The latter of each pair would be regarded as a *thema*, the former would not. Assuming an independent existence of *themas* raises the questions about how they come about, or how they relate to their "real-world" counterparts, the answers to which cannot easily be derived from the FRSAD conceptual model.

Does a *thema* exist before works refer to it as a subject, or does it come into being when its first appellation, a *nomen*, is established in a scheme? Indeed, the entity-relationship model of the basic FRSAD entities seems to indicate that *themas* do exist without a *nomen* (the cardinality of their relationship is many-to-many), and, also, that they exist independently of schemes (a *thema* cannot be associated with a scheme). On the other hand, the conceptual model seems to also indicate at times that "controlled vocabularies [...] enable the establishment of complex *themas*"[5], which seems

4 FRSAD 2010: 41.
5 FRSAD 2010: 18.

to presume a more intricate link between *nomens* and *themas* than mere appellation.

The FRSAD Working Group tries to address this ontological problem in passing in their discussion of views on "aboutness," shortly characterizing nominalist vs. realist viewpoints. They hesitantly conclude that, while user expectations ultimately suggest acting "in accordance with assumptions that are consistent with some version of the realist viewpoint," the group does not see the need to "take a philosophical position on the nature of aboutness"[6].

The model created by the group, however, seems to suggest a clear adoption of the realist viewpoint. The adoption of a *thema* entity fits well with their definition of realism as the "assumption that subjects are real things that exist separately from the linguistic expressions that we use to name them,"[7] i.e., independently from the *nomens* used as appellations of *themas*. However, this seems to clash with another general assumption of the group, namely thinking of "subject-ness" as a role of "everything that the user of a library catalogue might view as a 'subject'"[8], i.e., potentially *any* object.

If combined with a realist position, this stance seems to entail that whenever someone writes a book about any object, the substance of that object would somehow be altered to now include the property of "subject-ness." This object would be required to become an instance of the *thema* entity in order to function as a subject of this work, as works can only have *themas* as subjects. It can be argued that this paradoxical situation is somewhat mitigated by the group's confinement of *themas* to the library domain (especially in the discussions of complex *themas*), but it nevertheless seems likely that these assumptions are mutually exclusive. Either *themas* exist independently from beliefs, practices, conceptual schemes, etc., or they can be a role of *any* object.

While each of these interpretations may be upheld separately, together they fundamentally challenge the viability of an independent *thema* entity in the FRSAD model. If *themas* (only) exist independently, yet there is nothing that cannot be used as a subject of a work, *themas* become a superfluous entity of the domain. Since every real-world object has (potentially) a corresponding *thema* associated with it, the set of all *themas* acts essentially as "a Map of the Empire whose size was that of the Empire, and which coincided point for point with it."[9]. Interpreted in this way, there is no need or ground to specifically define subjects as special concept entities (i.e., *the-*

6 FRSAD 2010: 11.
7 Ibid.
8 FRSAD 2010: 16.
9 Borges 1999: 325.

mas as skos:Concepts) vs. as relationships that exist directly between works and real-world entities, as merely an aspect under which persons, places, concepts, etc., could be viewed. For example, it seems not at all clear in FRSAD example if an object can be both a foaf:Person and a *thema* at the same time. Or, if these are mutually disjoint sets, how is a *thema*/skos:Concept like "Thomas-Mann-as-a-subject" to be connected to the foaf:Person Thomas Mann?

As a consequence of this interpretation of the *thema* entity and its ontological status in the FRSAD model, an alternative SKOS alignment has to be considered. When adopting the viewpoint that it makes little sense to align *thema* with skos:Concept, because everything can be a *thema*, not just abstract entities (or abstract versions of concrete entities), it should make more sense to align *thema* with a much broader entity, namely, owl:Thing, the class representing "the set of all individuals"[10].

Under this alternative view, *nomen*, still interpreted as skosxl:Labels, would then be associated directly with instances of owl:Thing, which might be places, events, and also, among other things, skos:Concepts (see Figure 2).

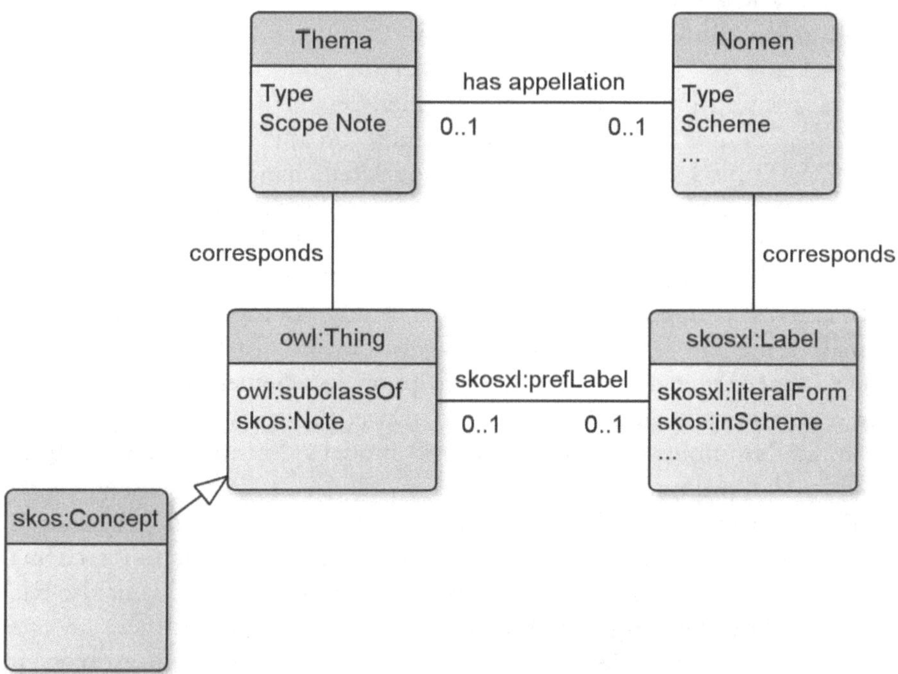

Figure 2: *Thema* viewed as owl:Thing

10 OWL 2 Syntax 2009.

To assess what kind of ontological commitment this interpretation of FRSAD is making, what things are parts of its ontological baggage, we have to reach a clearer understanding of how the definition of *thema* was motivated by the FRSAD Working Group in the first place. Could a SKOS model based on owl:Thing satisfy these requirements?

The *thema* entity seems to primarily support two tasks. Firstly, it enables the attachment of hierarchical and associative relationships to a subject for the benefit of exploratory tasks of information seekers[11]. Secondly, it seems to promote *nomen* interoperability for the benefit of creators of knowledge organization systems. Two vocabularies may make explicit that two different *nomens* are indeed appellations of the same *thema*, so that works that have subject access points corresponding to either one of these *nomens* can be assumed to have the same aboutness.

While this aligns closely with assumptions expressed in SKOS about the possibility of reusing concepts across schemes by asserting different skos:inScheme properties, it also inherits the same issues pointed out by Tennis and Sutton[12], who argue that, because a skos:Concept changes semantically when it is established as part of a scheme, SKOS needs to provide a mechanism to account for a skos:Concept *as conceptualized* in a specific scheme vs. the "platonic" version of the concept. As in FRSAD, semantic relationships in SKOS are assigned on the concept level, and (in principle) cannot be changed or augmented on the scheme level. In fact, the FRSAD model allows for no scheme-related change at all, as *themas* are never part of any scheme (e.g., a specific controlled vocabulary).

Although semantic interoperability seems to have been the reason to define *themas* as being independent of value encoding schemes or element vocabularies, it is not at all apparent whether this assumption is viable. Does it make sense for *thema*-like entities to exist outside of schemes? It could be argued that *themas* are, in fact, on life support in schemes, with no convincing reason to exist outside of them. To answer this question, we have to reexamine the implications of the FRSAD model's decision of confining semantic relationships to the *thema* level.

If, as imagined by FRSAD, a *thema* is not scheme-specific, then its semantic definition is not dependent on some conceptualization in a scheme. This begs the question, however, how is it determined which semantic relationships hold (and don't hold) for a given *thema* or when these become true or false? Also, as discussed above, what brings *themas* into existence in the first place? Is it the act of initial baptism by a *nomen* in a scheme, or are

11 FRSAD 2010: 37.
12 Tennis & Sutton 2008.

themas envisioned by the FRSAD model to exist as non-physical, non-mental, abstract objects?

In FRSAD as interpreted by using owl:Thing for *thema*, we would assume that all semantic relationships associated with *themas* either hold in the actual world, or they don't hold at all. This alignment does not give room to the assumption of an independent realm of subjects, but instead encourages a direct conceptualization of the world. "Subject-ness" or "*thema-ness*" would not be regarded as essential properties that only abstract entities like *themas* posses, but as merely a specific way how controlled vocabularies conceptualize and refer to all kinds of things. Contrary to a statement in FRSAD, where, "following Hjørland"[13], the nominalistic view on aboutness is equated with idealism, I would argue that such an (undoubtedly nominalistic) interpretation of *thema* would not deny the independent existence of *themas*, but rather require that they are particular and concrete, not abstract.

An alignment based on owl:Thing would imply that all things conceptualized in controlled vocabularies and other subject schemes are in the world not as *themas*, which can also be typed as places, concepts, situations, or processes, but instead as places, concepts, situations, or processes, all of which can also be *themas*. Ultimately, this leads to the assumption that library knowledge organization systems are creating conceptualizations of slices of the world, not requiring or inventing their own abstract realm of subjects separated from them. These conceptualizations, on the other hand, are firmly anchored in schemes. Different schemes may assert different semantic relationships to the things they describe, contrary to the assumption of *themas* that can only be named in different way across schemes. It seems implausible that every controlled vocabulary has the same conceptualization of "World War II" (as its interpretation as a skos:Concept *thema* would suggest), only establishing different names for it. On the other hand, it seems as least as implausible that each and every concept scheme that uses "World War II" would appellate a different (i.e., its own) version or sense of the "World War II" *thema*. The map is indeed *not* the territory, but is also not confined to an independent realm of *themas* defined by library domain vocabularies.

4. *FRSAD, Library KOS, and the claim of the Semantic Web*

If everything can potentially be a subject, there is no convincing reason to confine *thema* to something that only makes sense for communicating inside the library domain. The main challenge to this model arises from practices and the architecture of the Semantic Web.

---

13 FRSAD 2010: 10.

The main benefit of the Semantic Web and the lure of (library) linked data seems to be precisely that data creators from many disciplines can use the exact same tools to contribute to different areas of the data map. While this requires linked data providers to address complex identification problems to find common ground across disciplines and relating identifiers in order to find links between concrete objects across data sets, it enables the collection of their diverse, sometimes conflicting, conceptualizations of real-world entities.

The FRSAD model does not preclude this for subject authority data, as *themas* can be connected to conceptualizations from other domains, but it introduces an unnecessary layer of intermediacy into this dialog. Instead of clearly relating concepts to *things* that other disciplines may be also talking about, the FRSAD model seems to assume that library knowledge organization systems merely describe an exclusive realm of abstract *themas*. This controversy about the aboutness of subject authority data among information scientist can therefore also be seen in FRSAD. As just one of many examples, Gemberling reports on the difficulties to resolve the "ambiguity between subjects and names"[14] for buildings under Library of Congress' rules for authority headings establishment. He writes that "a drive towards conceptual consistency demands that buildings be established either as names or subjects, while the practical needs of library work call for flexibility."[15] FRSAD seems to merely reflect this ambiguity instead of trying to make a decision. Instead, as I hope to have shown, FRSAD places the burden of this decision on the implementers.

When interpreting FRSAD, implementers will have to decide between two main options: either a *thema* is regarded as essentially scheme-specific, with its semantic relationships asserted by the scheme (i.e., every *nomen* creates a different *thema*, which is only connected to that *nomen*). Or a *thema* is something else entirely, and its semantic relationships are grounded in the physical world. In the end, both interpretations seem possible in FRSAD and have benefits and drawbacks, but, as I have tried to argue, are mutually exclusive.

Thema, as (under-)specified in the FRSAD model, seems in this regard to behave exactly like counterfeit money. It signifies the indeterminate state of an entity that ceases to exist when determined what it really is. Counterfeit money is either real money or worthless paper. A *thema* seems to be either a particular and concrete external entity (a person, a concept, a place, etc.) or a specific conceptualization of such an external entity in a scheme.

The Semantic Web tries to "solve" this problem, perhaps too naïvely, by clearly taking one side of this debate. In the context of web architecture,

---

14 Gemberling 2010: 448.

15 Ibid.

RDF statements can be assertions about things that are not web documents (called *non-information resources* or *real-world objects*), rather than about abstract *themas*, which may be in some way connected to real-world objects. These assertions may originate from different agencies or schemes and may be conflicting, but this can be handled on subsequent levels of provenance and inference, not the level of a domain model.

5. *Conclusion*

The goal of the paper was neither an exhaustive analysis of the concrete philosophical stance of the FRSAD Working Group, nor an attempt at discerning the underlying "aboutness" paradigm of FRSAD (realism, nominalism, etc.). I was merely trying to shed some light on the difficulty of deciding between these viewpoints in order to correctly interpret the FRSAD model. Precisely this decision seems mandatory for using the FRSAD model for controlled vocabularies on the Semantic Web. Is *thema* meant to be skos:Concept or owl:Thing? What exactly *does* subject authority data represent: the world of subjects, or subjects in the world?

I believe that the changing nature of the KO environment – namely the growing influence of Semantic Web formalisms – forces domain modeling efforts to address these questions much more rigorously than they had to in the past, when a domain model like FRSAD would have been little more than an exercise on paper. We are now facing the challenge that, in order to express these models in languages with transparent ontological commitments (like OWL), there has to be the potential to align them unambiguously.

The introduction of *thema* into FRSAD as an ambiguous entity makes these tasks harder and only defers other difficult questions of alias management and resource identity. *Thema* claims to be broader than the confinement of a scheme, but at the same time it seems unclear how actual reuse outside of a scheme should happen or how relations to entities outside of the subject authority domain should be handled.

Acknowledgement

I would like to thank my colleague Jeff Young from OCLC Research, who was the first to doubt that *thema* maps neatly to skos:Concept.

References

Web Documents were accessed on June 17, 2011.

Borges, Jorge Luis. (1999). Collected Fictions. Translated by Andrew Hurley. New York: Penguin Books.

Functional Requirements for Subject Authority Data (FRSAD): A Conceptual Model. (2010). IFLA Working Group on the Functional Requirements for Subject Authority Records (FRSAR). Edited by Marcia Lei Zeng; Maja Žumer; Athena Salaba. Available at: http://www.ifla.org/files/classification-and-indexing/functional-requirements-for-subject-authority-data/frsad-final-report.pdf

Gemberling, Ted. (2010). Thema and FRBR's third group. In: Cataloging and Classification Quarterly 48 (5) : 445-449.

Green, Rebecca; Panzer, Michael. (2011). Relationships in the Notational Hierarchy of the Dewey Decimal Classification. In: Proceedings of the International UDC Seminar 2011. Würzburg: Ergon. [Forthcoming].

OWL 2 Web Ontology Language: Structural Specification and Functional-style Syntax. (2009). W3C Recommendation 27 October 2009. Edited by Boris Motik; Peter F. Patel-Schneider; Bijan Parsia. Available at: http://www.w3.org/TR/2009/REC-owl2-syntax-20091027/.

SKOS Simple Knowledge Organization System Reference. (2009). W3C Recommendation 18 August 2009. Edited by Alistair Miles; Sean Bechhofer. Available at: http://www.w3.org/TR/2009/REC-skos-reference-20090818/.

Tennis, Joseph T.; Sutton, Stuart A. (2008). Extending the Simple Knowledge Organization System for Concept Management in Vocabulary Development Applications. In: Journal of the American Society for Information Science and Technology 59 (1) : 25-37.

Integrating Semantic Interoperability into FRSAD

Felix Boteram

Abstract: Since its launch in 1998, the initiative introducing the Functional Requirements of Bibliographic Records (FRBR) has provided and established a new standard for the representation of bibliographic data. Following the success of the Functional Requirements for Bibliographic Records, a number of related modules have been developed, complementing the initial standard. One of the most recent and promising efforts in this field is the initiative surrounding the development and approval of the Functional Requirements for Subject Authority Data (FRSAD). FRSAD is a specification of the requirements for modelling subject authority data, based on a conceptual model, which combines various theoretical aspects and technical modelling strategies. This article analyses the model's adaptability and appropriateness in an environment of heterogeneous and distributed systems and makes some suggestions for further improvements.

1. Semantic interoperability as a general requirement

As networks and interconnected structures have become a universal metaphor in a large variety of fields and the connectivity of distributed systems seems to be taken for granted, the idea of interoperability is equally prominent. Integrating interoperability with all its various aspects is crucial, particularly when developing and establishing new standards for the representation of bibliographic information and subject authority data; indeed every model or framework for the representation of subject authority data should include the interoperability aspect on a technical, structural and conceptual level.

Whereas interoperability on a technical and structural level is well-defined in established standards for protocols and specifications for encoding, exchanging and processing information, the ideas behind the term of semantic interoperability are far less clear. Sometimes it is understood as interoperability between metadata schemes, sometimes as interoperability between controlled terms in indexing languages and sometimes as interoperability between document-specific subject-indexing data. As these types of interoperability are often intertwined and additionally the methods used are similar, they are often subsumed under the same term.[1] This may also be supported

---

1 Cf. Zeng & Chan 2010.

by the fact that they are all suited to improving the functionality and efficiency of information retrieval and knowledge exploration in heterogeneous information systems, be it cross-institutional library catalogues or web-based retrieval systems. However, distinguishing them is necessary as they have to support different functionalities when looked at in detail.

In the context of Semantic Web technologies, semantic interoperability is often considered as referring to fully machine-readable information and the modelling of this information. Connecting and functionally integrating a large number of decentralised and highly heterogeneous systems appears to be a task that can be managed entirely by algorithms operating in the background entirely unnoticed by the user and without actually requesting any intervention or additional information. This may be an efficient and appropriate approach when dealing with data that require technical or structural interoperability, but when dealing with semantic information, i.e. data relating to the meaning and the propositional content of an element of an indexing language, such a formal interoperability on the functional level has to be complemented by semantic interoperability on the conceptual level.

The functionality and efficiency of information retrieval and knowledge exploration depends on the structural characteristics and the semantic and syntactic expressiveness of the indexing languages used to describe and represent the content of the items in the collections or repositories. Whereas retrieval processes are mainly based upon machine-processing and machine-interpretation of data, processes of knowledge exploration are also accompanied by intellectual interpretation of the semantic data on behalf of the information seeker. In heterogeneous information spaces, semantic interoperability between concept schemes enhances the functionalities of individual concept schemes in respect of subject retrieval and knowledge exploration. According to Hubrich[2] three levels of semantic interoperability can be distinguished which correspond to different retrieval levels; word-based, conceptual and differentiated interoperability. Besides, when using mappings for the retrieval of information resources, differences between the entities modelled in indexing languages and the indexing data have to be taken into account.

A conceptual model for subject authority data that integrates interoperability should specify all the different types of conceptual entities and the characteristics of the existing relationships. It is the skilful combination of the definition of conceptual entities and their integration into a differentiated relational structure that provides true expressivity and functionality of a subject heading authority file and this facilitates relevant statements about

2 Hubrich 2011.

their similarity. This article analyses the adaptability and appropriateness of the *Functional Requirements for Subject Authority Data (FRSAD)*[3] in an environment of heterogeneous and distributed systems and makes some suggestions for further improvement. It develops and suggests a possible strategy and discusses necessary preparatory steps to integrate the aspect of interoperability into FRSAD. It discusses the requirements for a system that allows for valid and useful statements and expressive propositions on structural and semantic similarities between individual conceptual entities from different indexing languages.

2. *Interoperability in FRSAD*

The model of the *Functional Requirements for Subject Authority Data (FRSAD)* was designed to specify the functional requirements for the description and representation of the elements of subject indexing languages, especially controlled vocabularies, in the context of the *Functional Requirements for Bibliographic Records (FRBR)*[4]. This expansion and specification of functional requirements facilitates the integration of subject information into the basic model of FRBR. The latest version of FRSAD was eventually finalised after a long, co-operative process of developing, discussing and re-writing several different drafts.[5] The introduction and promotion of a comprehensive model of subject authority files in the now finalised version offers a good fundament and an interesting starting point for further developments.

As FRSAD is based on an Entity-Relationship (ER) model, it does not focus exclusively on the individual conceptual entities represented as isolated terms or classes of verbal or classificatory indexing languages, but also encompasses and represents the relations between these entities and the semantic expressivity of the resulting relational structure. Thus it provides a basis for the adequate representation of the complexity and multidimensionality of the relational structure of a subject field for information retrieval and knowledge organisation. The use of a relational model of subject representation also allows for the integration of semantic information that transcends the meaning of the individual concept; this is a technical and structural prerequisite as many machine-assisted strategies and functionalities in information retrieval and exploration rely on the interpretation of information invested in the relational structure. Logical characteristics in-

3 IFLA Working Group on the Functional Requirements for Subject Authority Records 2009 and 2010.

4 IFLA Study Group on the Functional Requirements for Bibliographic Records 1998.

5 See also Žumer 2011.

vested in specified relations may be used to draw inferences in order to reveal implicit knowledge which might be relevant for the retrieval process.

Particularly when consolidating or re-designing vocabularies of existing conventional indexing languages, whose terms feature little or no formalised information on the meaning, scope and usage of the individual terms, the formalisation of certain features of semantic relations interconnecting all terms can provide valuable additional information on the coherence of the individual terms in individual thematic clusters.

As modern retrieval and exploration strategies are most likely to be implemented in distributed and heterogeneous repositories, a description model for subject authority data should always provide strategies to interconnect these systems efficiently. Although the ER model does allow for differentiated inter-system relations to be modelled, a specific inventory of intersystem relations is not provided in FRSAD. As intersystem relations differ significantly from inter-concept relations in respect of their specific characteristics and derived functionalities[6], such an extended inventory is necessary for the adequate representation of conceptual similarities or equivalence between elements pertaining to different systems.

Even though the importance of semantic interoperability is well recognised, it is not extensively dealt with within the draft and the final report. The interoperability between the FRSAD model and common metadata schemes for the representation of data in the web is only briefly addressed in a separate section in the appendix of the final report; basic similarities in respect of the meaning of the main concepts of FRSAD on the one hand, and the SKOS, OWL and the DCMI Abstract Model on the other, are sketched.[7] Unfortunately, issues of semantic interoperability between various concept schemes are only casually mentioned twice in the main text in connection with the terms *thema* and *nomen*.[8]

Thema and *nomen* are a terminological mainstay of the conceptual model of FRSAD. The precise definition of the *themata* and *nomina* of the individual indexing languages is facilitated by an internal differentiation of these entities into the concepts they represent, the word or sign used to represent these concepts on the representational layer and the object they refer to in the real world. This triangular relational layout, which constitutes the terminological and conceptual centrepiece of the original conceptual model, takes up the

6 Cf. Boteram & Hubrich 2010.

7 IFLA Working Group on the Functional Requirements for Subject Authority Records 2010: 49f. In the former draft, this section was part of the main text (IFLA Working Group on the Functional Requirements for Subject Authority Records 2009: 67–69). See also Zeng & Žumer 2009.

8 Cf. IFLA Working Group on the Functional Requirements for Subject Authority Records 2010: 18 and 26.

basic idea of the semiotic triangle as introduced by Ogden and Richards[9]. In an analogy with the semiotic triangle, *thema* describes real-life objects, subjects and topics of information resources, i.e. *works*, which are represented by one or more *nomina* in form of specific signs or sequences of signs. FRSAD states that when mapping vocabularies, the "has as appellation/is appellation of" relation between *thema* and *nomen* may be a many-to-many relation: "Any *thema* may have more than one *nomen* [...] and any *nomen* may be the appellation of more than one *thema*."[10] This may be true if *nomina*, or the strings with which concepts are represented, are viewed independently from the concept schemes they were modelled in as it may be the case that they are accessed by machines without any additional information having been given. In many modern encoding schemes for the adequate representation of semantic data for web applications, however, the representations of concepts are viewed as an element of a specific concept scheme and are modelled correspondingly. This viewpoint is also taken up by FRSAD when schemes, in which *nomina* are established, are modelled as attributes of *nomen*.[11] Against this background, the statement that any *nomen* can refer to more than one *thema*[12] seems to be questionable. More clarity would help with describing issues of semantic interoperability; the *thema-nomen* model of FRSAD provides a valuable fundament for issues of semantic interoperability. By distinguishing concepts or subjects from the terms used to address them, it allows the distinguishing between word-based and concept-based interoperability. These two types of interoperability support different retrieval functionalities:

Word-based interoperability refers to the terms on the representational level, supporting word-based queries, whereas propositions on concept-based interoperability access and take into account the meaning of concepts, facilitating conceptual queries in globally-distributed systems.[13] FRSAD correctly points out that among

> the efforts to achieve global sharing and use of subject authority data, some efforts have focused on *nomen*, e.g. translated metadata vocabulary, a symmetrical multilingual thesaurus, or a multi-access index to a vocabulary. However, most efforts have focused on the conceptual level, e.g. mappings between two thesauri or between a classification scheme and a thesaurus.[14]

9 Ogden & Richards 1923.
10 IFLA Working Group on the Functional Requirements for Subject Authority Records 2010: 26.
11 IFLA Working Group on the Functional Requirements for Subject Authority Records 2010: 22.
12 Ibid.: 26.
13 Cf. Hubrich 2011.
14 IFLA Working Group on the Functional Requirements for Subject Authority Records 2010: 49.

Concept-based interoperability, however, may be created using different methods and different types of intersystem relations.

When using FRSAD to describe the conceptual entities of indexing languages and to access the semantic level, it is barely possible to establish concept-based interoperability by means of typed inter-system relations. Unfortunately, the entities and relations provided by FRSAD are not sufficient to precisely describe similarities and differences of conceptual entities of different indexing languages even on an implementation-independent abstract level.

3. *Enhancing FRSAD*

In order to make precise and logically valid propositions on the semantic interoperability between subject authority data as well as subject indexing data of different systems, all essential elements and contributing factors have to be taken into account. Defining the characteristics of the individual elements of an indexing language on the representational level is of primary importance. These elements constitute the terminological stock of both classificatory and verbal indexing languages and are the building blocks for any subject-strings. They also provide the fundaments for applications and functionalities of semantic interoperability.

Consequently, one important prerequisite for more differentiated statements on the degree of semantic similarity or equivalence of individual conceptual entities pertaining to different systems is the precise distinction and definition of the types of conceptual entities in the respective indexing languages.

The different characteristics of simple and complex, i.e. composite and synthetic entities have to be taken into account and have to be represented accordingly. The characteristics and interrelations of these entity types have to be specified in greater detail in order to facilitate more accurate and expressive statements regarding their commonalities and shared characteristics. A thorough understanding of these characteristics is a first step towards assessing semantic interoperability of individual conceptual entities and the respective systems in general. Therefore, the original model's scarce inventory has to be complemented and specified by various subtypes. The following section will elaborate on the suggested differentiation between simple and complex conceptual entities.

3.1 *Distinguishing between simple and complex conceptual entities*

Conceptual entities may be further differentiated into two major structural subtypes of conceptual entities; simple and complex conceptual (entities).

The model in its present state features a general (simple) conceptual entity which is not specified any further regarding its complexity or specificity. Taking a look at the wide range of different conceptual elements in existing systems – classifications as well as verbal subject authority files – it is apparent that a further differentiation is desirable in order to adequately assess and describe terms of varying complexity from various existing indexing languages. Therefore, we suggest a (first) differentiation which distinguishes simple (basic) and complex conceptual entities. As a result of this first move, a complex conceptual entity is introduced in which a complex concept referring to a complex object can be represented by a phrase. This is visualised in the right-hand triangle on Figure 1.

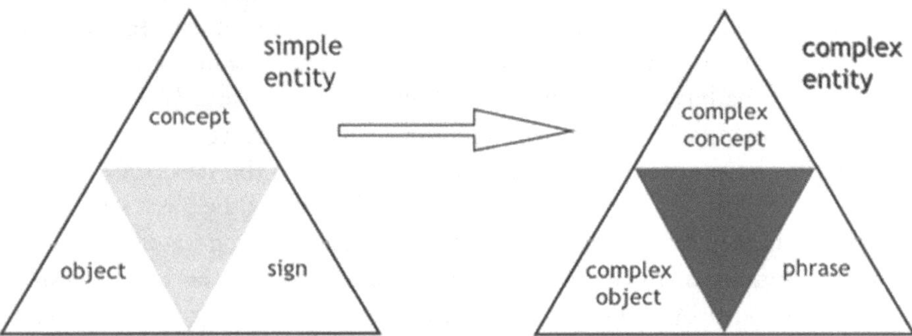

Figure 1: First distinction: Simple vs. complex entities

Every "conceptual entity" exists on a first, conceptual level merely as an inherently incommunicable abstract idea which can only become an element of a formalised system of an indexing language when receiving a formal realisation on the representational level. It is the formal realisations on the representational level which constitute the elements of an indexing language. This distinction becomes particularly relevant when handling varying levels of complexity of the conceptual entities belonging to different systems. Although this may be the case for a large number of complex conceptual entities, the degree and kind of complexity on the conceptual level does not have to correspond with the complexity on the representational level. Although there seems to be interdependence, there is no such thing as a well-defined formal correlation between the complexity of a conceptual entity on the conceptual level and its realisation on the representational level. This has to be taken into account when assessing the conceptual entities' varying levels of complexity as an important step towards a concise and relevant statement on the semantic similarity of conceptual entities.

3.2 *Distinguishing between (indexing) language-specific and document-specific entities*

The resulting subtypes may be further differentiated by making a second major distinction between entities representing concepts as elements of an indexing language and document-specific concepts. With this second differentiation, an additional dimension or aspect is introduced which complements the aforementioned first modification; this will help to understand and express whether the conceptual entities are used to describe individual concepts as parts of an independent indexing-language or whether these entities are used as elements and immediate constituents to form specific syntagms designed to describe complex conceptual entities on the document level. Establishing this second dichotomy allows for an additional distinction which in turn can be used to represent topics of documents either as basic concepts or synthetic constructions. This distinction between individual concepts as elements of an indexing language on the one hand, and a combination of these elements for the description of the topics of specific documents in a collection on the other, is vital for the correct understanding of various types of semantic interoperability.

The specificity of the differentiation of conceptual entities can be systematically enhanced by using a strategy of combining two consecutive differentiations: A first/An initial distinction between simple and complex concepts and their representation is complemented by a second major distinction between entities representing concepts as elements of an indexing language and document-specific concepts. This results in a set of four structural subtypes of conceptual entities. The relations and interdependencies between these four subtypes can be arranged as shown in Figure 2 which illustrates their interdependencies and the possible combinations of the simple and complex characteristics represented on the horizontal axis with the characteristics of language-specific and document-specific indexing on the vertical axis.

3.3 *Differentiating between coordinative and syntagmatic constructions of complex concepts*

Defining additional entity types derived from the original model by a process of differentiation in respect of their complexity enhances the inventories of existing conceptual entities with newly-defined structural elements. This facilitates the integration of more complex concepts and the phrases used to represent these on the level of formal representation.

When developing strategies designed to facilitate semantic interoperability, providing information and making relevant and formalised propositions

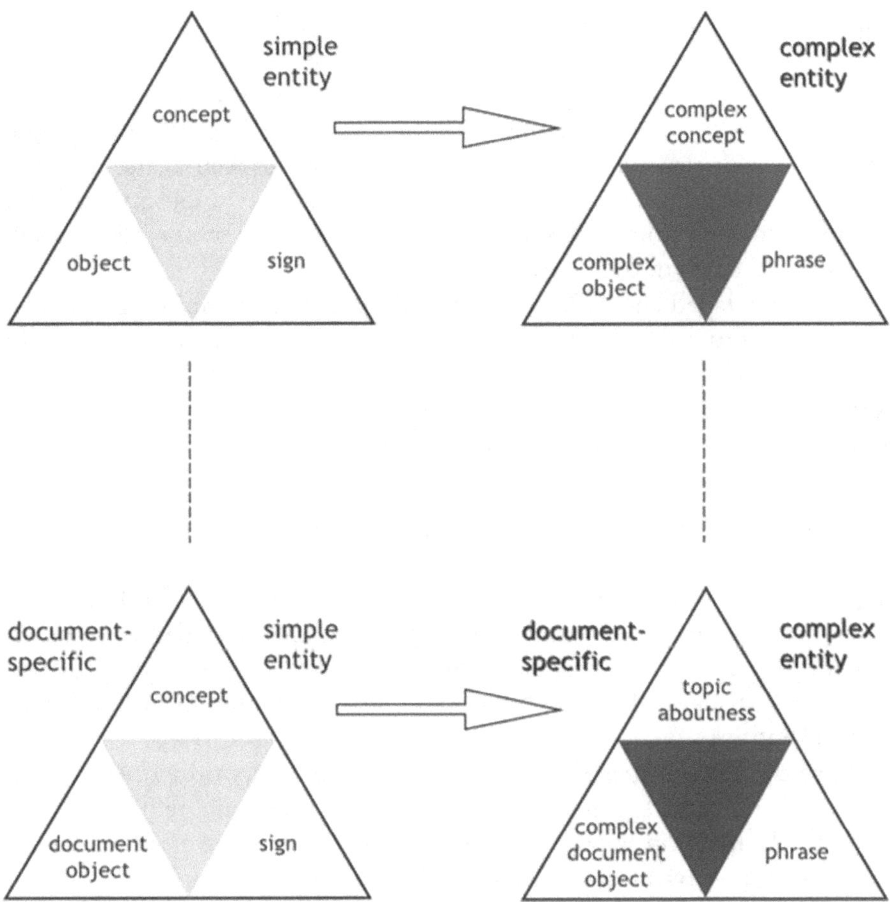

Figure 2: Second distinction: (Indexing) language-specific vs. document-specific entities

in respect of similarities and interdependencies between complex concepts, represented by syntagmatic constructions, is particularly difficult – if not even impossible – to handle. Unlike complex concepts, whose individual elements are combined in a simple coordinative process, syntagmatic expressions include highly functional syntactic elements for the combination of individual concepts into expressive and differentiated conceptual propositions. The syntactic elements determine the interrelation of the individual conceptual elements thereby combining them into highly complex concepts whose propositional content always exceeds the sum total of the individual elements of the concept.

Particularly in German, where compounding is a ubiquitous and very productive strategy of word formation, the entities' conceptual complexity does not necessarily correspond to the complexity of their formal representation; the distinction between complex conceptual entities represented by a single, albeit complex compound and those represented by complex terms or classes combining several elements is less clear. Therefore, these elements require a more precise definition and an adequate formal representation. This structural and functional similarity, as well as the structural analogy between compound words of considerable complexity and syntagms, requires a strict differentiation between the structural types and subtypes as described in this article.

Once a detailed and differentiated analysis of these various types of conceptual entities has been established, these types can be used to provide intersystem interoperability by making relevant, precise, detailed and – if possible, formalised – statements on the commonalities and differences of conceptual entities pertaining to different systems.

4. Types and specifications of interoperability

If intersystem interoperability is expected to transcend the technical and structural level to actually reach the conceptual level, detailed information on the semantic content of the intersystem relations has to be provided, taking into account the complex semantics of compound or synthetic conceptual entities.

How can these statements on the semantic similarity or conceptual congruency be designed to meet the technical and functional requirements of the overall model in which they are supposed to be integrated? The objective is to find ways of making propositions on semantic similarities and interdependencies between conceptual entities and to transform these into relevant and adequate mappings between the individual elements of various indexing-languages.

These statements should contain information on the structural and typological characteristics of the systems involved, the logical properties needed for machine-assisted or machine-based processes and – in order to facilitate the understanding of the thematic entities on the document level – information about the formative principles of simple, coordinative or even powerful syntagmatic constructions used to model the aboutness of documents with the help of FRSAD in the greater context of FRBR.

The suggestions and perspectives developed and discussed in this article were originally developed as an extension and specification of one of the earlier drafts[15] of the FRSAD model and were also submitted to the IFLA

[15] IFLA Working Group on the Functional Requirements for Subject Authority Records 2009.

working group on FRSAD as a reply to the invitation to contribute to the conception and development of the model. Their primary objective was to facilitate a better understanding of semantic interoperability and the requirements that have to be met in order to make reasonable and relevant propositions on the interoperability between systems and their individual elements. Although the suggestions brought forward in this article are theoretical and specific to the relevant models, the general principles and ideas in respect of the necessity and functional potential of taking semantic interoperability into consideration are valid for heterogeneous knowledge organisation systems and indexing languages. Implementing these new ideas into an existing framework will require further research and persistence.

Only if further research is undertaken and collaborative efforts strengthened, will the integration of these suggestions and their implementation in the context of heterogeneous, distributed systems be possible. Had these considerations, suggestions and the integration of the suggested modifications been incorporated into the draft during the course of the revision process, it might have actually increased the possibilities of modelling the aboutness.[16] Furthermore, it might have also provided a good starting point for further semantic interoperability between different conceptual entities belonging to linguistically, structurally and typologically heterogeneous systems in the context of various distributed, interconnected and eventually interoperable systems.

References

Web documents were accessed on 31st May 2011.

Boteram, Felix; Hubrich, Jessica. (2010). Specifying Intersystem Relations: Requirements, Strategies, Issues. Knowledge Organization, 37 (3) : 216–222.

Hubrich, Jessica. (2011). Intersystem Relations: Characteristics and Functionalities. In this volume.

IFLA Study Group on the Functional Requirements for Bibliographic Records (ed.). (1998). Functional Requirements for Bibliographic Records. Final report. München: K.G. Saur. Version as amended and corrected through February 2009 available at: http://www.ifla.org/files/cataloguing/frbr/frbr_2008.pdf.

IFLA Working Group on the Functional Requirements for Subject Authority Records (FRSAR). (2010). Functional Requirements for Subject Au-

16 Cf. Žumer 2011.

thority Data (FRSAD): A Conceptual Model. Approved by the Standing Committee of the IFLA Section on Classification and Indexing. Available at: http://www.ifla.org/files/classification-and-indexing/functional-requirements-for-subject-authority-data/frsad-final-report.pdf.

IFLA Working Group on the Functional Requirements for Subject Authority Records (FRSAR). (2009). Functional Requirements for Subject Authority Data (FRSAD): A Conceptual Model. 2nd Draft. Available at: http://nkos.slis.kent.edu/FRSAR/report090623.pdf.

Odgen, Charles Kay; Richards, Ivor Armstrong. (1923). The Meaning of Meaning: A Study of the Influence of Language Upon Thought and of the Science of Symbolism. London: Routledge & Kegan Paul.

Zeng, Marcia Lei; Chan, Lois Mai. (2010). Semantic Interoperability. In: Encyclopaedia of Library and Information Science. 4645–4662.

Zeng, Marcia Lei; Žumer, Maja. (2009). Introducing FRSAD and Mapping it with SKOS and Other Models. In: World Library and Information Congress. 75th IFLA General Conference and Council 23-27 August 2009, Milan, Italy. Available at: http://www.ifla.org/files/hq/papers/ifla75/200-zeng-en.pdf

Žumer, Maja. (2011). Challenges of Modelling the Aboutness. In this volume.

Index of Authors

Felix Boteram

Librarian and research assistant working for the Reseda project at the Institute of Information Management at the Cologne University of Applied Sciences, Germany

Stella G Dextre Clarke

Independent consultant specializing in the design and implementation of thesauri and other knowledge organization structures
Project Leader ISO NP 25964

Gordon Dunsire

Head of the Centre for Digital Library Research at the University of Strathclyde in Glasgow, Scotland
Member of the FRBR Review Group, Consultant to the FRBR Namespace project

Claudia Effenberger

Librarian and information scientist working at the German National Library

Winfried Gödert

Professor for Subject Indexing and Information Retrieval at the Institute for Information Science at the Cologne University of Applied Sciences, Germany
Leader of the CrissCross project on behalf of the Cologne University of Applied Sciences
Leader of the Reseda project

Julia Hauser

Librarian working at the German National Library IT Department on representing data in the Semantic Web

Jessica Hubrich

Team leader of the CrissCross project
Research assistant at the Institute of Information Management at the Cologne University of Applied Sciences, Germany

Jan-Helge Jacobs

Librarian and research assistant working for the CrissCross project at the Institute of Information Management at the Cologne University of Applied Sciences, Germany
Now working at the department of subject indexing at the German National Library

Yvonne Jahns

Senior research librarian for work and economics at the department of subject indexing at the German National Library

Helga Karg

Research librarian for law at the department of subject indexing at the German National Library
Leader of the CrissCross project on behalf of the German National Library

Philipp Mayr

Postdoctoral researcher and team lead at the department Knowledge Technologies for the Social Sciences at GESIS – Leibniz Institute for the Social Sciences in Bonn, Germany
Visiting professor for knowledge representation at the Department of Information Science and Engineering at the University of Applied Sciences in Darmstadt, Germany

Tina Mengel

Translator and research assistant working for the CrissCross project at the Institute of Information Management at the Cologne University of Applied Sciences, Germany
Translator of the updates of the Dewey Decimal Classification (DDC) for the German version of the DDC
Now working at the department of subject indexing at the German National Library

Katrin Müller

Librarian and research assistant working for the CrissCross project at the Institute of Information Management at the Cologne University of Applied Sciences, Germany
Now working at the department Data Archives for Social Sciences at GESIS – Leibniz Institute for the Social Sciences in Bonn, Germany

Peter Mutschke

Research associate at the department Knowledge Technologies for the Social Sciences at GESIS – Leibniz Institute for the Social Sciences in Bonn, Germany

Michael Panzer

Assistant editor of the Dewey Decimal Classification (DDC) and technical advisor for Dewey research projects and web services at the OCLC Online Library Center, Inc., USA

Philipp Schaer

Research associate and head of the department Knowledge Technologies for the Social Sciences at GESIS – Leibniz Institute for the Social Sciences in Bonn, Germany

Dagobert Soergel

Professor and Chair at the Department of Library and Information Studies at the Graduate School of Education at the University at Buffalo, USA
Professor Emeritus at the College of Information Studies at the University of Maryland, USA

Maja Žumer

Professor of Information Science at the University of Ljubljana, Slovenia
Member of the FRBR Review Group, chair of the FRSAR Working Group